THE CONSERVATIVE RESURGENCE AND THE PRESS

Medill School of Journalism
VISIONS *of the* AMERICAN PRESS

GENERAL EDITOR
David Abrahamson

Selected titles in this series

MAURINE H. BEASLEY
First Ladies and the Press: The Unfinished Partnership of the Media Age

PATRICIA BRADLEY
Women and the Press: The Struggle for Equality

DAVID A. COPELAND
The Idea of a Free Press: The Enlightenment and Its Unruly Legacy

MICHAEL SWEENEY
The Military and the Press: An Uneasy Truce

PATRICK S. WASHBURN
The African American Newspaper: Voice of Freedom

DAVID R. SPENCER
The Yellow Journalism: The Press and America's Emergence as World Power

KARLA GOWER
Public Relations and the Press: The Troubled Embrace

TOM GOLDSTEIN
Journalism and Truth: Strange Bedfellows

MARK NEUZIL
The Environment and the Press: From Adventure Writing to Advocacy

THE CONSERVATIVE RESURGENCE AND THE PRESS
THE MEDIA'S ROLE IN THE RISE OF THE RIGHT

James Brian McPherson

Foreword by Sidney Blumenthal

MEDILL SCHOOL OF JOURNALISM

Northwestern University Press
Evanston, Illinois

Northwestern University Press
www.nupress.northwestern.edu

Printed in the United States of America

10 9 8 7 6 5 4 3 2 1

Library of Congress Cataloging-in-Publication Data

McPherson, James Brian, 1958–
    The conservative resurgence and the press : the media's role in the rise of
the Right / James Brian McPherson ; foreword by Sidney Blumenthal.
        p. cm. — (Medill School of Journalism visions of the American press)
    "Medill School of Journalism."
    Includes bibliographical references and index.
    ISBN-13: 978-0-8101-2332-8 (pbk. : alk. paper)
    ISBN-10: 0-8101-2332-0 (pbk. : alk. paper)
    1. Mass media—Political aspects—United States. 2. Conservatism—United
States—History—20th century. 3. Conservatism—United States—History—
21st century. 4. United States—Politics and government—20th century.
5. United States—Politics and government—21st century. I. Medill School of
Journalism. II. Title. III. Series: Visions of the American press.
P95.82.U6M385 2008
320.520973—dc22

                                                                    2008000294

♾ The paper used in this publication meets the minimum requirements of the
American National Standard for Information Sciences—Permanence of Paper
for Printed Library Materials, ANSI Z39.48-1992.

To my wife, Joanna, who makes it all possible and worth doing

CONTENTS

FOREWORD

Sidney Blumenthal

The story of the role of the press in the fortunes of conservatism in America, a tale so ably told by James Brian McPherson in this volume, has its origins in the 1930s. At the height of the New Deal, conservative Republicans dominated the press. From William Randolph Hearst's vast properties to Father Charles Coughlin's radio show, from the *New York Herald Tribune* to the *Chicago Tribune,* from the *Los Angeles Times* to *Time* magazine, media opinion was overwhelmingly organized against Franklin D. Roosevelt and the Democratic Party. Newspapers sympathetic to the New Deal were few and far between. In 1940, the eastern Republican media establishment largely hatched the candidacy of Wendell Willkie, who became the Republican nominee. For more than a generation afterward, from 1940 on, the majority of newspapers editorially endorsed Republican candidates for president. In 1964, however, when Barry Goldwater, avatar of the new Right, seized the helm of the party, the weight of newspaper endorsements tilted for the first time to the Democrat. The origins of modern conservative media, and their allegations about liberal bias in news coverage, can be traced to that moment of shock, when the traditional press seemed to slip out of the Republicans' grasp.

Conservatives felt disenfranchised and disoriented by the shifts in media technology, the public's news habits and their impact on politics. By 1963, the majority of Americans used television as their principal source of news rather than newspapers. A Roper poll showed that 36 percent regarded television as a more reliable source, compared with 24 percent who favored print. Edward R. Murrow, the leading liberal commentator, was deprived of his hour-long CBS public-affairs program, *See It Now*, after his courageous stand against the demagogy of Senator Joseph McCarthy, but the half-hour network newscasts were innovative, professional, and objective. They served as a national source of information overriding the influence of provincial Republican newspapers and radio broadcasts that used to dominate political media. And conservatives were dismayed and angered. "I can no longer stand silently by and watch the shabby treatment Goldwater is getting from most of the news media," wrote John S. Knight, editor and publisher of two prominent Republican newspapers, the *Detroit Free Press* and the *Chicago Daily News,* in a syndicated editorial.

With the election of Richard Nixon in 1968, the assault on the news media became fixed as an elemental goal, partly out of partisanship and partly out of Nixon's deeply rooted social resentment of those he considered elites. Vice President Spiro Agnew was sent out to discredit news media as a whole, calling them "nattering nabobs of negativism." Nixon encouraged eccentric billionaires Ross Perot and Richard Mellon Scaife to purchase the *Washington Post* and CBS, zany plots that came to nothing. Nixon's resignation in the Watergate scandal only intensified conservative hatred of the media, whose investigations into his corruption were instrumental in his fall.

After Nixon, conservatives began to assault not just the news media but conventional journalistic standards, which supposedly had a built-in proliberal prejudice. Yet despite concerted agitation from conservative activists such as Reed Irvine (Accuracy in Media) and Edith Ephron (author of *The News Twisters*), contemporary conservative media remained relatively small and self-contained until the late 1980s. In 1987, the Reagan administration's Federal

Communications Commission abolished the Fairness Doctrine, which since 1949 had stipulated that broadcasters allow for balanced and equitable treatment of controversial issues on the airwaves. The Democratic-controlled Congress reacted by voting for legislation reauthorizing the doctrine. But President Reagan vetoed it. With that, the floodgates opened for right-wing talk radio.

By 1993, after the election of Democratic president Bill Clinton, hundreds of conservative talk radio shows blanketed the country. The preeminent conservative journal, *National Review,* featured the most popular right-wing talk show host, Rush Limbaugh, on its cover as the "Leader of the Opposition." In Clinton's early years, Limbaugh helped lead the charge in blocking universal health care and touting the Clinton pseudoscandals. "Whitewater is about health care," Limbaugh boasted.

The advent in 1990 of Fox News, a conservative cable TV news channel owned and operated by buccaneering mogul Rupert Murdoch (also publisher of the tabloid *New York Post*) and directed by its news president Roger Ailes (a longtime Republican media consultant) augmented and amplified right-wing talk radio. Reporting on Fox News has been handled like a Republican political campaign, strategically calculated for maximum partisan advantage, often with blatant disregard for fact.

Conservative media is not another aspect of the mainstream media. It operates according to radically different imperatives, methods, and goals. The conservative media serves as the essential medium bonding and mobilizing the conservative wing of the Republican Party. Tuning in is elemental in the forging of the conservative identity. Conservative media is an echo chamber for collectively issued talking points and storylines. It presents an alternative narrative of events as they occur, often a mélange of distortion and opinion, the intent of which is to discredit any contrary version.

The sensibility of conservative media is not that it is media like other media but merely more conservative. Rather, it combines the nostalgic partisanship of the vicious Republican press of the past with an inverted Leninist relativism about fact assimilated from neoconservatism, which retains the mind-set of its Communist origins. "Leninism was a tragedy in its Bolshevik version, and it has returned as farce when practiced by the United States," wrote the political philosopher Francis Fukuyama, himself a former ardent neoconservative, in a 2006 article in the *New York Times*.

Conservative media does not see itself as a reverse mirror image of the mainstream media but as its dedicated foe. Its core mission is to destroy the professionalism that has defined journalism since the mid-twentieth century. Undermining the mainstream media is a deliberate and relentless effort, and conservative media is a battering ram against traditional journalistic standards. One way it has pushed the boundaries of its influence is to foster the notion that objectivity and fairness consists in acknowledging the conservative Republican position as at least half of the political spectrum. Every issue and event must be reported as though it has two sides and only two sides: the hard-right Republicans and the liberals (a category including all nonideologically conservative journalists). This polarizing technique systematically destroys journalistic objectivity, the responsibility to determine fact, and substitutes a distorted pseudoreality in which the extremist fringe has an exaggerated purchase on the truth.

Conservatives stigmatize the press's adjudication of fact and truth as partisanship, special pleading, or liberal bias. They browbeat the press into accepting that objectivity consists of presenting a conservative point of view and another one labeled "liberal," which subsumes what was formerly considered objective reporting. Under this political pressure, reportorial authority has been gradually abdicated. Professional reporters are cast as liberal, threatening their ability to act as purveyors of news and transforming them into opinionated commentators equal to the conservative ones. Facts dissolve, becoming fragments of opinion. In the Leninist equation, might determines right.

Conservative media also has had a major impact by channeling its stories into the mainstream media. For example, nearly all the Clinton scandals were set in motion by right-wing groups, floated through conservative media organs, from the *Washington Times* (owned by Sun Myung Moon, the South Korean would-be messiah) to the *American Spectator,* then hyped by Rush Limbaugh and pushed by conservative activists. Finally, the network news organizations and major newspapers pulled on the threads laid out for them, ultimately leading years later to journalistic dead ends but in the meantime paying rich political rewards to the Republican Right, culminating in the impeachment trial of President Clinton.

Conservative media has become a transmission belt for activists and its own brand of celebrities. The career of Ann Coulter, one of the Right's foremost provocateurs, is a case in point. She began as a right-wing campus activist, joined the Federalist Society, and received training at the National Journalism Center, a conservative group devoted to equipping activists with polemical skills and a gloss of journalistic knowledge. After working at a right-wing legal group, the Center for Individual Rights, she wrote her first book, *High Crimes and Misdemeanors: The Case Against Bill Clinton,* for the conservative Regnery Publishing. Regnery also owns the Conservative Book Club and the conservative weekly *Human Events,* which heavily promoted the book. Bulk buying by unidentified benefactors lifted it onto the best-seller lists. "Journalism is war by other means," Coulter wrote in a subsequent book,

Slander. Her many scurrilous accusations against liberals and journalists (one and the same in her books) have disintegrated under scrutiny. Though her reformulation of the Leninist conception of journalism may be crude, she honestly reflects much of the conservative media method.

Colonization of mainstream media is yet another significant strategy for extending the influence of conservative media. By replacing the idea of objective reporting, assessment of the facts, with a standard of objectivity measured according to how much ground is ceded to conservatives, the Right has succeeded in gaining footholds within major news organizations. The appointment of William Kristol as a columnist at the *New York Times* is the latest fruit of this strategy. Upon his naming, a *Times* editor extolled him as a "respected conservative intellectual," a fanciful description of someone who had abandoned an academic career out of indifference, written not a single article or book of intellectual consequence, and as editor of the neoconservative *Weekly Standard* regularly incited polemical distortion and even contempt for fact. His legitimacy really derived as a source for *Times* reporters, when he was Vice President Dan Quayle's chief of staff and Republican operative. No matter; his elevation to the prime real estate of the *Times'* op-ed page was explained as a natural reward for his intellectual merit and the newspaper's never-ending quest for balance. In the past, the *Times'* notion of balance among its columnists meant that it would have someone who had been a serious political correspondent. Now that definition has migrated to mean that its op-ed pages must include not one (David Brooks) but two neoconservatives.

It was ironic that the *Times* added Kristol just as the neoconservatism he espouses had been thoroughly discredited. The fall from grace after President George W. Bush's reelection in 2004, when neoconservatism and conservative media seemed omnipotent, was swift. And in the Republican presidential nominating contest of 2008, conservative media divided just like the party. The arc of its influence follows that of the Republican Right to which it is organically attached. As post-Bush conservatives scramble to paste together their fragmented movement and party, conservative media reinforce the attitudes that have led to its disrepute and disorganization. Like the Right generally, conservative media may rest its hopes on another political cycle in which it can get back to the basics of demonizing liberal media.

Perhaps an equally open question, as Professor McPherson suggests, is what role the American press, taken as whole, will play in this process in the future. On one hand, it can continue to be a vehicle for a notably destructive sort of partisanship. Or, on the other, it can rise to the nobler purposes so essential to a well-informed—and therefore self-governing—citizenry.

PREFACE

Most Americans will never have the privilege of demanding answers from their elected leaders with the expectation that answers will come via any means other than a form letter with a mechanical signature. Few will experience the adrenaline rush of uncovering and exposing bureaucratic wrongdoing in a way that changes government for the better. Most cannot experience the satisfaction of having found the perfect illustrative quote or poignant phrase. Few will see the results of their daily efforts—the glorious successes and the dismal failures—flash before the eyes of thousands of readers or viewers.

Those who criticize journalists as ego-driven are right, to some degree. No one without a healthy ego would survive the abuse heaped on media professionals, let alone thrive on it. And no one without such an ego would believe so strongly, as a good journalist does, that he might protect others by pointing out problems. Having worked as a journalist and as a professor of journalism, I love the press. Or at least I love the idea of the press, as I believe it is supposed to work. I also happen to care about politics and appreciate the relationship between good journalism and effective self-government.

The United States is fortunate to have a lot of good journalists. Most never become household names or earn large salaries. Many are much better at their craft than I ever was. Still, relatively few are as good as I should have been, or as they could be, though they are not entirely to blame for the shortcomings of the press.

Those shortcomings were part of my motivation for returning to school to become a teacher of journalism and part of the motivation for this book.

One of my greatest frustrations is the lack of historical and political context common to news stories, including stories ostensibly about politics. Because of time constraints, newsroom conventions, a lack of historical appreciation, and sometimes carelessness or laziness, the news media tend to treat any unusual event as essentially unprecedented, unless the same type of event has happened very recently. Recognizable examples might include an outbreak of a new virus, a terrorist attack on American soil, sexual misconduct by a politician, or a devastating hurricane. Many such events are obviously newsworthy even if they lack historical uniqueness, but knowing how similar events have occurred and been dealt with in the past would provide a more complete story, and might even help decrease the magnitude of such events in the future.

On the other hand, also troubling is that if some unusual event—a church burning, a shark attack, a school shooting, or the murder of a pretty white woman, for example—has happened even once in recent months, journalists now treat it as part of a trend. Yet rarely do the media compare the number of similar incidents that have occurred during comparable time spans in the past, nor do they compare the dangers they choose to cover to other more common tragedies. As a result, probably few Americans would guess that their child is more likely to drown in a toilet than to be eaten by a shark, that today's first grader probably is less likely to be a victim of a violent crime at school than her parents were, and that almost none of the thousands of American children who are shot to death each year die in their schools.

The events discussed in this book would be classified as recent history—too recent, for example, for a full understanding of what those events will mean for the future of either American democracy or American journalism. Even so, based on the results of the 2006 congressional and gubernatorial elections, some might be tempted to believe that a book tracing the relationship between the press and the post–World War II rise of conservatism already is outdated. After all, despite Republicans' claims about the supposed liberalism of their Democratic opponents (and of virtually anyone else who disagreed with the Republicans in power, for that matter), most of those Democrats won. But Democratic does not necessarily mean liberal, any more than Republican means conservative. In fact, both parties have shifted to the political Right in recent decades. Conservatives still control every branch (executive, legislative, and judicial) of the federal government even if Democrats now hold a slight congressional majority. Incidentally, the shift in national politics reflects what has occurred to a more moderate extent to the country as a whole and to the American news media. Conservatism has won, at least for now.

If recent events do happen to signify a shift back toward liberalism, perhaps this book can point out the sorts of indicators that journalists and political scientists might consider when trying to understand—or, more importantly, to explain—that shift. Most of the recent conservative resurgence went largely unnoticed and unreported by the press until after it had occurred. Preoccupied with day-to-day events, journalists tend to bounce from story to story without noticing or explaining the larger political landscape that surrounds them and their audiences. Democracy matters, they argue, while rarely explaining how modern American democracy works. Or fails to work. Slightly more often, journalists try to point out the importance of their own First Amendment protections. Yet they have failed to convince most Americans *why* a free press should matter, and the actions of the news media often further diminish their already ineffective argument.

This book's subtitle—*The Media's Role in the Rise of the Right*—has a straightforward meaning, using "right" in the simple context of political orientation to reflect that the American press has become more conservative during recent decades. I had considered a more ironic (but ultimately less clear) subtitle, *Getting the News Right*. In that case, "right" would have had a second meaning, as a synonym for "correct." For me, that more complicated definition reflects irony, skepticism, and hope. The irony comes from the fact that, partly because conservatives have unceasingly criticized the supposed liberalism of the press, in some respects the American news media probably now cover politics worse—less correctly or less "right"—than they once did. I am skeptical that the corporate mainstream news media will soon change for the better or that Americans will become more discerning about their media or political needs. Yet I retain a bit of hope, fueled by the fact that a few members of the mainstream press and alternative media do a decent job of covering politics, and others try. The necessary tools for good political journalism mostly are in place, and perhaps journalists can learn from the past.

ACKNOWLEDGMENTS

Many people made this book possible. David Abrahamson has been a friend and a generous and insightful editor. He, Jessica Paumier, Mairead Case, and unknown others at Northwestern University Press helped make the process much easier than is typically the case and made the book much better than it would have been without their contributions.

Brother Guy served as first proofreader and a valuable sounding board. Parents Jim and Edna, sister Carol, and "kids" and in-laws—Kathy, Gary, Grace, Brooke, Ruthie, Larry, Sheila, Lee, and Rosemary—all demonstrated patience with my efforts. Teddy the dog and Tony the cat lay on either side of me during most of the writing, providing moral support and occasional welcome distraction.

Whitworth University provided research funding and sabbatical time to write, and its librarians provided valuable research assistance. My students, most of them young conservatives, continually ask necessary questions and provide regular insights.

Most importantly, my wife, Joanna, now has indexed two of my books and has been my best editor and my best friend for more than twenty-seven years.

THE CONSERVATIVE RESURGENCE AND THE PRESS

ONE

THE NEW CONSERVATISM AND PRIOR MOVEMENTS

In what originally was called one of the first political kidnappings in American history, a man claiming to belong to a group called the American Revolutionary Army grabbed an *Atlanta Constitution* editor in 1974 and held him for a seven-hundred-thousand-dollar ransom.[1] The kidnapper, who was quickly captured and found to be acting alone, had said the money would be used "to combat excessive liberalism of the press."[2] And though that year—the same year in which Watergate revelations helped end the presidency of Richard Nixon—was one of the high points for American journalism, the Atlanta kidnapper was hardly the only American dismayed by press behavior at the time. The newspaper noted afterward that it had received letters from "nice little old ladies who wrote:'I am glad you will have to pay the ransom....The way you have persecuted the President has been awful. . . . God evens things out.'"[3]

Regardless of the perspective of the Almighty, the so-called liberal press has been a favorite target of conservatives for at least a half century. That criticism continues despite the fact that the mainstream news media (like all branches of the federal government, also targets of conservative complaints) have grown increasingly conservative during recent decades and, in most respects, now are more conservative than liberal. One indication of that conservative emphasis might be seen simply in the use of the contrasting terms: most conservatives take pride in calling themselves conservatives, while, somewhat ironically, many liberals hark back to a major social movement of a century ago and have taken to calling themselves progressives. Of course, few institutions or individuals hold consistent conservative or liberal views on all issues. For example, contemporary conservatives tend to be more opposed than liberals to abortion and more supportive of the death penalty, yet many Americans support or oppose both. Despite some definitive issues and simplistic portrayals by politicians, conservatives and liberals alike usually favor strong families, safe streets, and good schools. President Bill Clinton was lambasted as a liberal by Republican opponents, yet he drew criticism for "stealing" and implementing supposedly Republican ideas such as deficit reduction, international free trade, welfare reform, increased numbers of police officers, and charter schools. "Conservative" president George W. Bush supported a No Child Left Behind education program and the Department of Homeland Security, both originally Democratic ideas.

It also is important to recognize that the meanings of *conservative* and *liberal* have changed over time. The Founding Fathers generally accepted the then-liberal view (now often referred to as *classical liberalism*) that favored limited government along with individual freedom and responsibility. Their conservative side was expressed through the formation of a style of government that, because of federalism and the separation of powers, made rapid change relatively difficult. For most of American history, conservatives have been those who believed in adhering to the status quo and typically held views sometimes perceived as isolationist, with relatively little use for foreign entanglements beyond business ventures. Both early and modern conservatives have tended to be Christian (joined by conservative Jews in recent decades), concerned about social morality, and promoters of free enterprise. Especially at the national level, conservative Republicans once were viewed as pro-business elites who could not understand the needs of blue-collar workers, while in more recent times Democrats have been portrayed as pro-government liberal elites who cannot understand or relate to most Americans. Noting that people use "word weapons" to stereotype their opponents, one legal scholar offers this definition: "Critics of media bias generally use 'liberal' to mean people who are reluctant to use military force; support government regulation of the economy; favor programs to aid the poor and disadvantaged; are tolerant of abortion, homosexuality, and sex outside of marriage; and are skeptical about institutions such as religion, the military, and the traditional family."[4]

Contemporary neoconservatives have less faith in government-sponsored social programs than do modern liberals but are more willing to let the government legislate "moral" issues such as abortion, pornography, and homosexuality. Conversely, political philosopher Michael Sandel wrote more than twenty years ago, "Liberals often take pride in defending what they oppose—pornography, for example, or unpopular views." Sandel also argued that conservatives "sometimes exploit this distinction by ignoring it. They charge that those who would allow abortions favour abortions, that opponents of school prayer oppose prayer, and that those who defend the rights of Communists sympathize with their cause."[5] Today he might substitute the word "terrorists" for "Communists," but otherwise the statement still rings true.

In perhaps the most recent definitional shifts, modern *neocon-*

servatives also are somewhat more willing than liberals or more traditional conservatives to use American military force abroad (as evidenced by the George W. "Bush doctrine" of "preemptive war" adopted as part of national security policy in 2002 and used the following year in Iraq). They also seem more willing to trade some of their privacy as individuals for perceived security and to overlook or even favor deficit spending by the government. It also should be pointed out that most political experts differentiate between modern neoconservatives and more traditional conservatives, sometimes called *paleoconservatives.* In large part because of party divisions, however, that supposed conservative divide essentially has become a distinction without a difference. With most issues, the neoconservatives have won and traditional conservatives have acquiesced. "From the late 1970s on it became increasingly hard to disentangle neoconservatism from other, more traditional varieties of American conservatism, whether based on small-government libertarianism, religious or social conservatism, or American nationalism," wrote Francis Fukuyama, a noted one-time neoconservative who later rejected the movement. According to Fukuyama, "Many neoconservative ideas were wholeheartedly adopted by mainstream conservatives. . . . But the second reason for this convergence is that many neoconservatives began adopting policy positions of traditional conservatives."[6]

The next chapter further discusses the shift from the traditional conservatism of the 1950s to the neoconservatism that gained prominence in the 1990s. Unless stated otherwise, this book will use contemporary understandings of conservatism and liberalism.

One obvious way in which the media clearly have become more conservative in recent years is exemplified by how much conservatives control the public airwaves. Talk radio programs provide the most obvious example, especially since the arrival of bombastic conservative commentator Rush Limbaugh in the 1980s. Limbaugh freely mixed news with opinion and distortion, delivered with a caustic wit. His popularity spawned numerous imitators, almost all of them also conservatives, and most American cities soon had stations devoted entirely to talk radio.[7] Those programs should be differentiated from the news media, but many Americans—and the networks themselves—often fail to make that distinction. Besides, many of those commentators can be heard, and increasingly seen, on broadcast networks that claim to primarily deliver news. Fox News is the most blatant television example, with its most popular program hosted by Bill O'Reilly. Popular conservative Sean Hannity cohosts another Fox show, paired with quieter, less well-known, and more liberal Alan Colmes. Oliver North, who once lied to Congress about the illegal sale of weapons to Iran, has a show on Fox News. Like other conservatives, columnist and radio host Tony Snow regularly criticized George W. Bush for acting too much like a Democrat with some issues. But Snow went from hosting a Fox News program and serving as Limbaugh's primary guest host to become Bush's press secretary (and headlining fund-raisers for Republican congressional candidates at the same time, perhaps the first White House press secretary to so actively participate in partisan electoral politics). Though commonly recognized as less conservative than Fox, MSNBC offers one show hosted by noted liberal Keith Olbermann but two programs hosted by conservatives Tucker Carlson and Joe Scarborough. The same network hired Michael Savage, perhaps the most vicious of the right-wing commentators (Ann Coulter is the possible exception). MSNBC fired Savage less than a year later when he told a homosexual caller: "Oh, you're one of the sodomites. You should only get AIDS and die, you pig."[8] Conservative radio personality Laura Ingraham, who once served as a speechwriter for Ronald Reagan, hosted another MSNBC program. Conservative commentator Glenn Beck began hosting a show on CNN in 2006.

Of course, many political personalities—including not only politicians but also party regulars and some media figures—have learned two keys to enhancing their own popularity. The first is that audiences appreciate simple messages, regardless of how misleading. The second is that almost everyone dislikes some aspects of the media, making the press an easy target. The interesting but troubling result, judging by the widespread popularity of media bashing among some broadcast personalities and by the decreasing number of Americans who read newspapers, is that probably most of the Americans who criticize the "liberalism" of the *New York Times* have never actually read it. Conversely, based on the *Times'* perceived influence among those same commentators, and among politicians and academics, it also is a safe bet that the most influential critics who complain about the newspaper's editorial slant still peruse it regularly and probably believe most of what they read within it. *National Review,* perhaps the most important conservative magazine in the United States for the past fifty years, noted in 1986 that although the magazine's editors "have used the *New York Times* as our favorite pincushion. . . . The brightness of the Grey Lady, its appetite for the news, for features, for supplements, the sheer universality of its coverage make it the outstanding newspaper in the world."[9] Of course, the *National Review* could afford to be magnanimous—by then, conservatism reigned in American politics, as it would for at least the next two decades.

That conservative control brings up another key point: conservative critics tend to contradict themselves when making the "liberal media" argument. In their efforts to combat pornography and other "harmful" content, they logically argue that if the media had no influence, advertising would cease to exist. Yet one might reasonably wonder, if the news media are liberal, and if the media have significant influence, how could the United States end up with conservatives controlling all three branches of the federal government and most state governments? It seems that conservative critics either must be wrong about the media having much influence or they must be wrong about the idea that whichever media wield influence are liberal in nature.

In the case of newspapers, most people read local publications that concern themselves more with regional issues than with national affairs, and it is in local and regional issues that newspapers can have the greatest influence.[10] For better or worse, in that way the press may find itself in the same position as Congress: voters commonly give Congress low ratings, but they approve of their own representatives. Similarly, readers and viewers may like their own local news outlets more than they appreciate the news media as a perceived whole. If so, especially if they rely on nonprint media, they may have things backward. After all, the national media know that their mistakes will be caught and highlighted, a situation made truer with the recent rise of Internet bloggers. But local media provide much less news and probably less accuracy than their national counterparts, especially for the unfortunate majority of Americans who rely primarily on television for their news. In most regions of the country, local television news has degenerated into a mishmash of lurid but largely irrelevant crime stories, video of fires and car crashes, briefs plagiarized from newspapers, video news releases from government and corporate sponsors, weather graphics, local sports, and on-air "happy talk."[11] Local radio programming has largely disappeared altogether, swallowed up by conglomeration and cost cutting. The lack of meaningful coverage has negative effects beyond the individual news consumers and media credibility. "Because local news avoids a lot of important items, including city council meetings, policy decisions, and local initiatives—in short, the blueprints of local democracy—we are civically poorer," one media scholar notes.[12]

Another problem involves what might be seen as the most important kind of "hard news": what one viewer perceives as good investigative journalism or necessary questioning of authority, another sees as bias. Perhaps that complaint has some basis in fact, considering that one is more likely to find fault (and to seek it in the first place) with one's enemies than with one's friends. When the *Chicago Tribune* became perhaps the best investigative newspaper in the country during the 1960s, it did so as a conservative newspaper uncovering corruption in the city's Democratic power structure.[13] When the *New York Times* and the *Washington Post* fought the Nixon administration to publish the Pentagon Papers in 1971, then as the *Post* began digging into Watergate, the two newspapers were among the relatively few in the country that would not endorse Richard Nixon's reelection as president.[14] At one time, most American cities had two or more daily newspapers—one might be more liberal, one more conservative. But outside of New York City and Washington, D.C., almost no cities still have competing dailies. In the few cities that have two dailies, typically the two share business operations through a joint operating agreement (discussed in more detail in chapter 7).

Those who complain about a liberal bias among the news media point to surveys showing that most journalists identify themselves as more liberal than their audiences. For example, in one guide to media bias sponsored by the conservative Media Research Center, the authors hyperbolically state: "No one would accept the statement of a Ku Klux Klansman, in line for a judgeship, that he was capable of applying the civil rights laws objectively, without regard to his personal opinions. Yet the argument is advanced by the members of the media that a reporter can cover George Bush fairly even if he believes Bush is a tool of fascist warmongers and racist plutocrats."[15] The supposed members of the media who advance that hypothetical argument are not identified, nor is there any evidence that any mainstream reporter ever considered Bush to be in league with Fascists or racists. One also might argue that it is difficult to imagine a Klansman being in line for a judgeship. Still, the central point has some merit—no one is truly unbiased—though as one scholar notes, "Despite claims by the left and the right, journalists do not generally hold extreme political positions, unless we count the extreme center."[16] A 2006 national survey found that most journalists describe themselves as moderates, though very few describe themselves as conservatives.[17] Journalists do tend to lean left, in part because many of them enter journalism as a means to help bring about positive social reform. Even so, most contemporary journalists recognize that bias exists and likely would agree with historian Peter Novick that objectivity is an admirable but ultimately unreachable goal.[18] They try to overcome potential biases by striving for balance or fairness to all sides. In attempting to avoid charges of bias they may even be inclined to bend over backward to be especially fair to those with whom they disagree. Obvious examples of liberal bias can be found, but so can examples of conservative bias—as another media watchdog, the liberal Fairness and Accuracy in Reporting, regularly points out. One of that organization's founders also produced a guide to detecting bias, published in the same year as the Media Research Center book, arguing that "mass media are often little more than vehicles through which those in power pontificate to the American public."[19]

Interestingly, both books argue that one way to fight bias would be to increase competition among newspapers so that biases could be more clearly identified by readers. Many journalists and media scholars also agree that public discourse probably would benefit from more two-newspaper cities, though the competitive demands of such an occurrence would be unlikely to bring the news media closer to objectivity. As more and more American cities became one-newspaper towns, surviving newspapers typically tried to appeal to as many readers as possible by maintaining a middle-of-the-road perspective. The fact that the papers draw criticism from liberals and conservatives alike suggests that they have been largely successful in claiming that middle ground. Or perhaps in standing by while others fight over the ground. As one media scholar argues, " 'Passivity' is a better word than 'objectivity' or 'fairness' to describe the professional stance of the press." That passivity leads to three common types of newsgathering: passing along public-relations propaganda as news, "normalizing" spontaneous events by presenting them in familiar terms, and reporting conflict without appropriate context.[20] In fact, no studies have convincingly demonstrated that the political leanings of reporters affect their coverage. Besides, most publishers and station managers (and most corporate advertisers and media owners) are more conservative than reporters, and for many critics the ideology of those who finance the media is far more important than the ideologies of the journalists.[21]

Despite the formation of foundations and the publication of books that attempt to prove consistent bias toward either the liberal or conservative end of the spectrum, those attempts tend to be contradictory and more obviously biased than are the mainstream media themselves. "Academic research can be found to support almost any perspective on media bias, from liberal bias to conservative bias, to no bias at all. . . . Vast attention and consideration is paid to addressing a partisan bias for which there is little evidence," one political scientist notes.[22] The lack of evidence never has kept critics from all sides at bay, of course. As one journalism historian has pointed out, "Virtually since the first edition came off the first flat-bed press, critics have chronicled with alarm how the media are often scurrilous, fantastical, pandering, titillating, vengeful, irresponsible, left-wing, right-wing, tub thumping and subversive."[23] The media are not helped by the fact that they frequently fail to do an adequate job of educating readers or viewers about why journalists do what they do, or about the need for a free press.[24]

Even without trying to analyze the biases of individual journalists or their messages, some obvious tendencies have emerged. Though those tendencies do not necessarily correspond to overt partisan biases, in most cases they do reflect a broader kind of conservative bias—a reflection that shows American journalism to be wary of change or those who promote change, while promoting a pro-business, pro-community, pro–status quo, pro–American perspective. (Business aspects are discussed further in chapter 7.) Almost thirty years ago sociologist Herbert J. Gans identified eight all-American values that influenced news content for networks and major newsmagazines. He called those values ethnocentricism, altruistic democracy, responsible capitalism, small-town pastoralism, individualism, moderation, social order, and national leadership.[25] No political student would have trouble applying any of those same themes to the speeches of Ronald Reagan (the focus of chapter 4). The fact is American journalists are Americans first and journalists second, and they generally believe in the same general values as other Americans. One book about media theories argues:

> Fundamental is a belief in the value of the capitalist economic system, private ownership, pursuit of profit by self-interested en-

trepreneurs, and free markets. This system is intertwined with the Protestant ethic and the value of individual achievement. The companion political values center around liberal democracy, a system in which all people are presumed to have equal worth and a right to share in their own governance, making decisions based on rational self interest.[26]

From a political perspective, the majority of American newspapers have endorsed Republican candidates over Democrats in most presidential elections (1964, 1992, and 2004 being the only exceptions since those two parties gained political dominance) and have historically favored Republicans over Democrats in most state and federal elections. That trend began to shift somewhat in the 1960s, and by the 1990s the Democratic candidates had a slight endorsement advantage for the first time.[27]

Regardless, though the editorial pages of newspapers may show a liberal bias such as that apparent with the *New York Times* or the *Washington Post* (though both of those papers supported the Iraq War), or a conservative bias such as that illustrated by the *Wall Street Journal* or the *Washington Times,* most newspapers strive for balance. That attempt to achieve balance or fairness creates another problem that can only be deemed conservative, if conservatism is taken to mean resistant to change: journalists tend to contact and quote a limited spectrum of sources who are disproportionately white and male, and to exclude perspectives beyond two main sides, which they then try to balance equally. "They attempt to chain opinions to their opposites, hoping, it seems, that these beasts will annihilate each other, leaving what passes in journalistic thinking for the truth," one media scholar writes. "Some events and issues, after all, are unbalanced, and the effort to balance them in itself adds a kind of bias."[28]

Particularly in Washington, political reporters hobnob with politicians, attending the same functions. It is true, as conservative former CBS newsman Bernard Goldberg argues in a book-length criticism of press liberalism (which also compares network news to the mafia), that national journalists in particular are likely to be out of touch with the everyday lives of their readers and viewers. These journalists often have more in common with their sources than they do with their audiences.[29] Especially in recent decades, most political sources are conservatives. Regardless of any liberal tendencies that journalists may have, most of the people whose views they pass on likely counter those perspectives. Even the most elite American journalists, the members of the Washington press corps, reflect their work environment. As former Lyndon Johnson press secretary George Reedy wrote more than three decades ago, "Like all elites, they have a tendency to pomposity and an overly developed self-esteem, but, generally speaking, it seems to me that most of them have traveled a much more difficult road in arriving at their present status than have their counterparts in law and government."[30] Reedy also discounted the idea that journalists act in concert to promote any agenda, liberal or otherwise: "In terms of social cohesion, these correspondents are just about like any other similar group of professionals. They are clannish, clique-ridden, jealous of each other, and usually in total ignorance of the other segments of the press with which they are not in contact."[31]

Some of Goldberg's other complaints, such as his claims that the news media focus too much on entertainment values and that too many crime victims made visible are white females, have more obvious validity. But those shortcomings more accurately reflect a conservative, protect-the-power-structure bias than a liberal bias. Those problems may also help explain why a 2003 University of

Maryland study found that roughly half of Americans wrongly believed that the United States had found evidence of close ties between Saddam Hussein and al-Qaeda. More than 20 percent of Americans surveyed believed that weapons of mass destruction—a significant Bush administration rationale for the Iraq War before it began—had been found in Iraq, that Iraq was involved in the 9/11 attacks on New York and Washington, and that most of the world supported the U.S. war effort. None of those beliefs were true, though all four contributed to support for the neoconservative cause. News users who relied primarily on Fox were the most misinformed of the respondents, while those who relied heavily on public television and radio had the fewest misconceptions.[32]

While modern news media are more conservative than liberal, the dominant political and social views of the press have shifted back and forth at various times in history. It is important to recognize that in the United States those swings have not been particularly wide in comparison to the media of other nations but have ranged between somewhat liberal and somewhat conservative perspectives. Even during their most extreme phases, mainstream American news media have never openly advocated socialism, anarchy, or any form of totalitarian government. Importantly, press media shifts have tended to reflect the mood of the country as a whole—though perhaps mainstream journalists rarely have been as extreme in their positions as have political leaders or, for that matter, as extreme as the American people whom both politicians and journalists try to serve. As one media scholar noted more than two decades ago, "The mainstream press has traditionally spoken to and for the homogenous middle."[33] At various times in American history the middle has shifted toward the right or toward the left, but the mainstream news media, despite an oft-expressed desire to lead public discourse (perhaps while simultaneously maintaining some perhaps-contradictory sense of objectivity), typically have been reactive. Though the media might point out individual problems that signal larger social issues and help bring those larger issues to the forefront of general consciousness, the press generally has been in tune with its times—or a bit behind. One former journalist has written:

> The average news staff has settled into a routine of chasing ambulances and fires, news releases and social news, city council meetings, Lions Club lunches, and visits to the local Chamber, School Board, or Legislature for their stories, making believe that they are really hard-hitting "investigative" journalists just because on occasion they may stumble onto a story that others have known for years. . . . The reality is that a gung-ho "I'm-gonna-win-a-Pulitzer" reporter, often encouraged by desk-bound editors, will clumsily dig into a story that is little more than a flea bite upon society's ass, and overlook the story that can tear at its heart.[34]

Meanwhile, nonmainstream, alternative media nibble at the edges of political thought, often unnoticed except by those who seek them out, sometimes helping to nudge other media in one direction or the other.[35] Sometimes those alternative media (in conjunction with other societal factors) may help push other media and the nation as a whole toward becoming more liberal or more conservative. The rest of this chapter offers a broader historical view to help illustrate those changes. Later chapters demonstrate that even if conservatives may once have had justifiable complaints about media liberalism, any such complaints have become outdated. Those who make such charges today are either misguided or dishonest.

With the possible exception of the first short-lived newspaper, the American news media started out as conservatives. Newspapers were produced by businessmen (and a few women) who made most of their living from job printing—the printing of pamphlets, fliers, and other materials for other people. Newspapers were expensive, purchased by elites with the financial means to buy them and the education to read them. The very first, Benjamin Harris's 1690 *Publick Occurrences, Both Forreign and Domestick,* might be viewed as a liberal, change-promoting rabble-rouser, though it actually was born during a period of societal and governmental turmoil and its single issue established little.[36] A devout Anabaptist who had been jailed at least twice in England for publishing his views before fleeing to Boston, Harris established a prosperous business as a printer and bookseller. Though Harris's professed goal was to give a "faithful relation" of events and to help curb colonial gossip, a story about a sex scandal in the French royal family helped prompt authorities to shut down his newspaper four days after it appeared.[37] Other factors also played a part in the suppression, including fear of criticism among those in authority. The order stated, "The Governour and Council having had the perusal of the said Pamphlet, and finding that therein is contained Reflections of a very high nature: As also sundry doubtful and uncertain Reports, do hereby manifest and declare their high Resentment and Disallowance of said Pamphlet, and Order that the same be Suppressed and called in; strickly forbidding any person or persons for the future to Set forth any thing in Print without License first obtained from those that are or shall be appointed by the Government to grant the same."[38] The controversy did not hurt Harris, who continued to succeed as a publisher in Boston and later published at least three newspapers in England.[39] Still, demonstrating the degree to which pre-Revolutionary printers acquiesced to governmental regulation, the next American newspaper did not come out for another four-teen years. That newspaper, the *Boston News-Letter,* prominently carried the words "Published by Authority" just below the front-page nameplate. And while most local news was relegated to the back pages, "the governor's activities always made front page sto-ries."[40] Because authorities worried about maintaining their own positions in the colonies, one historian notes, "It comes as no surprise, therefore, to discover that a license was apt to be issued only to a printer who favored the ruling elite."[41] Though dull writing played a part, the *Boston News-Letter* gained little popular support largely because of its government ties, which also led to the newspaper ignoring some of the most important news in the colony at the time. Two media historians write: "Most of the Pu-ritan citizenry . . . held the *News-Letter* in low regard. The Puritan leadership seemed, at best, to accord the paper scornful tolera-tion as a mouthpiece of the royal government, about which they could do little but ridicule."[42]

The first three American newspapers, and eight of the first fif-teen, were published in Boston. The *News-Letter* became more in-teresting and more informative after the third, the *Boston Gazette,* arrived in 1719 to provide competition. The *Gazette* was no anti-establishment publication, however. Published by new postmaster William Brooker, the *Gazette* was viewed as the official publica-tion of the colonial governor, while the *News-Letter* generally took the side of the elected assembly. At times, both newspapers pub-lished material from both sides, and neither was religiously con-servative enough for a Massachusetts minority who believed that the Anglican Church was the only true church and that religion and the state should be bound together. Those beliefs, along with smallpox, helped prompt the formation of another Boston news-paper, the *New-England Courant,* in 1721. For all practical purposes, the printers by that time were ignoring licensing requirements, though later *Courant* editor James Franklin was jailed. His younger brother, Benjamin, took over the paper for a time.[43]

More newspapers meant a broader range of ideas, some of which involved the life-and-death issue of smallpox. The disease hit Boston several times, killing more than eight hundred people during a 1721 outbreak. Puritan leader Cotton Mather, perhaps the best writer in the colonies, had learned about experiments in which small amounts of the disease were injected into healthy people. Mather argued in pamphlets and in the *Boston News-Letter* that inoculation should be tried, but he persuaded only one of the city's ten doctors—who quickly became a target of the majority, who opposed the inoculations. Among those opposed were the Anglicans, who started the *Courant* largely to attack Mather and other proponents of immunization. They lost the argument when people were able to contrast the survival rates of those immunized with those who had not been. The *Courant* did not last long. For one thing, Puritans outnumbered Anglicans. For another, the *Courant,* which shifted from common newswriting to attack essays, often seemed shrill. It did, however, provide an antiroyal voice.[44]

The contrasting religious and scientific views offered a preview of the party press system that would arrive after the Revolutionary War. During the buildup to war, however, many printers were spurred to action by the 1765 imposition of the Stamp Act: "For the first time in the short history of America, and perhaps for the first time in the history of the world, an unexpected ingredient was added to the taxation recipe: a completely unified mass media in protest."[45] In addition, because the Stamp Act (a tax on paper) affected newspapers directly, all of the coverage of the tax was negative, and the consistent coverage created a new "mass media" phenomenon. After the tax was repealed in 1766 "America had won a victory over the hated Stamp Act, at least in part through the unison efforts of the mass media. For the first time in America, it was as though everyone, everywhere, at the same time, had a chance to see a controversial issue through the eyes of his or her neighbor, as reported in the press."[46] New taxes and new battles would soon come, though, and the press was not as unified with those issues. Printers did realize that an end of British rule would also end licensing by the crown, prompting many to oppose the British.[47] As relations with England deteriorated, some editors tried to avoid taking sides. Others were pro-British and tried to tell both sides of the story. Until war broke out: "As American forces and British troops opened fire at Lexington and Concord, the entire press in America, both Loyal and Patriot, would choose the philosophy of the Patriots: one-sided, biased, persuasive news coverage. The practice would serve well during the war."[48] A few Loyalist newspapers continued to support the British, but most soon adopted a patriotic stance that would become familiar: "By and large, the American media as an institution have generally been in favor of American military actions and have sought to encourage public support and to bolster morale through their coverage of events," notes one media historian.[49] Former war reporter William Prochnau has referred to "jingoist propaganda" on the part of the press as "an inevitable by-product of war."[50]

After the revolution, party politics soon became part of the new nation. Printers quickly aligned themselves with political parties as a means of trying to guarantee their own survival. Parties relied on newspapers to get out their messages, and when in power, the parties awarded printing contracts to loyal publications. For the party press papers, bias was both obvious and expected. William Cobbett, a leading Philadelphia editor of the time, accurately described a common belief of the period when he called anyone who professed to be an unbiased editor instead to be "a poor passive fool, and not an editor."[51] Publishing during a time of considerable political conflict, editors of the period believed they "would have failed in their devotion to truth and in their duty to serve the best interests of their country had they not stood up for their political convictions," notes one historian.[52]

Such partisanship could irritate government officials and cause serious problems for those involved with printing. The most dramatic example came when Democratic-Republican vice president Aaron Burr killed Federalist Alexander Hamilton in an 1804 duel that stemmed in part from a trial over libel law. However, printers were more affected six years earlier by the Sedition Act of 1798, approved by a mostly Federalist Congress and President John Adams. More than two centuries later, some strong supporters of the Iraq War might agree with at least some aspects of the act. It called for a fine of up to two thousand dollars and a jail term of up to two years for anyone who "shall write, print, utter or publish, or shall cause or procure to be written, printed, uttered or published, or shall knowingly and willingly aid in writing, printing, uttering or publishing any false, scandalous malicious writing against the government of the United States, or either house of the Congress of the United States, or the President of the United States, with intent to defame said government, or to bring them, or either of them, into contempt or disrepute."[53] Many Democratic-Republicans (also sometimes referred to simply as Republicans or as Anti-Federalists) of the time supported the French Revolution, while Federalists, who held most of the power in the United States, feared that the ideals of that revolution might catch fire in America and perhaps sweep them from power. The Sedition Act, one of four acts aimed at perceived foreign threats that were passed at the same time, was portrayed as a means of protecting national security. Most newspapers were aligned with the Federalists and apparently sensed no danger to press freedom from the new law. Democratic-Republican printers, on the other hand, recognized the threat they faced. To their credit, few of them were cowed. Twenty-five arrests led to ten convictions (eight involving newspapers) for violations of the act. After Democratic-Republican Thomas Jefferson won the election in 1800, he let the measure lapse and pardoned all those convicted under it.[54]

Overt bias in newspapers faded significantly with the arrival of the penny press in the 1830s. Editors such as Benjamin Day, Horace Greeley, William Cullen Bryant (better known as a poet), and James Gordon Bennett found that cheap newspapers—priced at a penny or two—aimed at a broad swath of readers could be extremely popular and profitable. The new publications relied on reporters, including foreign correspondents and a few women, more than had their predecessors. Political bias became less visible in news stories, with the strongest opinions relegated to editorials. The penny papers also brought frank language, humor, sensationalized crime news, business and sports pages, and increased use of illustrations. Increased readership meant publishers could charge more for advertising, and heavy advertisers gained increasing influence. Though political parties and other groups continued to produce their own publications—and some small-town papers were started with subsidies from merchants expressly to be community boosters—more Americans read newspapers than ever before, and the penny papers quickly became the "mainstream media" in a changed world.[55] Incidentally, despite its reputation today as a publication read by elites, the *New York Times* also was a penny paper, though more conservative than its sensationalistic New York brethren. The penny papers had permanently impacted the news media. As one historian has noted about Day's

New York Sun, "Large numbers of readers and advertisers, rather than political and business elites, determined the paper's sensibilities and taste."[56] That has remained somewhat true for more than 170 years, for newspapers and the broadcast media that followed, though business factors have played an increasing role (as discussed in more detail in chapter 7).

Perhaps the time when Americans most rely on the news media is during war. "War is not healthy for children and other living things, but it sells newspapers," notes one historian.[57] Wartime also has prompted the most obvious consistent prejudice for the American news media: a pro-war bias, or at least a pro-government bias during times of war. The Civil War may have been the lone exception, though of course the nation as a whole was seriously divided at the time. Virtually all southern newspapers were strongly pro-Confederacy during the war, but northern publications were less consistent. Many supported Abraham Lincoln and the war, but so-called Copperhead papers were based in the North but supported the South. Lincoln, like leaders to follow, had few apparent qualms about imposing censorship. He turned control of telegraph wires over to the secretary of war. Despite the disagreements, one historian writes, "By war's end, the front pages of much of the Northern press had become a repeater service for the war department."[58]

Other American wars have been easier to characterize as "us versus them" and have produced a more consistent pro-America, pro-war bias. The sensationalistic yellow journalism papers of William Randolph Hearst and Joseph Pulitzer have been credited with helping push the United States into the Spanish-American War in 1898. Some reporters on the battlefield fired weapons or acted as spies, and Hearst even captured some Spanish sailors with his own yacht.[59] During World War I, World War II, and the Korean War, newspapers and other media quickly supported the war effort, generally having little tolerance for war protestors while going along (sometimes grudgingly) with censorship restrictions. World War I brought the Espionage Act, which allowed the U.S. postmaster to prevent the mailing of publications that were deemed treasonable or seditious. *The Nation* magazine was one of the few publications that were at least briefly denied mailing privileges. Most were radical, Socialist, or German-language publications. Their suppression often was supported by the mainstream press, as was the internment of Japanese Americans in camps during World War II.[60]

Even during the Vietnam War, most of the press supported the military action longer than did the majority of Americans, sometimes making fun of "peaceniks" but usually reporting the war matter-of-factly. At least one newspaper refused to put antiwar rallies on its front page, and some newspapers carried a syndicated promilitary comic strip, *Tales of the Green Berets.*[61] Later, things did change as the war became more unpopular, and the news media may have reflected an antiwar bias. Television reporter Liz Trotta later wrote, "If you did twenty interviews in the field with GIs, chances were those who knocked the war would survive the editor's scissors."[62] With more recent wars, however, the press did little to oppose the government or the military effort. Flag lapel pins on anchors and flag graphics swirled about the television screen during the first weeks of the Iraq War—a war apparently based on faulty intelligence, but in which the news media did little to check administration officials' prewar claims. "The country could have profited from a much more searching examination of the so-called preemption doctrine," a *Columbia Journalism Review* critic lamented.[63] Reporters were embedded with military units and sometimes found themselves unable to "shake the sense that we were cheerleaders on the team bus," one journalist noted.[64] Another later wrote: "The result was reportage, not journalism, for there was no way to investigate and tell the complete story. The major stories of the Iraq invasion were those that the media missed: the absence of weapons of mass destruction despite purported intelligence information that they existed; the failure of the civilian and military leadership to plan for irregular warfare and for stabilizing the peace; and the existence of abuses at Abu Ghraib and other detention centers."[65] Even years after it began, television news programs regularly showed what might have been the most iconic video image of the war, footage of an apparent crowd of Iraqis pulling down a statue of Saddam Hussein. Almost none of those programs noted that the close proximity of the cameras had made the crowd look larger than it was or that the "spontaneous" event was instigated and partly conducted by the U.S. military.[66]

American media have shown a pro–status quo bias in areas outside of war coverage, as well. For example, the press generally ignored or helped promote government-promoted Red Scares of the 1920s and 1950s until Joseph McCarthy's unsubstantiated anti-communism rhetoric became too virulent to ignore. Newspapers themselves suffered during the Great Depression because of economic issues and new competition from radio, and they did a poor job of covering the national economic situation, in part to avoid hurting consumer confidence. Most newspaper publishers were and are Republicans, and the vast majority of papers opposed Franklin D. Roosevelt in his presidential campaigns. Hearst and other publishers even tried to link the president to Communists. Reporters liked the president better than their bosses did, helping Roosevelt gain support for his New Deal programs, but Roosevelt's distrust of the press helped prompt him to bypass

newspapers to talk directly to his "fellow Americans" through radio "fireside chats."[67] Later the press also was slow to cover civil
rights issues, until television images of protests and riots brought
race issues to the attention of Americans throughout the country.

One time in history in which the most important news media
might clearly have been characterized as liberal—seeking significant social and political change—was early in the twentieth century, with the progressive movement and the muckrakers. Those
journalists drew their movement's name from a speech by President Theodore Roosevelt, referring to a passage from John Bun-
yan's seventeenth-century work *The Pilgrim's Progress:* "You may
recall the Man with the Muckrake, the man who could look no
way but downward, with a muckrake in his hands; who was offered a celestial crown for his muckrake, but who would neither
look up nor regard the crown he was offered, but continued to
rake to himself the filth of the floor."[68] In words that ring true today if directed more at radio personalities, political pundits, bloggers, and interest groups than at the mainstream press, Roosevelt
also warned, "Gross and reckless assaults on character—whether
on the stump or in the newspaper, magazine or book—create a
morbid and vicious public sentiment, and at the same time act as a
profound deterrent to able men of normal sensitiveness and tend
to prevent them from entering public service at any price."[69]

Some newspapers engaged in social reform efforts, particularly
addressing social problems in major cities, but the most important
of the muckrakers worked for inexpensive popular national magazines such as *McClure's, Cosmopolitan,* and *Collier's.* Ida Tarbell,
Lincoln Steffens, Ray Stannard Baker, David Graham Phillips, and
others wrote lengthy, meticulously researched articles that brought
attention to political and business corruption and to other issues,
in what one historian calls "a bold attempt to shape reality in the

way the journalists thought it should be—by showing truth as it already was."[70] Hundreds of muckraking articles appeared during a period of just over a decade. Some of those articles prompted major reforms, including the Pure Food and Drug Act. Even so, newspapers—the other part of that era's mainstream media—were much more conservative than magazines. Many newspapers relied heavily on advertising from sometimes-dangerous patent medicines, one of the muckrakers' most important targets. Newspapers also found themselves targeted, particularly in a 1911 fifteen-part *Collier's* series.[71] Some muckrakers produced books, the most famous of which was Upton Sinclair's meatpacking exposé, *The Jungle.* Sinclair later produced one of the most notable book-length critiques of American journalism, *The Brass Check,* which compared journalism to prostitution.[72]

The most recent period in which the mainstream American news media might be viewed as more liberal than conservative came during the 1960s and 1970s. How that increased liberalism came about, and then how conservatism came back to the prominence it had achieved by early in the twenty-first century, is discussed in the following chapters.

TWO

ROOTS OF POLITICAL
RESURGENCE

At the end of World War II, relative liberalism reigned in American politics. Though Republicans almost always controlled the White House and both houses of Congress from 1896 to 1932, Franklin D. Roosevelt, the president who engineered the New Deal, was elected four times. After his death, his former vice president ended World War II with a bang to end all bangs and was on his way to narrowly winning the presidency on his own. "Our boys" were home from the war, and—after some initial problems with shortages and strikes that helped Republicans temporarily gain control of Congress in 1946—the U.S. economy was strong. Americans were buying homes and cars in unprecedented numbers, and television was about to sweep the nation. The last Republican president was remembered (largely unfairly) as the president who had led the nation into the Great Depression, and the most prominent Republicans were mostly easterners who represented the liberal side of their party. Republican conservatives viewed even the next GOP president, Dwight D. Eisenhower, as a liberal. They favored the nomination of Ohio senator Robert Taft, who narrowly lost to Eisenhower in the primary. Two years earlier, renowned literary critic and essayist Lionel Trilling had written:

> In the United States at this time liberalism is not only the dominant but even the sole intellectual tradition. For it is the plain fact that there are no conservative or reactionary ideas in general circulation. This does not mean, of course, that there is no impulse to conservatism or to reaction. Such impulses are certainly very strong, perhaps even stronger than most of us know. But the conservative impulse and the reactionary impulse do not, with some isolated and some ecclesiastical exceptions, express themselves in ideas but only in action or in irritable mental gestures which seek to resemble ideas.[1]

Trillings's quote has been repeated by numerous writers since he first penned it, but in fact the "isolated and ecclesiastical exceptions" had already planted the seeds for a new conservative revolution that would continue to grow for the next half-century. That growth has been so impressive, in fact, that a critic in recent years might have been tempted to reuse the quote, replacing each usage of "conservative" with "liberal" and vice versa. But the conservative movement was slow to be recognized—or to organize, as noted by two of some of its earliest members, Richard Viguerie and David Franke: "Grass roots anarchy would be a better description of the state of the conservative non-movement in 1955. Probably 90 percent of all Americans didn't know that these grumblers existed, even if they shared many of their gripes."[2]

Incidentally, many conservatives somewhat misremember their history. For example, Elliot Abrams, who served George W. Bush as deputy national security adviser, wrote, "It was in the McCarthy era that the iron triangle of liberal bureaucrats, a liberal press, and liberal Democrats in control of Congress was first evident."[3] In fact, in 1952 the Republicans regained control of the White House and both houses of Congress. On the other hand, conservatives considered many of their Republican brethren to be too liberal (a feeling some contemporary conservatives share about their own colleagues). "To counteract this Liberal Establishment, which conservatives believed encompassed both political parties, they deliberately created the Counter-Establishment," movement critic Sidney Blumenthal wrote years later. "By constructing their own establishment, piece by piece, they hoped to supplant the liberals."[4]

Political movements require two main elements: true believers committed to waging war—culturally, militarily, or both—even when individual battles are lost, and societal factors that make the more apathetic and sometimes fearful masses willing to go along with change. The progressive movement, the Great Depression, and two world wars provided those elements for American liberalism in the first half of the twentieth century. Attitudes and events that followed World War II provided the same elements for conservatives. U.S. prosperity and optimism were generally high after the war, making true believers especially important early on in the conservative revolution. But in some respects the timing was right for political change. Historian David Halberstam has called the period "a mean time" in which "the nation was ready for witch-hunts," while "Republican politicians had been out of power for too long, and their postwar political rhetoric had a basic purpose and tone: It was about getting even."[5] Perhaps ironically, the most important of those believers, known as the neoconservatives, defected from the liberal camp. Neoconservative founder Irving Kristol famously called himself a liberal "mugged by reality."

Even before World War II began, conservatives protested Roosevelt's New Deal policies—policies they viewed as an unwarranted and dangerous expansion of state power. ("Big government" still strikes a chord with many conservatives, even drawing complaints from many who otherwise supported the governments of Ronald Reagan and George W. Bush.) The fears about bureaucratic intrusion did not overly concern neoconservatives, however. "We were all children of the depression, most of us from lower-middle-class or working-class families, a significant number of us urban Jews for whom the 1930s had been years of desperation, and we felt a measure of loyalty to the spirit of the New Deal if not to all its programs and policies," Kristol wrote decades later. "Nor did we see it as representing any kind of 'statist' or socialist threat to the American democracy."[6]

That statist threat feared by traditional conservatives was represented by economist Friedrich Hayek, author of the 1944 book *The Road to Serfdom,* and by Russell Kirk, who wrote *The Conservative Mind: From Burke to Santayana* in 1953. Kirk later stated: "A nation is no stronger than the numerous little communities of which it is composed. A central administration, or a corps of select managers and civil servants, however well intentioned and well trained, cannot confer justice and prosperity and tranquility upon a mass of men and women deprived of their old responsibilities."[7] Incidentally, Hayek and Kirk are both often credited with breathing some life into conservatives after World War II, though as one political scientist has noted, those conservatives were "neither organized nor coherent in any real sense," though they generally shared "a commitment to local liberties and limited government."[8]

Conservatives found more allies soon after the defeat of the Nazis and the Japanese in World War II as they increasingly raised the alarm against a perceived new menace that began to stir the fears of Americans. "Unable to make headway by attacking Democrats on domestic New Deal legislation, Republicans and conservatives more and more emphasized Democratic and liberal softness on communism, both the Soviet threat abroad and subversion at home," one political scientist writes. "They in effect chose to run against the spirit and leadership of liberalism, not its economic substance, by accusing liberals of softness, even treason, on the issue of communism."[9] The chairman of the Republican National Committee said the 1946 election represented a choice between "Communism and Republicanism."[10] That year the official Republic publication, the *Republican News,* carried a front-page illustration of a Russian bear wearing Democratic donkey ears.[11] The issue became so quickly and tightly tied to the Republicans that Democrats spent decades, even through the Vietnam War, trying to prove they were not "soft" on communism (not long after the fall of the Soviet Union, conservative Republicans found political success in accusing Democrats of being equally soft on terrorism). Conservatives who previously had rejected Harry Truman's interventionist policies abroad were turned by the idea of a spreading Soviet empire. One historian notes:

> After 1947, the skeptical, noninterventionist Republican majority endorsed the Cold War, authorizing military and economic aid to Greece and Turkey, passing the Marshall Plan, developing the national security apparatus (the Central Intelligence Agency, National Security Agency, Department of Defense), and ratifying the North Atlantic Treaty Organization (NATO), America's first military alliance since an alliance with France was abrogated in 1800. Nonintervention was dead.[12]

Communism never seriously threatened the United States from within, but foreign threats loomed. China, an American ally against the Japanese in World War II, fell to a Communist government in 1949. The Soviet Union tested an atomic bomb the same year (Americans Ethel and Julius Rosenberg later were executed for helping the Soviets learn American nuclear secrets), and its reach was spreading throughout Eastern Europe. The Soviet Union was widely perceived to be seeking world domination (not long after Americans had helped the Soviets squash similar ambitions on the part of Adolph Hitler). The United States led a multinational force in stemming Communist aggression in Korea in 1950.

Whittaker Chambers and the Alger Hiss case gave American anti-Communists more ammunition on the domestic front. Called to testify before the House Un-American Activities Committee in 1948, Chambers, an editor for *Time* magazine, admitted that years earlier he had served as a Soviet spy before repudiating communism. Using language similar to that used a few years later by Wisconsin senator Joseph McCarthy (discussed in more detail in the next chapter), Chambers claimed to have knowledge of a secret cell of Communists working in the U.S. government. One of the people he named as a former Communist was Hiss, a former law clerk for famed Supreme Court justice Oliver Wendell Holmes who had served in several New Deal administrative positions. Hiss denied any Communist ties, but one HUAC member—first-term Republican congressman Richard Nixon—did not believe Hiss. The investigation was carried over to a three-person subcommittee, where Hiss and Chambers repeated their contradictory assertions. After Chambers repeated the accusation that Hiss had been a Communist on *Meet the Press* (then a radio program), Hiss sued for slander. During the slander trial, Chambers produced documents that indicated that both he and Hiss had secretly worked for the Soviets. In 1950, after two trials, a jury found Hiss guilty of perjury, and he served almost four years in prison. He continued to maintain his innocence until his death in 1996 at age ninety-two. Scholars who have since examined the case have split on the question of whether he was guilty, but anti-Communists began using his name as a rallying cry even before his conviction.[13] Though Chambers admitted his own involvement with the Soviets and the evidence clearly showed that he had perjured himself before HUAC, he was not charged. He died in 1961, and in 1984 President Ronald Reagan awarded him the Medal of Freedom, saying, "At a critical moment in our Nation's history, Whittaker Chambers stood alone against the brooding terrors of our age."[14]

Chambers hardly "stood alone," of course, as many Americans—both liberals and conservatives—participated in the nation's latest Red Scare. Reagan himself, then president of the Screen Actors Guild, became a confidential informant for the FBI in 1947 and freely testified before the House Un-American Activities Committee that same year. Asked whether he had "observed or noted within the organization a clique of either communists or fascists who were attempting to exert influence or pressure on the guild," Reagan responded, "There has been a small group within the Screen Actors Guild which has consistently opposed the policy of the guild board and officers of the guild, as evidenced by the vote on various issues. That small clique referred to has been suspected of more or less following the tactics that we associate with the Communist Party." The tactics are not described, and Reagan admitted not knowing whether any members actually were Communists.[15] But a few months earlier, according to FBI records, Reagan had gone to the agency with the names of six Screen Actors Guild members who he thought were acting like Communists and stated that he believed Congress should outlaw the Communist Party.[16]

HUAC had begun its work the year that Reagan first testified and had called numerous entertainers to appear. Some of those who refused were jailed or left the country. In 1950 *Red Channels: The Communist Influence in Radio and Television* listed more than one hundred people who supposedly had Communist sympathies. The more famous names included composer Leonard Bernstein, singer Lena Horne, poet Langston Hughes, playwright Arthur Miller, journalist Howard K. Smith, and actor/director Orson Welles. That document and other blacklists, naming more than two hundred entertainment figures in all, cost numerous entertainers their jobs. A few killed themselves. The mainstream news media cowered.[17] Even fictional tough-guy detective Mike Hammer decided to "stop chasing the garden variety of gangsters and corrupt pols and concentrate instead on stopping domestic Communist subversion."[18]

Communism provided an enemy perfect to appeal to the fears of Americans. "There was no obvious rule-of-thumb for isolating Communists by dress, customs, language, or religion; nor like Japanese-Americans during World War II, could they be rounded up and incarcerated by look," one former journalist writes. Because of that ability to blend in, for some anti-Communists, "The less evidence there was of their presence, the more obvious it was that they or their sympathizers were secretly at work in society. Declining Party membership throughout the 1950s made them more, not less dangerous."[19] Such concerns helped prompt the formation of Christian Echoes National Ministry, which produced a publication titled *Christian Crusade*. In 1957 *Christian Crusade* began offering "intelligence reports" about supposed Communist influence in American churches. The following year, ardent anti-Communist Robert Welch formed the far-right John Birch Society, which would go so far as to accuse Republican president and

World War II hero Dwight D. Eisenhower of Communist sympathies. Postwar communism also provided a strengthened focus for the American Legion, which lists as one of its purposes to "perpetuate a one hundred percent Americanism."[20] The organization's newsletter, *Firing Line,* in the 1950s was devoted almost exclusively to fighting communism at home and "to supply[ing] Legionnaires with solid facts on all aspects of the complex and highly deceptive problem of domestic subversion."[21]

The ability to link the Soviets with godlessness also helped draw support for anti-communism and to build bridges that would strengthen the conservative movement as a whole. "The Communist vision is the vision of Man without God," Chambers argued.[22] For conservative writer William Rusher, Chambers's 1953 book "expressed, as well as it is ever likely to be expressed, the fundamental clash between communism and the root principles of Judaeo-Christian civilization. *Witness* made it brilliantly clear why a thoughtful individual might well devote his life to resisting the triumph of communism."[23] The American Legion effort and *Christian Crusade* provided two examples of the link between Christians and anti-communism. Another was the *Christian Anti-Communism Crusade News Letter,* which began to appear in the mid-1950s. Founder Frederick Charles Schwarz testified before a congressional committee in 1957 that Communists "planned to take over the United States by 1973, not by destroying but by utilizing American factories, schools, and other property."[24]

Oddly, several former Communists besides Chambers led much of the attack against communism, while becoming the forerunners of the neoconservative movement. "They underwent a complete political transformation and yet remained the same," one critic noted. The former Communists "changed from true believers into true believers. They became crusaders against what had been the object of their passionate devotion. Still, they retained their desire for total victory."[25] Irving Kristol widely is viewed as the godfather of the neoconservative movement and apparently was the first self-described neoconservative, but New York University philosophy professors Sidney Hook and James Burnham shared many of the same ideas and preceded him. Like Hook and Burnham, Kristol was a former Communist who became disenchanted with communism, then adamantly opposed it. He was part of a group of people who, in the words of one historian, were "twice alienated—first from the norms of white middle-class life in America, with its dominant Protestant values, and, second, from the religious life of their Jewish parents." Yet they also had "a lust for ideas and a craving to make a mark on the world of thought," a craving that they first fulfilled with ventures into socialism and communism.[26] Two other New York Jews, Norman Podhoretz and Nathan Glazer, also helped shape and define the neoconservative movement. Podhoretz edited *Commentary* magazine and wrote books, doing "as much as anyone to give neoconservatism its notoriety."[27] Glazer became a sociologist at the University of California—where he encountered and rejected the free speech movement—and then at Harvard. He also helped edit *Commentary* before joining Kristol as coeditor of the *Public Interest*.

While neoconservatives joined paleoconservatives in battling communism, the neocons still considered themselves to be liberals (and often Democrats). William F. Buckley also became friends with Chambers, but he never considered himself to be anything other than a conservative. Buckley became one of the most important figures in a rising conservative resurgence at a young age. In 1951, a year after his graduation from Yale, he published *God and Man at Yale,* a critique of the liberal faculty and administration at his alma mater. The book was mentioned in *Time, Newsweek, Life,* and other publications and quickly found favor with conservatives—even more so after some liberals attacked it. One offended Yale trustee wrote in the *Saturday Review of Literature* that the book "is one that has the glow and appeal of a fiery cross on a hillside at night. There will undoubtedly be robed figures who gather to it, but the hoods will not be academic. They will cover the face."[28] Four years later, at the age of twenty-nine, Buckley became co-founder, primary stockholder, editor in chief, and publisher of a new conservative publication, *National Review* (discussed further in chapter 6). Like the neoconservatives, Buckley opposed communism; unlike the neoconservatives, he focused heavily on traditionally libertarian concerns. A member of a wealthy family, he considered the capitalism versus communism argument to be more important than the democracy versus communism conflict.

Buckley, Chambers, Hayek, and Kirk were among several authors whose books helped motivate and stimulate conservatives. *McCarthy and His Enemies,* written by Buckley and L. Brent Bozell, and Burnham's *The Web of Subversion* both appeared in 1954. James J. Kilpatrick's *The Sovereign States* came out in 1957, followed two years later by Buckley's *Up from Liberalism.* Reaching a wider audience than any of those political philosophers, fiction writer Ayn Rand popularized libertarianism with *The Fountainhead* in 1943 and *Atlas Shrugged* in 1957. Those books and various magazines (discussed further in chapter 6) provided a voice for conservatives, even if they were mostly talking to each other. A number of dedicated conservative organizations appeared, including the American Enterprise Institute, Americans for Constitutional Action, Young Americans for Freedom, and the Intercollegiate Society of Individualists. The groups and publications helped hold together conservatives until a string of other volatile social factors, combined with a bitter defeat for a favorite conservative candidate, arose to provide rallying points for conservatives and to worry even mainstream Americans who paid much less attention to politics.

The candidate upon whom many conservatives placed their best hope for political revival was Barry Goldwater, a plainspoken Arizona senator whose 1961 book *The Conscience of a Conservative* (written largely by Bozell) sold millions of copies. Besides his willingness to confront liberalism, as a westerner, Goldwater was outside of the more liberal northeastern hierarchy that controlled the Republican Party. Phyllis Schlafly wrote a best seller titled *A Choice Not an Echo* that supported Goldwater's presidential campaign, and Goldwater quickly became the conservative choice to battle "eastern liberal" Nelson Rockefeller for the Republican nomination in 1964. Goldwater entered the race reluctantly, spurred by a "draft Goldwater" movement that began in 1961. By the time he won that battle, however, he knew he would not face another Eastern liberal in the presidential race: John F. Kennedy had been assassinated, and Texan Lyndon Johnson would be the Democratic nominee. Goldwater had given up his Senate seat to run for the presidency but was reelected to the Senate four years later.

In part because of his perceived extremism coupled with an abrupt nature, Goldwater carried only 39 percent of the vote and six states—his own, and five southern states—in the presidential election. Still, his campaign did demonstrate a number of positives for conservatives, including the fact that a substantial part of America identified with the conservative message and that they could win control of the Republican Party. "On any serious accounting, 1964 was the most important and truly seminal year for American conservatism since the founding of *National Review*," one conservative later wrote. "Before 1964, conservatism was at best a political theory in the process of becoming a political movement; after 1964, and directly as a result of it, conservatism increasingly became the acknowledged political alternative to the regnant liberalism—almost fated, in fact, to replace it sooner or later."[29] Among other things, Goldwater's campaign launched the political career of Ronald Reagan (discussed in chapter 4). It brought new voters into the party, and thousands of Goldwater's supporters found their names on mailing lists that in the future would be used to revolutionize political campaigns (discussed in chapter 5).

Outside of the obvious political realm a number of social factors also were beginning to help conservatives, at least in the long run. Civil rights became an important national issue, especially after the Supreme Court's 1954 decision in *Brown v. Board of Education*. Until the decision, most American newspaper readers might have been justified in thinking their nation's people were monochromatic. Newspapers not only ignored race issues, they almost entirely ignored nonwhites. On the rare occasions that blacks made the papers, usually in crime stories, they were identified by race. At least one southern newspaper ordered its photographers not to shoot photos of blacks; African Americans were cut from crowd shots. *Brown* showed that almost one hundred years after the Civil War, the United States remained a divided nation. So did its newspapers: most northern newspapers supported the Supreme Court decision, while southern papers overwhelmingly opposed it. Southern states also continued to fight or sometimes ignore the *Brown* decision until federal troops arrived to enforce it. Northern journalists poured into the South to cover civil rights events and often found themselves viewed as part of the enforcement mechanism of integration—a justifiable view to some extent because many of those reporters apparently viewed themselves that way. At the very least, their prointegration sympathies were clear.

A few journalists staged photos to make the situation seem even more dramatic.[30]

Unfortunately, when the American press began to cover race issues, it usually did so in terms of conflict. School districts in which integration proceeded smoothly drew less attention than the locations where violence seemed possible. Besides, plenty of conflict existed. Some of the most dramatic pictures on television and in newspapers showed crowds of enraged whites screaming at badly outnumbered young blacks who wanted to attend school. Civil rights leaders began to stage demonstrations that would draw cameras, and Americans throughout the country saw African Americans attacked with dogs, rocks, fists, and fire hoses. For middle-class citizens of a postwar nation, many of whom lived in the suburbs or small towns and believed that the United States had settled into a bucolic land of plenty, nightly news coverage of civil rights clashes provided harsh evidence that all was not well in America. The clashes forced federal officials to act and brought new civil rights legislation, but not all of the underlying issues were resolved. Some school districts still were trying to avoid or overturn integration almost fifty years later, and large numbers of white southerners began sending their children to private schools.[31]

The most important new legislation was the 1964 Civil Rights Act proposed by John F. Kennedy and signed into law by Lyndon Johnson after Kennedy's assassination, followed the next year by the Voting Rights Act. The bills abolished the Jim Crow laws of the segregated South, outlawing discrimination based on color, race, religion, sex, or national origin. New laws applied to schools, public facilities, housing, and job hiring, outlawing "whites only" restaurants and hotels. The Civil Rights Act also angered many southerners, including some in the Senate who staged an eighty-three-day filibuster, the longest in Senate history, to try to block the bill. West Virginia Democrat Robert Byrd and two other Democrats joined twenty-one southern Republicans and five others—including Goldwater, who was about to become the Republican presidential nominee—in an unsuccessful attempt to prolong the filibuster. Democratic senators Byrd, Albert Gore Sr. of Tennessee, and J. William Fulbright of Arkansas voted with other southern Democrats against the final version of the bill, but 73 percent of senators and 70 percent of the House of Representatives passed it. The passage had an important political effect that has continued even with recent elections. The Republican Party denounced the law at its 1964 national convention, and the South, once solidly Democratic, began to shift toward the Republicans. Though most African Americans had favored Democrats anyway, the margin widened to the point where Ronald Reagan apparently became only the second Republican presidential candidate (Goldwater was the first) not to bother making a direct appeal to black voters.[32] After becoming president, Reagan continued to offer little to African Americans, with one critic going so far as to write:

> The Reagan Administration's policies on affirmative action exemplify the "new racism." Despite that Administration's pro-civil rights rhetoric, its policies rolled back both the practice of affirmative action and the enforcement of civil rights laws. In addition to opposing affirmative action, the Reagan Administration initially supported tax exemptions for the private, segregated academies set up in the South to avoid legally mandated integration in the public schools. It supported South Africa at a time when U.S. Blacks and others were urging a boycott of its apartheid regime. It opposed school busing, a strong Voting Rights

Act, and the celebration of Martin Luther King, Jr.'s birthday as a national holiday.[33]

Regardless of Reagan's feelings two decades later, there is no denying that many of the 1960s opponents of the Civil Rights Act were racists. Many cities, including the nation's capital, boasted numerous neighborhood associations that existed primarily to "protect" their neighborhoods from integration. Even so, other conservatives based their opposition on other issues. States' rights proponents argued that the federal government had no business involving itself so heavily in the affairs of individual states, regardless of how pure the motives of federal legislators might be. Even some who supported the civil rights movement opposed what many liberals saw as logical expansions of the Civil Rights Act: Johnson's Great Society initiatives that led to welfare, affirmative action programs, and school programs that bused some black children away from their own neighborhoods into white neighborhoods while busing some white children to schools in black neighborhoods. "If a man finds himself saving less money, he may not know enough to blame the government; but when a school bus comes to cart his kids across town, he knows exactly who the villains are," one conservative later wrote.[34] Some even argued that busing was used as a means of keeping children away from their homes for longer periods of time, decreasing the potential influence of parents.[35] Goldwater apparently worried about the rise of affirmative action and a resulting increase in bureaucracy. He agreed with other traditional conservatives that a potential socialistic redistribution of wealth might result and argued that civil liberties were a local affair. However, partisan politics rarely deals in complexities, and conservatives often felt they were characterized unfairly regardless of their motivations. "It was a defining moment in American history," one avowedly conservative historian writes. "Because the leader of the conservative movement voted against major civil rights legislation, albeit for constitutional reasons, conservatives have been tarred ever since as racists and bigots."[36]

Of course, part of that criticism came after the presidential election of 1968, when Nixon used his now-famous Southern Strategy to win the presidency. The plan is visible in a 1969 book, *The Emerging Republican Majority,* by Kevin P. Phillips, a Nixon campaign strategist who has been called "by far the most influential of the New Right theoreticians."[37] Phillips recognized that conservative power was shifting to the South, the West, and to some degree the Midwest.[38] Conservative writer M. Stanton Evans had noted some of the same themes while predicting increasing conservative strength in *The Future of Conservatism,* published in 1968.[39] Critics called Nixon's strategy cynical race-baiting, none more strongly than Democratic presidential candidate Howard Dean in 2004, when he said Nixon had won the White House "in a shameful way—by dividing Americans against one another, stirring up racial prejudices and bringing out the worst in people." Dean said other conservatives, especially Ronald Reagan, have copied Nixon's strategy to expand the power of the Republican Party.[40] Some Americans, including at least one Nixon aide, saw no particular problem with a largely divided America. "The Little Italys, the Chinatowns, the Irish, Polish, Jewish and other ethnic communities of the nation's cities are not social problems," wrote Patrick Buchanan. "The social problem crying out for relief is the existence of a minority of zealots, with disproportionate power, who will not desist from using government to coerce people into involuntary social associations they do not want."[41] Conversely, when they perceived immigration from Mexico and Latin Amer-

ica to be a threat four decades later, many of those same people favored legally making English the "official language" of the United
States.

The passage of the 1964 Civil Rights Act did not end racial conflict in America. Just a year later, the Watts section of Los Angeles exploded into flames as rioting killed more than thirty people
and injured more than one thousand others. Hundreds of build-
ings were destroyed, and almost four thousand people were arrested. The front page of the *Los Angeles Times* proclaimed: "21,000
Troops, Police Wage Guerrilla War."[42] Other American cities also
experienced 1960s race riots, brought to the nation via television. Not all of the coverage was well received. "With its insatia-
ble appetite for live drama, television turned the riots into some
kind of Roman spectacle," one critic wrote. "Not only did television exacerbate an already inflammatory situation, but also, by
turning the riots into a Happening, may also have helped prolong them."[43] Numerous journalists since have been criticized for
helping prolong events ranging from demonstrations to international terrorism.[44]

Brown v. Board of Education angered some southern conservatives. But a 1962 Supreme Court decision infuriated Christian
conservatives throughout the country, while further increasing
private school enrollments. *Engel v. Vitale* ruled that a government
could not compose even a "voluntary" prayer for public school
students to recite. Many Christians viewed the decision as a move
to "push God out" of the schools and, especially after other decisions broadened the prayer restriction, as an attack on their values,
as one history of conservatism notes:

> Religious conservatives took for granted school prayer at athletic
> events and pastoral sermons at baccalaureate services until they

suddenly had the rug of religious security pulled from beneath them. Since many of these people believed that America was founded on Christian principles, they saw these actions as hostile to the very core of their national experience. . . . Conservatives contended that the very nature of the Judeo-Christian tradition was the explanation for why the American public developed as it did.[45]

At about the same time as the school prayer decision, an old issue came back to reinvigorate Christians. The teaching of evolution has always offended many Christians with a more fundamentalist view of the world, and at various times in history those concerns have become more visible. One such period came during the 1920s, highlighted in 1925 by the so-called Scopes Monkey Trial, in which a Tennessee jury convicted a teacher of violating state law by teaching evolution. Clarence Darrow defended teacher John Scopes, while three-time Democratic presidential candidate William Jennings Bryan represented the state.[46] Evolution opponents got another boost in the early 1960s from Henry M. Morris, an engineer with a literal interpretation of the biblical book of Genesis. He and seminary teacher John C. Whitcomb Jr. wrote a 1961 book titled *The Genesis Flood,* and Morris helped found the Creation Research Society in 1963. The book "was probably the most significant creationist work since the 1920s for a simple reason: It looked scientific," one historian has noted.[47] After the Supreme Court once again offended conservative Christians by tossing out an Arkansas antievolution bill in 1968, creationists began to demand equal time for creationism—sometimes euphemistically labeled scientific creationism, creation science, or, in recent years, intelligent design. In other words, they said, teachers should be required to devote as much discussion to creation as to lessons about evolution.

Further definition of church-state issues also frustrated Christians. Copies of the Ten Commandments came down from public classroom walls, and religious displays were banned from town squares.[48] As they became more politically involved, Christians faced the possibility of having their churches and religious schools lose tax-exempt status. Even so, the recognized political involvement of Christians was fairly negligible until the 1970s. Many viewed political involvement as a waste of time, or as a corrupting, unchristian influence. Outside of religious programming, the most visible Christians on American television screens were liberals engaged in civil rights protests, voter-registration drives, and antiwar activities—Christians practicing a "social gospel" that had contributed to a split in American Protestantism.[49] More extreme were the "Jesus freaks," a segment of the 1960s hippie movement. As for conservative Christians, they tended to agree with Baptist minister Jerry Falwell, who proclaimed in 1965 (as a critique of Martin Luther King Jr. and other civil rights activists) that preachers were "not called to be politicians, but soul-winners."[50] The values of evangelical Christians, one historian writes, "stressed individual salvation and the futility of attempting to improve the world through social action."[51]

Social action became the answer, however, with a Supreme Court decision that did more than anything else to bring Christians into political activism: *Roe v. Wade* in 1973. The decision granted women nationwide the right to first-trimester abortions. It also brought conservative Protestants—who as recently as 1960 had worried about the election of a Catholic president, and who traditionally had distrusted the Catholic Church—into an alliance with conservative Catholics. "Those who regularly attended church, particularly Catholics and Baptists, regarded the fetus as a living child. Abortion was murder," one historian notes.[52] *Triumph,* a monthly Catholic publication, published its next issue with an all-black cover and every page bordered in black "in funereal acknowledgment of the unborn who would be killed as a result of this decision."[53] Members of the three-million-member Missouri Synod of the Lutheran church testified before a House of Representatives subcommittee in seeking a repeal of *Roe*. Hundreds of antiabortion groups popped up throughout the country.[54] Even some liberal legal scholars questioned the decision, which many considered to have been wrongly decided by an activist court. Some said the court had allowed itself to become overly politicized with *Griswold v. Connecticut* eight years earlier, when it found a "right of privacy" in the Constitution to justify striking down a Connecticut law that banned contraceptives. "The Warren Court operated on the principle of first deciding what is right and what is wrong, and then finding a constitutional pretext for doing good works," conservative writer George Will wrote about the *Griswold* decision.[55] The *Roe* case drew much more heat.

Incidentally, neoconservatives generally supported the civil rights movement, considered themselves to be liberals, and usually voted as Democrats. But as moral issues began to concern Christians, those same issues also appealed to neoconservatives. Kristol wrote: "It was primarily the neoconservative criticism of welfare for corrupting the souls of its recipients, as against the traditional conservative emphasis on the waste of taxpayers' money, that helped make welfare reform a major issue for religious conservatives. Similarly, the troubled condition of the modern family was a concern of both secular neoconservatives and Christian conservatives, before it became a popular conservative topic."[56] Other family and social issues, including the increasing acceptance and popularity of pornography and the sexual revolution made possible in part by the arrival of the birth-control pill in the 1960s, also strengthened the ties among various branches of conservatism while drawing increased support for their cause.

The women's movement was already well under way by the time of the *Roe* decision. The Civil Rights Act established the Equal Employment Opportunity Commission, which immediately began to hear workplace complaints from women. The complaints apparently had little impact at first, and the commission granted exceptions such as one that allowed newspapers to advertise jobs by gender.[57] For example, a typical newspaper ad (listed under HELP WANTED—MEN) read: "Six-day, afternoon paper, not afraid to tackle real depth reporting, needs a *man* who wants to direct reporters who do more than skim the surface. Not a job for a faint-hearted news*man* afraid to use a copy pencil. Right salary for dedicated news*man*"[58] (emphasis added). Even so, one university journalism department chairman noted that in 1965, close to half of journalism students were women, compared to "six or seven to one" just fifteen years earlier. "Journalism may be losing its manly spirit," he complained, while predicting that the trend would continue. "They won't go away; they're women," he argued. "Any officer who has worked with women in uniform, regardless of rank, knows that most of them need a male colleague looking over their shoulders or available for such duty on short notice. Journeyman reporters who have covered a story with a woman know the pattern."[59] Women did not "go away," of course; they continued to gain influence—not always with the blessing of conservatives. As late as 1986, one leading conservative magazine noted: "Women are running for office in record numbers. The good news is that most of the best ones are Republicans."[60] The reader is left to wonder if the first sentence constitutes the bad news.

The National Organization for Women was founded in 1966. A few women's liberation publications began to appear in the early

1970s. Feminists staged a 1970 sit-in at the offices of the *Ladies' Home Journal,* which as a result agreed to turn over eight pages of its August issue to the activists. Gloria Steinem brought feminism to the masses with *Ms.* magazine in 1972. "The strength of this new 'magazine for women' was its ability to be both a women's magazine, which had a place on the battlefield with existing women's magazines, and a resource within the women's movement, a mass circulation text that could connect women to a national community of feminism," one historian notes.[61] In 1972 Congress passed the Equal Rights Amendment, which stated simply, "Equality of rights under the law shall not be denied or abridged by the United States or by any state on account of sex." Thirty-eight states then needed to pass the amendment for it to be made part of the U.S. Constitution, and twenty-two did so the same year, followed by eight in 1973, three in 1974, and one in 1975.[62]

By then, conservative opposition had arisen. Phyllis Schlafly, the political activist mother of six who in 1964 had written *A Choice Not an Echo* supporting the presidential campaign of Barry Goldwater, led much of the opposition to the amendment. Congressional passage of the ERA prompted Schlafly to start a national organization, Stop ERA (which in 1975 became Eagle Forum), to fight what she called "the principle legislative goal of the radical feminists."[63] A Catholic, she involved evangelical Protestants and Orthodox Jews in the effort. She devoted numerous issues of her monthly newsletter, the *Phyllis Schlafly Report,* to the ERA, arguing that the 1964 Civil Rights Act already protected women from discrimination and that the ERA could not guarantee equal pay but that it would strip women of rights they already had. She and her supporters claimed the ERA might deny spousal support for women, allow women to be drafted, increase abortions (and require federal funding of them), and lead to unisex restrooms and same-sex marriages. Women's rights became identified with liberals and Democrats, despite the fact that the Democratic Party failed to include a plank favoring an equal rights amendment in its national convention platform until 1972, the same year in which Congress passed the ERA. Meanwhile, nine consecutive Republican convention platforms, from 1944 to 1976, included statements favoring equal rights for women (the 1980 GOP platform did an about-face, maintaining that the Equal Rights Amendment violated traditional values).[64] Many of feminism's critics considered the women's movement and *Roe v. Wade* to be inseparable.

An even more tenuous connection may have been the relevance of equal rights for women to same-sex marriages, but linking the two touched on another recent fear that had arisen for conservative Christians. Homosexuals, once less visible to most Americans even than African Americans, became visible in the 1960s. A gay subculture had existed in American cities for at least two decades by that time, and although President Dwight D. Eisenhower issued a federal order banning homosexuals from holding government jobs, most Americans barely knew homosexuality existed. Most gays remained hidden, or "in the closet." The news media generally ignored the issue until what became known as the 1969 Stonewall Riot triggered the beginning of the U.S. gay rights movement. Police regularly raided gay bars, but when New York police hit the Stonewall Inn to enforce a liquor license violation, some patrons—including several drag queens, or men dressed as women—attacked the police officers. "Queens, princesses and ladies-in-waiting began hurling anything they could get their polished, manicured fingernails on.... The war was on," reported the tabloid *New York Daily News.*[65] The more reserved *New York Times* stated, "Hundreds of young men went on a rampage . . . after a force of plainclothesmen raided a bar that police said was wellknown [*sic*] for its homosexual clientele."[66] Street demonstrations continued for several days, and the alternative newspaper the *Village Voice* concluded one of its first Stonewall articles with: "Watch out. The liberation is under way."[67] The incident led to the formation of several gay and lesbian organizations, some of which worked to become more visible in the press. In 1973 the American Psychological Association voted to declassify homosexuality as a mental illness, and many states decriminalized homosexual behavior, to the consternation of social conservatives (though not all conservatives, some of whom believed that laws against homosexual behavior represented an unconstitutional state intrusion).

A final social and political factor that helped motivate some conservatives was the Vietnam War—especially the opposition to it, which stirred anti-Communist and pro-American sentiment. Television and newspaper pictures of protests and hippies burning draft cards contributed to feelings that some liberals were unpatriotic and that America might be spinning out of control. Mainstream journalists joined in criticizing the liberal activists. One reporter wrote about working "under cover" as a "peacenik," taking part in "demonstrations against the war in Viet Nam, against poverty and against 'police brutality.'"[68] His twelve-part series ran in more than fifty newspapers around the country. In 1970 National Guardsmen shot and killed four Kent State University students during an antiwar demonstration, and police officers killed two students during a demonstration at Jackson State College.

Liberals in particular mourned when Robert F. Kennedy and Martin Luther King Jr. both were assassinated in 1968, and that year's Democratic Convention in Chicago erupted in widely televised violence. Still, a *Chicago Tribune* editorial that year captured the feelings of many conservatives about the entire period of the

1960s and 1970s, while managing to blame the deaths of King and Kennedy on parental permissiveness and rising liberal tolerance for drugs, coed dormitories, immodest dress, and free speech movements—signs that "moral values are at the lowest level since the decadence of Rome."[69]

THREE

THE FADING OF REFORM JOURNALISM

Besides the political reasons discussed in the previous chapter, some critics cite the supposedly liberal nature of the press as one reason for the rise of conservatism. According to that argument, conservative activism came partly as a reaction to the excesses of the liberal media. For example, magazine publisher William Rusher wrote: "Prior to 1964 there were only three avenues of national communication in extensive use for political purposes: the major television networks, the major newsmagazines, and (arguably) one or two newspapers that commanded national attention. With exceptions that do nothing to modify the essential point, all of these avenues were under liberal control."[1] Despite those claims and the fact that the press provides a convenient and easily identifiable scapegoat, little evidence exists for such an argument—unless "liberal" simply means more liberal than the critics. Though the mainstream press did become more liberal in some ways than it had been in the past, so did America as a whole. Where the majority of public opinion leads, the press typically follows. Regardless, shifts in the news media, even the liberal shifts, probably benefited conservatives far more than liberals.

Conservatives sometimes criticize the news media for engaging in crusades, trying to improve on the status quo while simultaneously undermining authority. Yet journalists recognize that some authority deserves to be undermined. Many in the press see their primary role as that of watchdog, protecting an often-unappreciative public from the potential excesses of government, corporations, or other institutions. Typical American citizens have neither the time nor resources (nor, unfortunately, the interest) to participate directly in most of the institutional decisions that impact their lives. They must rely on the press to keep them informed about what they should know so they can choose to act when and if they must.[2] Incidentally, conservative newspapers have been at least as likely as others to engage in critical investigative journalism. Despite a somewhat atypical stance opposing the death penalty in recent years, the *Chicago Tribune* has long been considered one of the most important conservative voices in the country. It once carried the front-page slogan "The American Paper for Americans." Yet even before most other newspapers regularly engaged in investigative reporting, the *Tribune* regularly used its editorials to congratulate itself for uncovering abuses in city government. An editorial page credo ran almost daily for about forty years beginning in 1962, stating: "The newspaper is an institution developed by modern civilization to present the news of the day, to foster commerce and industry, to inform and lead public opinion, and *to furnish that check upon government which no constitution has ever been able to provide*" (emphasis added).[3] Besides referring to its credo, the newspaper also sometimes referred to itself as "a watchman on the wall."[4] *New York Times v. Sullivan* was resolved in 1964 in favor of the *Times,* giving the media the right to cover public officials more vigorously with a significantly reduced threat of facing libel charges. The decision prompted the *Chicago Tribune* to join other newspapers around the country in expressing pro-watchdog sentiments.[5] The 1960s *Tribune* agreed with the *Seattle Post-Intelligencer,* which editorialized, "Without the ceaseless vigilance of independent watchdogs, without the right to criticize, expose and admonish, no free press is worthy of the name."[6]

Despite their editorial expressions of glee over support for the watchdog function of the press, before the 1960s most of the news media did little to fulfill that function.[7] During most of the first half of the twentieth century, newspapers mostly tried to cover events as they happened, sticking to facts about the events. When conflict arose, reporters dutifully reported claims from both sides of the conflict, rarely going so far as to investigate the issues themselves or to try to explain to readers the significance of the issues. That began to change after World War II, as a new "war"—the cold war—gained political and social prominence. Though newspapers tended to reflect the same fears about communism that were expressed elsewhere in society, interpretive reporting began to gain in popularity. "For many editors, interpretation seemed to go hand-in-hand with clearer, simpler writing as a means to make a complex world understandable," one historian writes.[8] Of course, one reporter's interpretation may differ from the perspectives of critics on both sides of an issue. Another problem is that most journalists lack expertise in many of the things they cover, increasing the possibility of misinterpretation.

Largely because of the cold war, the government became more secretive at the same time that increasing bureaucracy was making government functions increasingly complicated. Then Wisconsin senator Joseph McCarthy began engaging in a dishonest early 1950s anti-communism crusade, claiming that "Reds" had infiltrated the State Department, the military, and the press. Because McCarthy's claims—almost all unproven—were so dramatic, and because he was a U.S. senator, the news media reported the claims. They sometimes doubted the veracity of the statements, but "felt trapped by the journalistic conventions that required them to report every charge, no matter how outrageous."[9]

To escape the trap, some reporters turned to increased interpretation. CBS newsman Edward R. Murrow was best remembered for exposing McCarthy, even before the popular 2005 movie titled *Good Night, and Good Luck*. But Murrow was far from the first to question the senator's motives. The *New York Times,* the *Washington Post,* the *Christian Science Monitor,* the *Baltimore Sun,* the *Milwaukee Journal,* and the *Oregonian* all frustrated McCarthy at times because of their coverage before Murrow's famous broadcast, and Murrow himself believed he should have taken on the senator sooner. By the time he did, McCarthy's theatrics in the nation's first televised Senate hearings had already turned many Americans against him. Many conservatives—and many newspapers, for that matter—were more critical of the questioning press than of McCarthy.[10] Senate colleagues censured McCarthy, but his fellow Republicans split evenly on the censure resolution. Conservatives outside the Senate also had mixed emotions. "He may have been a demagogue, they felt, but he was *our* demagogue," one avowed conservative later wrote about feelings in the 1950s. "After all, Communism is so much worse."[11] Some conservatives—including Irving Kristol, who would become the first self-described neoconservative—called McCarthy a "vulgar demagogue" and strongly disagreed with McCarthy's tactics but still thought liberals were worse.[12] World War I hero Eddie Rickenbacker predicted that someday the country would erect a monument to McCarthy, and the late senator remained a hero to some conservative groups. "For most of these groups, McCarthy is a martyr and liberalism is evil because, so they say, it leads to socialism, which leads to communism," one reporter wrote in 1962.[13]

Three other factors in the middle decades of the twentieth century contributed to increased interpretation in mainstream newspapers: television, literary journalism, and alternative newspapers. Even before almost all of America's afternoon newspapers died and twenty-four-hour cable news arrived newspaper editors realized that they could not keep up with the immediacy or visual impact of television news. However, they could offer much more depth than television and greater understanding of events through interpretation. Some of those distinctions disappeared later, as television reporters also began increasingly to rely on interpretation. Also, as technology helped prompt more and better print photos, newspaper stories became shorter.[14]

Literary journalism was mostly a magazine phenomenon of the 1960s and 1970s, but it helped blur the lines between news and entertainment. Writers such as Joan Didion, Thomas Wolfe, Norman Mailer, and John McPhee wrote stories, often in first-person narrative, to discuss social problems through the eyes of individuals affected by those problems. They immersed themselves in their stories rather than maintaining the distance common to newspapers, and they used popular fiction techniques such as plot, pacing, and dialogue (sometimes re-created or imagined).[15] Though newspaper feature writers rarely went to the lengths that the literary journalists did, their writing did become looser. News features became more common, as did historical and political context. In addition, critics lumped newspapers with the magazines that commonly employed literary journalism. For better or worse, all were considered part of "the media." And from the perspective of conservatives, it usually was worse.[16]

Even more troubling for conservatives and for many involved

with mainstream newspapers was another relatively new part of the media: the alternative press, especially the so-called underground press. It gained attention at about the same time as literary journalism. Offset printing made publication much cheaper and easier than the use of hot lead printing, and smaller publications were among the first to take advantage of the new technology. Because of the social turmoil of the period—and, notably, because of liberal activists' frustration with being shut out of what they perceived to be the conservative mainstream media—many of those activists started their own publications. Hundreds or thousands of alternative newspapers appeared during a socially tumultuous period of little more than a decade. The Vietnam War was the most popular topic, but issues such as racial equality, women's rights, law enforcement, environmental issues, legalization of marijuana, and the conservatism of mainstream news media also drew significant attention from the upstarts.[17] Like conservatives, liberals also felt that their concerns were ignored or given only cursory, typically critical attention. One syndicated writer for alternative publications captured the general feeling of liberals at the time when he wrote, "Big-city dailies are a corrupt advertising medium; they've forfeited their right to be called newspapers."[18]

Alternative newspapers most irritated many Americans because of how much attention those papers paid to sex, drugs, and rock music. Some editors were arrested on pornography charges, and many of the publications relied heavily on sex-oriented advertising (at the time, many daily newspapers accepted advertising for adult movie theaters, which also angered conservatives). Some also turned to pornographic editorial content. Most did not last long, but some of the more serious and better-funded publications did hang on for a few years. New York's *Village Voice* and the *Texas Observer* still survive. Other notable alternative publications included the *Berkeley Barb,* with a circulation of eighty-five thousand readers, and the *Los Angeles Free Press,* which lasted a decade and boasted a top circulation of ninety thousand readers. The *Free Press* once published the names of all known narcotics officers in Los Angeles, San Francisco, San Diego, and Santa Ana.[19]

Mainstream newspapers sometimes denigrated and mostly ignored the alternative papers, but the newcomers did push other newspapers into paying more attention to some issues. Sometimes alternative papers uncovered problems that larger publications then followed up on, and some mainstream reporters used the alternative papers to keep track of counterculture ideas and activities.[20] The increased attention played into complaints about the liberal media. As well-known conservative commentator Patrick J. Buchanan complained, "It is the big media which serves as the publicity arm for the movements of liberalism and the left— i.e., civil rights, consumerists, environmentalists, women liberationists—at the expense of the concerns and issues raised by the right."[21] The complaint may have some merit, if mainstream media were following the lead of the alternative publications; after all, liberals produced almost all of the upstarts. Still, the "concerns of the right" clearly were less newsworthy than those of the left simply because journalists rarely cover *ideas* from any perspective, and liberals' concerns were more likely to involve *events* such as protests, riots, and lawsuits. The nation was in social turmoil on a variety of fronts, and most of the new concerns stemmed from liberal concerns about issues such as the Vietnam-era draft and equality for women, African Americans, and homosexuals. Unable to ignore those issues, the press found itself in a can't-win situation: it was covering them too much for the liking of conservatives, too little for liberals. Unfortunately, the lack of coverage of ideas also meant that protests and riots were covered in spot-news fashion, with relatively little examination of why the events took place. "The more militant the demonstration, the more extreme the protest, the more belligerent the form of dissent, the greater the likelihood it will be aired on the evening news," Buchanan pointed out.[22] One result was that the protests and demonstrations seemed more widespread than they actually were, with one conservative writer maintaining, "The number of students who ever demonstrated or marched or could by any public act have been taken to be 'radical' or 'hippie' never exceeded 2 percent."[23] Though others estimate higher figures—former Supreme Court nominee Robert Bork claimed that radicals "made up two-thirds of the student body" at Yale while he was there, making life "close to intolerable"—the fact is that even most young Americans were not engaged in public protests.[24]

Concerns about equality also spread to the press in another way. Editorial staffs were overwhelmingly male and glaringly white, a fact that became more obvious when the news media tried to cover civil rights issues. In 1952 mainstream newspapers employed a total of twelve black reporters and editors. Even after an effort to increase those numbers, fewer than two hundred African Americans worked on the editorial staffs of the nation's 1,749 newspapers in 1968. Fewer than 2 percent of that year's journalism majors were black, about one graduate for every seven newspapers in the country.[25] Women fared little better, particularly in comparison to their population. Some were hired and made up about 10 percent of the *New York Times'* six-thousand-person editorial staff. None of those women were editors or managers, however, and in 1974 a group of them filed a lawsuit, *Boylan v. New York Times,* in an attempt to gain such jobs. The so-called liberal *Times* settled the lawsuit four years later, just before it went to trial. Other news organizations also faced lawsuits over their exclusion of women and minorities during the same period. Not surprisingly, broadening the representation of those who could be reporters and editors also broadened definitions of news. Poverty, child care, birth control, the growing women's movement, and other issues became more newsworthy and were addressed more often and more seriously than they would have been with all-male, all-white editorial staffs. And television news began to look different, with women and minorities showing up for the first time at TV news desks.[26]

Interestingly, in recent years conservative Christians have claimed that they are underrepresented in newsrooms. They call for an increase in the number of avowedly Christian reporters, especially for religious stories. "If the news industry of this country were really interested in promoting diversity it would mean placing more emphasis upon religion, hiring reporters who have taken the time to learn their beat, even hiring as journalists graduates of divinity schools and religious studies programs, and insisting upon accurate and truly balanced reporting," writes one former reporter who now works for a conservative political organization. "Otherwise, the news industry is just handing us a line about their interest in 'diversity.'"[27]

To some degree, Christians who make such calls may have a point. After all, the news media found that their failure to employ African American journalists meant they could not adequately cover the civil rights movement, and definitions of news changed somewhat when newspapers and broadcast stations hired more women and minorities. Still, in the 1960s, the lack of minority and women reporters was obvious, while many reporters were (and are) Christians or were brought up in Christian households. Besides, seldom if ever do conservative Christian calls for increased religious diversity include demands for more Muslims, Jews, Hindus, or Buddhists in newsrooms. Nor do they tend to address the fact that even Christians of various denominations, or even within denominations, strongly disagree about some of the most potentially inflammatory issues in the news, such as abortion, gay rights, school prayer, and justifications for war.

Much to the dismay of many conservatives, the press probably reached its high point in terms of credibility during the turbulent 1970s. It did so for a number of reasons, beginning with the fact that Americans trusted their government less and sought new sources of institutional authority. Journalists also trusted government less. Though those who worked with John F. Kennedy liked the president, they tired of Kennedy's lies. Kennedy officials "managed" the news, blatantly lied to the press about the botched Bay of Pigs invasion in 1961, and criticized the media for failing to support the administration's cold war activities.[28] Lyndon Johnson's administration officials later lied about various aspects of the Vietnam War, and then President Richard Nixon, who had promised in 1969 to start withdrawing American troops, escalated the war the following year. Then came the Pentagon Papers case in 1971.

The forty-seven-volume report that became known as the Pentagon Papers revealed that American leaders had consistently misled Americans about the Vietnam War. By that time most of the public had turned against the war. Among them was historian Daniel Ellsberg, a Defense Department analyst who helped write part of the report. Ellsberg secretly copied most of the report and turned it over to the *New York Times,* which in June 1971 began a series based on the report. Claiming that the report could harm national security, the Justice Department asked the newspaper to stop publication of the series and then after publication of the third installment persuaded a court to grant a temporary restraining order halting further publication. The *Washington Post* and other newspapers obtained copies of the Pentagon Papers and also were prohibited from running articles. Just fifteen days after the injunction was filed, however, the Supreme Court decided in favor of the newspapers. The articles began to run anew, proving dishonesty on the part of government officials and winning the *New York Times* the Pulitzer Prize for Public Service.

Editorial writers throughout the country generally praised the court decision, though not all accepted the idea that the press could now freely attack government. Even the conservative *Chicago Tribune* supported the decision, though it also supported the administration's action to protect secret documents and criticized the Nixon administration for attempting "to defend the indefensible efforts of prior administrations."[29] While the Pentagon Papers series was not itself an example of investigative reporting because Ellsberg simply handed over a report after he and others compiled it, the incident did help spur an increase in investigative reporting at all levels. Other factors also contributed to the increase. Local investigative reporting became a Pulitzer Prize category in 1964 (though until 1970 only two winners in the category investigated organized government wrongdoing, while during the 1970s almost every winner did so).[30] National investigative reporting focused heavily on government. In one 1974 story, Seymour Hersh reported in the *New York Times* that the CIA "conducted a massive, illegal domestic intelligence operation during the Nixon Administration against the antiwar movement and other dissident groups in the United States," and that the agency maintained files "on at least 10,000 American citizens."[31]

Government actions actually helped journalists conduct more investigations. The 1966 passage of the Freedom of Information Act instituted the Federal Public Records Law and made investigation of the federal government somewhat easier. Though the

first court ruling under the law went against the press, later journalists would regularly use Freedom of Information requests to
pursue and uncover stories.[32] By the mid-1970s, Congress and every state had enacted open-meetings laws. Government agencies
tended to keep better records than private organizations, and new
open-records laws meant government organizations could keep
fewer of their records from journalists and the public. Comput-
ers became increasingly valuable, especially for *precision journalism,*
which relies heavily on statistics and social science research methods. For example, a 1968 *Miami Herald* series detailed high crime
rates, low arrest rates, and possible prosecutorial biases against
blacks and the poor. In another example the same year, the *Detroit
Free Press* won a Pulitzer Prize when it used survey data to better explain Detroit riots. Many reporters learned to compile and
analyze databases of information such as tax records, census data,
criminal records, and legal decisions.[33]

Concerns about press freedom and the issue of confidential sources helped prompt the 1970 formation of the Reporters
Committee for Freedom of the Press, an organization for working journalists who might face legal problems. The organization's
steering committee included several well-known national print
and broadcast journalists. In 1977 the group began publishing *News
Media and the Law,* one of a spate of publications devoted to press
issues to appear during the 1960s and 1970s. The Poynter Institute
was formed in 1975 to offer training for journalists and journalism teachers. The same year, a small group of journalists formed
Investigative Reporters and Editors (IRE), a national organization for investigative reporters. The Christian Church (Disciples
of Christ), which had actively supported freedom of information,
and a Lilly Endowment Grant helped fund the organization. A
year later, members from around the country descended upon

Phoenix, Arizona, to investigate the death of *Arizona Republic* reporter and IRE founding member Don Bolles, who died after a car bombing. Dozens of journalists from ten newspapers and television stations spent five months investigating the political corruption that led to Bolles's death, and many newspapers around the country published part or all of the resulting twenty-three-part series.[34]

In addition to considering the faults of those in government and other institutions, the press also examined its own behavior. News organizations and other donors funded the National News Council (modeled partly after the still-surviving Minnesota News Council) in 1973 to investigate complaints against the news media. The large Gannett media chain and CBS strongly supported the national council, but several news organizations refused. They included the *New York Times,* the *Wall Street Journal,* the *Chicago Tribune,* and the American Society of Newspaper Editors. Though it opposed the council, the *Chicago Tribune* joined the *Washington Post, Boston Globe,* and *Seattle Times* in adding ombudsmen or "reader's representatives." However, most newspapers did not. The ombudsman typically serves as a liaison between the newspaper and its readers, investigating reader complaints and then reporting in the newspaper what reporters or editors had done right or wrong.[35]

Even before the arrival of computer databases, other technological advances improved reporting and contributed to the rise in investigative journalism. Thanks to the arrival of fully automated photocopy machines, by the 1960s reporters and their sources could easily duplicate documents. Reporters found the cassette-tape recorder much more useful than bulky reel-to-reel machines. Technological improvements, new laws, *New York Times v. Sullivan,* and the Pentagon Papers case all made journalists more confident in taking on government. One result was that the Supreme Court decided more key First Amendment cases during the 1970s than during any other decade in American history. A more visible result for most Americans made two young *Washington Post* reporters famous while bringing down a president: Watergate.

The *Post* reported in a June 18, 1972, front-page story that five men had been arrested in a plot to bug the Democratic National Committee offices. Reporters Bob Woodward and Carl Bernstein, both younger than thirty years of age, ran their first story about the case the following day, noting that one of the burglars was "the salaried security coordinator for President Nixon's reelection committee."[36] The *Post* continued to run stories about the incident in the following months, though the stories had no apparent impact on Nixon's landslide reelection. Most newspapers had endorsed him in 1968, and even more did so in 1972. Nixon easily won reelection. He failed to win over one group, however: the working press. The largest newspaper employees' union, the Newspaper Guild, broke a forty-year tradition of neutrality to endorse Nixon's opponent in 1972. Nixon and the press distrusted each other throughout his political career. His own lack of charisma made him particularly vulnerable to journalists who were gaining more recognition of their own power. *Newsweek* magazine focused on the conflict with a 1973 cover story. Nixon once responded to a tough question from CBS newsman Dan Rather with, "Are you running for something?" Rather replied: "No, Mr. President. Are you?"[37] Few conservatives openly supported Nixon as his involvement with Watergate became clear, but the conflict between the president and the media prompted some conservatives to question the motives of the press in its Watergate coverage, even suggesting, "Many in the news media were hypocritical in their reaction to the crime . . . because reporters and columnists regularly used stolen information on grounds of the public's right to know, just as . . . those planning the Watergate burglary acted in the interest of national security."[38] In truth, those who planned and covered up the burglary did so far more because of partisan politics than because of national security concerns, and though most conservatives agreed that Nixon had to go, some were most disturbed by factors other than the crime involved. "While conservatives cared little that Nixon had bugged the Democrats' Watergate headquarters, they were disturbed about other moral lapses," one historian notes. "Nixon's foul language, captured on tape in all of its teamster-wannabe glory, destroyed his reputation among conservative clergy."[39]

In a preview of press difficulties to come, the Nixon administration used various ways to drive a wedge between the people and the media. Vice President Spiro Agnew and Senator Robert Dole led the attack, with Dole making veiled threats about not renewing the licenses of stations that criticized the administration. In one of his better-known quotes, Agnew once referred to journalists as liberal "nattering nabobs of negativism." Those who offended the administration could find themselves left off of the press plane for future trips. Nixon also tried to bypass reporters to talk directly to the American people through regular televised addresses, even as Watergate became a bigger issue in the media— and then through two nationally televised sets of congressional hearings. Nixon complained about the amount of time the media had devoted to the subject and about what he said were sensationalized reports. After it eventually became clear that Nixon had lied, he resigned in August 1974. The reporting of Woodward and Bernstein won the *Washington Post* a Pulitzer Prize.[40]

Though television news was beginning to slide into triviality in many respects by the 1970s, ABC countered the trend after

Iranian students took over the American embassy in Tehran and held fifty-two Americans hostage for 444 days. ABC soon began a series of nightly updates, hosted by Ted Koppel, immediately after the nightly news. On its 142nd day, the title of the program became *Nightline*. The constant coverage hurt Jimmy Carter's presidency, but *Nightline* became an American late-night institution with what the *Christian Science Monitor* called "the thinking man's alternative to late network viewing."[41]

Unfortunately, by the time *Nightline* aired, American journalism was fading in both its willingness to take on authority and in terms of credibility. Many factors contributed to the fade of reform journalism, including attacks from the Right, the rise of Ronald Reagan, and increasing emphasis by media organizations on business and entertainment. Some of those factors are discussed in more detail in later chapters, but other issues also played a role. For example, even other journalists did not always trust or respect alternative publications or literary journalism. When mainstream journalists began to use some of the same techniques, such as more analysis and more literary writing, they appeared to be less objective. In addition, views of their objectivity undoubtedly suffered among conservatives because so much investigative journalism seemed to target Republican administrations—an inevitable result of having those administrations in power for six of the past nine four-year terms. Besides, few outside of the extreme right of the political spectrum could argue that Bill Clinton, a Democrat more conservative than Richard Nixon in many respects, got a pass from the news media during his two terms. Inevitable tension exists, or should exist, between the news media and those in power, as perhaps illustrated by John F. Kennedy's pithy quote about his own relationship with the press: "I am reading more and enjoying it less."[42]

In truth, investigative journalism began to decline in relative frequency and quality after the mid-1970s partly because some mainstream news organizations became timid. Cowed by lawsuits, California news organizations left the investigation of Synanon, a religious cult, to the tiny *Point Reyes Light* (which won the Pulitzer Prize for Public Service in 1979). The federal government went to court in 1979 to prevent *Progressive* magazine, a leading American alternative publication for seventy years at that time, from running an article about the hydrogen bomb (with the inflammatory and somewhat misleading title, "The H-Bomb Secret: How We Got It; Why We're Telling It"). Many newspapers—including the *Washington Post,* which had helped drive Nixon from office just five years earlier—immediately sided with the government, despite the fact that no one outside of the government and the magazine knew what the article included. [43] "Rarely has the press been so reluctant to join an issue where its First Amendment protections are in danger," *Newsweek* noted.[44] *Progressive* editor Erwin Knoll was blunter. "Many of the mass media (though not all) proved themselves pathetically eager to support Government censorship," he later wrote. "Their notion was that the First Amendment stopped where 'national security' began."[45] The *Progressive* case demonstrated that even defining journalism had become problematic.

The press also caused itself other problems. Thanks to its success, it had become an influential authoritative institution—one that had spent much of its time teaching Americans not to trust institutions. Many Americans now considered the news media to be too powerful. For its part, the press did a generally poor job of self-protection. Failing to recognize that readers and viewers do not typically hold the same regard for a press watchdog function as do journalists, the media consistently have failed to adequately explain the importance of that function to readers. News media often appeared too defensive, with few hiring ombudsmen. The National News Council lasted just over a decade. Some newspapers began hiding their codes of ethics, afraid they might be used in court.[46]

As many in the news media became more skeptical about the political process, the tone of their stories began to change. Instead of letting partisan sources set the tone (positive, negative, or neutral), journalists did so, and that tone increasingly was negative. Television sound bites (the on-air bits of candidates' speeches) grew progressively shorter, from an average of more than half a minute in 1968 to about ten seconds two decades later. As they took more control over the message, journalists appeared more confrontational and sometimes arrogant. Because the press could not check all of the claims made by authorities—and often did not bother to check the ones they could—journalists turned to politicians' political opponents to counter claims. The result was what one political scientist called "news based on attack and counterattack." Unfortunately journalists also sometimes didn't bother contacting the opponents, instead expressing their own "unsubstantiated and unattributed refutations."[47] Even investigative journalism was viewed as too negative, with investigative journalists considered among the "chief disseminators of cultural pessimism."[48]

Tired of what they perceived as negativity by the media, Americans blamed the messenger. Most thought reporters cared more about getting good stories than about the possible harm to individuals. Constant exposure may have made it more difficult for Americans to separate isolated news incidents from the possibility of personal harm in their own lives, as demonstrated by the fact that even as crime rates went down, fears about crime went up. Some critics suggested changing the First Amendment or placing other restrictions on the media, and some argued that the press would do more good by assuming a supportive role rather than an adversarial one.[49]

Americans wearied of investigative journalism in part because too much of that journalism involved questionable methods. By the early 1980s anonymous attribution littered most network news stories and newsmagazine stories and much of the news carried by newspapers and wire services.[50] Even more controversial, though popular among many news organizations, was the use of hidden cameras or blatant deception. In 1978 the *Chicago Sun-Times* bought and operated a bar and then used hidden cameras to document the corruption of payoff-seeking city employees. Television new magazines later used hidden cameras to track the behavior of dishonest service workers or salespeople and then confronted the alleged wrongdoers with tape of their activities. The resulting stories cheapened investigative journalism by using questionable methods to uncover small-scale corruption by individuals with little actual power, rather than to reveal more important institutional wrongdoing. Later, ABC newsmagazine *Primetime Live* even faced a lawsuit over the issue when it sent producers with hidden cameras to work undercover at Food Lion supermarkets. The supermarket chain sued the show and ABC for trespass and fraud, and a federal jury awarded Food Lion $5.5 million. Many people, including many journalists, questioned using illegal acts as anything other than a last resort. Though most editors agreed with readers and viewers who said they opposed secretly recording sources, neither journalists nor the courts agreed on hard-and-fast standards, and as hidden devices became smaller and cheaper, their use continued to grow.[51]

Some journalists further hurt the credibility of their profession by going beyond questionable behavior to misrepresentation or outright lying. CBS settled out of court with General William Westmoreland, former commander of U.S. military forces in Vietnam, over a 1982 broadcast titled *The Uncounted Enemy: A Vietnam Deception* after the general claimed that the program distorted facts. A year later, *Time* settled with an Israeli official who said the magazine falsely implied that he encouraged a Lebanon massacre. The most famous case involved *Washington Post* reporter Janet Cooke, whose invented 1980 story about an eight-year-old heroin addict won a Pulitzer Prize. In later years, writers for major newspapers also plagiarized other publications or invented details. Some cameramen staged photos and passed them off as reality. Some of those incidents helped prompt the Society of Professional Journalists to amend its code of ethics to call plagiarism dishonest and unacceptable. It did not define plagiarism, however, and even editors disagreed about what constituted wrongdoing.[52]

Readers and viewers faced with media deception might have been tempted to ask journalists, "What were you thinking?" After 1979, they could: *Herbert v. Lando* established that a reporter's "state of mind" could be used in determining libel liability. Reporters might be asked to identify sources or turn over interview notes or tapes. Many editors became more careful and worried more about libel. Their fears were justified: one survey reported that two-thirds of newspapers were sued at least once between 1975 and 1981, and though the news media almost always won, libel suits could be expensive to defend and drew negative attention. Journalists had further reason to worry a few years later, after President Ronald Reagan appointed William Rehnquist, the justice considered least friendly to the First Amendment, as chief justice in 1986.[53] As chief justice, Rehnquist sided with government in First Amendment cases more frequently than his two most recent predecessors.[54]

Journalists were not entirely to blame for their problems, far from it, in fact. In addition to the existing critics who long had been eager to find philosophical wrongdoing by the press, new organizations arose during the 1980s to call attention to perceived media faults. Few of the new critics had the media's best interests at heart, and though they tended to call their activities nonpartisan, some were more obviously political than were journalists. The politically conservative Accuracy in Media (AIM) had been around since 1969, and in 1986 it was joined by the politically liberal Fairness and Accuracy in Reporting (FAIR). Both organizations "studied" the press to back their claims that the mainstream media were politically biased, though naturally the two organizations disagreed on whether that bias was liberal or conservative. In 1987 came the conservative Media Research Center (often called nonpartisan by conservatives), with the slogan "Bringing Political Balance and Responsibility to the Media." Less obvious in its political orientation but providing another critical voice was the research-oriented Center for Media and Public Affairs, founded in 1985. As attacks increased, individuals and organizations found it increasingly easy to blame the news media for a host of problems.[55]

Recent world events highlight the importance of another factor that unfairly hurt the credibility of the press: the view heavily promoted by conservatives that the press somehow helped "lose" the Vietnam War. In fact, the press probably covered the Vietnam War better than any other war involving American troops, and most of the mainstream media supported the war longer than most Americans who watched it on their television screens. But the realities shown by that coverage, coming night after night at a time before cable news options, did not help the administration or its war efforts. One dramatic example came in 1965 when viewers saw American soldiers using their lighters to burn down 150 houses. An enraged President Johnson called CBS News president Frank Stanton to demand, "Frank, are you trying to fuck me?" *New York Times* reporter David Halberstam infuriated Presidents Kennedy and Johnson with his coverage, and Kennedy ordered the CIA to check the reports for accuracy. In 1969 the *Cleveland Plain Dealer* and *Life* magazine ran stories and photos from My Lai, where American soldiers killed hundreds of Vietnamese civilians. Photos of a monk who immolated himself in protest, a young girl running after being hit by napalm, and the on-street assassination of a Vietcong suspect became iconic images of the war. Besides nightly news reports, the networks aired numerous Vietnam-related documentaries and hearings, some of which questioned U.S. policy. The news media regularly reported heavy and demoralizing death tolls in Vietnam and showed protest rallies at home. Eventually Walter Cronkite, America's most-trusted newsman, told Americans that the war seemed "mired in stalemate."[56] While the press coverage undoubtedly contributed to negative feelings toward the war, most scholars have concluded that the media had little or nothing to do with the outcome or with public opinion. As one historian noted simply, "Body counts mattered more than television."[57]

Another factor that hurt the press was a shifting emphasis of priorities in covering political news. The news media found it easier—and more popular among readers and viewers—to focus more on personalities than on procedures, especially when conflict or scandal was involved. For example, during the 1972 New Hampshire Democratic primary, front-runner Edmund Muskie appeared to cry while responding to a newspaper article that questioned his wife's mental health, and after widespread coverage of "Muskie's tears," his campaign faltered. In the same election, the press discovered that Democratic vice presidential candidate Thomas Eagleton had been treated for nervous exhaustion years before. The ensuing press coverage forced Eagleton to withdraw his candidacy.[58]

Those already in office also found that their private lives became newsworthy. For better or worse, politicians' alcohol use and sexual activities previously had been largely ignored by the press. But the *New York Times* and the *Washington Post* both reported when Congressman Wilbur Mills, chairman of the powerful House of Representatives' Ways and Means Committee, was arrested for drunken driving and a stripper ran from the car (police had to pull her from Washington's Tidal Basin). Two years later, another congressman would find himself in hot water after the *Post* reported: "For nearly two years, Rep. Wayne L. Hays (D-Ohio), powerful chairman of the House Administration Committee, has kept a woman on his staff who says she is paid $14,000 a year in public money to serve as his mistress. . . . 'I can't type, I can't file, I can't even answer the phone,' says Elizabeth Ray, 27, who began working for Hays in April 1974 as a clerk."[59]

As politicians found themselves embarrassed by news coverage about their sex lives, critics faulted the press for failing to explore and explain more serious political issues. "The crucial ingredient, it seems, is scandal—corporate, political, or personal," former senator J. William Fulbright wrote in 1975. "Where it is present, there is news, although the event may otherwise be inconsequential. Where it is lacking, the event may or not be news, depending in part, to be sure, on its intrinsic importance, but hardly less on competing events, the degree of controversy involved, and whether it involves something 'new'—new, that is, in the way of disclosure as distinguished from insight or perspective."[60]

Election stories began focusing more on election strategy than

on policy, while relying more on public opinion polls conducted by the media themselves. Those two "horse-race" trends continue. The increased reliance on polls ended up creating a cycle in which candidates who received the most media coverage
tended to do well in polls, and then poll front-runners, viewed
as the most credible candidates, received the most coverage. At
the same time, front-runners tended to get more negative coverage than trailing candidates received, which may have made races
closer and therefore more newsworthy. Polling provided plenty of
news, created by the news media themselves, but may also have
changed the electorate. "Americans used to read the newspaper to
help them form their opinions," media scholar Leo Bogart noted.
"Now newspapers and television tell them what their opinions
are."[61] Some publications generally gave presidential candidates
more favorable than unfavorable coverage, but in 1980 the coverage became primarily about bad news. Television news focused
on the positive for a bit longer, though its perspective also would
change. Meanwhile, the number of adults who said they read a
daily newspaper dropped from almost 78 percent in 1970 to fewer
than 64 percent by 1985.[62]

By the end of the 1970s Americans held the mainstream media
in the same low regard that they had for most politicians, be those
politicians liberal or conservative. Unlike the new media, however,
political conservatives had a cowboy riding in from the sunrise to
help save the day. Ronald Reagan would promise "morning in
America." Liberals and those who valued an adversarial press experienced a definite shift to "mourning in America."[63]

FOUR

REAGAN'S CULTURAL REVOLUTION

While Americans had relatively little respect for the media by the end of the 1970s, they also disdained politics and politicians. After the Watergate scandal forced Richard Nixon to resign, Vice President Gerald Ford—whom Nixon had appointed after Spiro Agnew resigned because of income tax charges—angered many by pardoning Nixon for any crimes he may have committed. Even before Watergate, Nixon had alienated many of his former conservative supporters by strengthening ties between the United States and the Communist regimes of China and the Soviet Union.[1] Of course liberals never liked Nixon. Though the pardon may have been a courageous act on Ford's part, critics viewed it as just another political backroom deal. It helped cost Ford the 1976 presidential election.

President Jimmy Carter then found himself faced with high inflation and an energy crisis, and he consistently failed to engender optimism that things would improve. His most memorable speech became known as the "malaise" speech, though that particular word came from the news media, not from the speech. In the July 1979 address, Carter reported that he had spent ten days speaking to all kinds of Americans, which "confirmed my belief in the decency and the strength and the wisdom of the American people." However, he immediately followed up those words with, "But it also bore out some of my longstanding concerns about our Nation's underlying problems."[2] He then seemed to blame the people for many of the problems they faced:

> I want to talk to you right now about a fundamental threat to American democracy. . . . The threat is nearly invisible in ordinary ways. It is a crisis of confidence. It is a crisis that strikes at the very heart and soul and spirit of our national will. We can see this crisis in the growing doubt about the meaning of our own lives and in the loss of a unity of purpose for our Nation. The erosion of our confidence in the future is threatening to destroy the social and the political fabric of America. . . . In a nation that was proud of hard work, strong families, close-knit communities, and our faith in God, too many of us now tend to worship self-indulgence and consumption. Human identity is no longer defined by what one does, but by what one owns.[3]

The speech actually boosted the president's approval ratings temporarily, but two days later Carter asked for the resignations of his entire cabinet and other senior staffers—thirty-four people in all. He then accepted five of the resignations. Four months later came the Iranian hostage crisis. (The hostages were released the day Ronald Reagan became president.) Throughout most of the 444-day ordeal, *Nightline* host Ted Koppel reminded nightly viewers of how long the crisis had lasted, intoning, for example, "It's the 357th day of America held hostage."[4] Then, in 1980, three years after irritating conservatives by telling a Notre Dame commencement audience that communism was not the serious threat it once had been, Carter frustrated many Americans by refusing to let U.S. athletes participate in the Moscow Olympics after the Soviet Union invaded Afghanistan.[5] Things became so bad that he faced the indignity of having to fend off a challenge from the more liberal Senator Ted Kennedy during the 1980 primaries. "Three quarters of all the criticism hurled at the president during the election season came from Kennedy and the Left," one historian notes. "Consequently, the GOP could afford to ignore Carter as he bled from Kennedy's knifing."[6] Incidentally, four years earlier Carter had benefited from the fact that Reagan drew support from conservatives while mounting a primary challenge of Ford, the sitting president of his own party.

Carter was widely viewed as a decent man but an inept, micromanaging president. There was little chance he would do much to stem the conservative political tide. "What made Jimmy Carter and much else possible was Watergate," argued a *National Review* editorial. "Carter will be seen historically as essentially an interim figure, something that was stuffed into a crack in the wall. . . . Carter was an aberration, historically considered, and with Reagan the anti-liberal revolution got back on the tracks and rolled once more."[7] Actually, Carter aided that revolution through more than his failures. Reagan became known for deregulating various industries, but Carter signed bills (pushed heavily by the liberal Senator Ted Kennedy) that deregulated airlines and interstate trucking.[8] Carter was more socially conservative than Ford, the Republican he replaced, and more conservative than his opponents in the Democratic primaries.[9] While running for president in 1976, the former Georgia governor freely admitted being a "born-again" Christian, and most white evangelical Christians voted for him. He then managed to anger those same evangelicals enough that most voted against him in 1980.[10] As conservative as he was personally, his politics left critics feeling betrayed. The Christian Right thought it knew what to expect from Carter. His evangelical Christianity was "*presumed, rightly or wrongly,* to carry with it a community of views on certain questions directly relevant to the particular religious commitment: support for the sanctity of marriage and the 'family values' in general; opposition to abortion; opposition to the use of drugs (and perhaps even alcohol); concern over the growth of pornography and sexual promiscuity; etc."[11] In fact, Carter differed from many Southern Baptists in that he did not believe in a literal interpretation of the Bible and believed religion and politics should be largely separate. He would not allow his personal religious beliefs to determine judicial appointments, and he supported the Equal Rights Amendment. The three-city (Baltimore, Minneapolis, and Los Angeles) 1980 White House Conference on Families let more than 1,500 delegates "examine the strengths of American families, the difficulties they face, and the ways in which family life is affected by public policies" but ended up—after battles between liberal factions and newly mobilized but outnumbered religiously conservative "pro-family" factions—supporting the ERA, abortion, and gay rights.[12] Perhaps most responsible for fraying ties with evangelical Christians was the IRS, under Carter's administration, beginning to examine the tax-exempt status of private schools—most of them Christian schools—more closely.[13] All of those factors combined to make conservative Christians look elsewhere for support, even if it meant turning to a divorced former Hollywood actor. "In the end, the Religious Right might never have emerged if Jimmy Carter's success had not prepared the ground for the evangelical entry into national politics," political writer E. J. Dionne Jr. wrote. "Carter's failure, in turn, allowed the Religious Right to emerge as Evangelicalism's loudest voice."[14]

Interestingly, while Carter kept religion and politics too separated for some of his critics, some Christians managed to tie an odd array of political issues to their faith, as perhaps best illustrated by a history of Christian broadcasting published by the National Religious Broadcasters (written by one of its members). Among more obvious faith-based reasons, a section explaining why evangelicals turned against Carter offers the following: "The president signed away the Panama Canal, recognized the Chinese communist regime of Mao Tse-tung, and offered arms concessions to the Soviet Union. Taxes were raised. New federal regulations tied business in knots."[15] The relevance of those issues to Christianity may be fuzzy, but they touched on obvious longtime concerns for traditional conservatives who joined with the Religious Right to finally put unabashed conservatism in "the promised land" of the White House. Conservatives rejoiced and liberals bemoaned that a Reagan presidency would mean, in one historian's words, "cutting benefits to poor people, lowering taxes for the wealthy, increasing the military budget, filling the federal court system with conservative judges."[16]

Some of those conservatives had envisioned a Reagan presidency since the seeming debacle of the 1964 Barry Goldwater defeat. The most inspirational speech of the Goldwater campaign came not from the candidate, but from the president of the Screen Actors Guild. Titled "A Time for Choosing," for many conservatives the nationally televised late-October address came to be known simply as "the Speech." Reagan noted that he had once been a Democrat and warned about a growing national debt and the "welfare state." He said Americans should be able to "opt out" of Social Security and compared the Johnson administration to socialism. He called the fight against communism in Vietnam a "war with the most dangerous enemy that has ever faced mankind in his long climb from the swamp to the stars." (Antievolution conservative Christians apparently ignored the bit about the "climb from the swamp" when they became Reagan supporters.)[17] The speech also offered the kind of stirring patriotic rhetoric that would later mark Reagan's presidency:

> If we lose freedom here, there is no place to escape to. This is the last stand on Earth. And this idea that government is beholden to the people, that it has no other source of power except to sovereign people, is still the newest and most unique idea in all the long history of man's relation to man. This is the issue of this election. Whether we believe in our capacity for self-government or whether we abandon the American revolution and confess that a little intellectual elite in a far-distant capital can plan our lives for us better than we can plan them ourselves.
>
> You and I are told increasingly that we have to choose between a left or right, but I would like to suggest that there is no such thing as a left or right. There is only an up or down—up to a man's age-old dream, the ultimate in individual freedom consistent with law and order—or down to the ant heap of totalitarianism, and regardless of their sincerity, their humanitarian motives, those who would trade our freedom for security have embarked on this downward course.[18]

Reagan spoke with the practiced air of someone who had spent years as a radio broadcaster, an actor, and a product pitchman. He had starred on television's *General Electric Theater* during the 1950s and served as a General Electric (GE) spokesman for eight years. He spoke at GE plants around the country and for numerous civic organizations. "His speech was always the same," recalled his publicity director. "He had it polished to perfection.

It was old American values—the ones I believe in, but it was like the Boy Scout code, you know, not very informative. But always lively, with entertaining stories."[19] GE was a conservative corporation, and Reagan peppered the speech with probusiness, antiregulation, antitax, and anti-communism views that appealed to local chambers of commerce. With some of those same themes, "A Time for Choosing" focused less on Goldwater the candidate than on conservative ideals—a focus perhaps to be expected for a relative "new believer" such as Reagan. A longtime Democrat whose father had been saved from destitution by the New Deal's Works Projects Administration, he became a conservative after becoming involved with the political struggles of the movie business. "Reagan was a premature neoconservative," one longtime observer wrote. "Like the neoconservatives, he first became personally disillusioned with the left and then attributed the world's fall to the left's activities and programs."[20]

After the Goldwater speech, for some conservatives Reagan immediately "seemed a more reasonable conservative advocate than the Republican presidential candidate."[21] He returned to the Old West set of *Death Valley Days,* the television program he hosted, but other conservatives immediately began discussing the idea of Reagan as California governor. Two years later, he ran against two-term Democratic governor Pat Brown. Reagan supporters found that along with his traditional views toward business and communism, he also appealed to so-called "values" voters at a time when those concerns were relatively new on the political front. "People do not know what they ought to think about relations between the sexes, about relations between parents and children, about relations between the citizen and government," Irving Kristol wrote during Reagan's gubernatorial campaign. Because of a national "crisis in values," Kristol suggested that numerous

California fathers "find Ronald Reagan's rhetorical emphasis on the traditional values quite appealing."[22] Reagan defeated Brown to become one of five new Republican governors elected in the West (Arizona, Nevada, New Mexico, and Alaska also replaced Democratic governors with Republicans), and within a year Reagan was being promoted as a future presidential candidate. While some traditional conservatives believed that an actor would never be a viable candidate, others recognized Reagan as the right man at the right time. One leading conservative author wrote in 1968, "[Reagan] projects the aura of excitement that has become so essential a part of the American process; he is skilled in the use of the electronic media, perhaps more effective on television than any other extant politician; he has the free and easy style necessary to the age, but combines it with a careful attention to the quality of his rhetoric."[23] Critics were less enamored with the rhetorical quality: "The typical Reagan speech was a mixture of hokum, bunkum, flapdoodle and balderdash of the type dished out daily by motivational speakers, along with mashed potatoes and turgid chicken breasts, at countless business luncheons in the Marriotts, Hyatts and Hiltons of America," one wrote years later.[24] Two years after becoming governor, Reagan ran a weak presidential campaign and was then reelected governor two years later. He left office in 1974 and ran against Ford in a close but unsuccessful 1976 bid for the GOP presidential nomination. After the loss Reagan spent the next couple of years hosting a weekly radio program, giving speeches for other GOP candidates, chairing a political-action committee that raised money for Republicans, and putting many of those Republicans politically in his debt.[25]

Reagan benefited from the fact that cable television had not yet exploded on the scene. Though a few cable stations were available in the 1970s, CNN did not arrive until 1980, and most cable programming came later. As a result, if Americans were watching television during the campaigns, more of them saw coverage of the candidates than in any election since. For example, more than 70 percent of viewers saw a 1980 Reagan-Carter debate, compared to fewer than 40 percent who tuned in to watch George H. W. Bush debate Michael Dukakis eight years later.[26] More than eighty million people watched the Reagan-Carter debate, eighteen million more than watched a "highly rated" George W. Bush–John Kerry debate in 2004.[27] More accustomed to dealing with the cameras than his political opponents were, Reagan rarely forgot that he was the star of his own show. When a debate moderator tried to quiet him before the 1980 New Hampshire primary, Reagan gave newscasters the evening's best sound bite—and himself an immediate boost in the polls—by barking, "I'm paying for this microphone." His main opponent, George H. W. Bush, sat stiffly and stared straight ahead as if watching his own presidential dreams pass ghostlike through the back wall of the room (he later became president after two terms as Reagan's vice president). In a debate with Carter, the most memorable line was Reagan's "There you go again," though apparently few noticed that he then declined to address Carter's point. Four years later, when the issue of age came up in a debate with Walter Mondale, the seventy-three-year-old Reagan drew the largest laugh when he promised, "I am not going to exploit, for political purposes, my opponent's youth and inexperience."[28]

Aided by a largely compliant press, Michael Deaver and other key Reagan staffers mastered the art of media politics. They adopted and tried to adhere to a "theme of the day." They worked to develop focus group–tested "power phrases" that could be used repeatedly in speeches. "When these power phrases are discovered, of course, they are timed to fourteen and one-half seconds to ensure getting them on the evening news shows," one rhetorical scholar noted.[29] Reagan and key staffers offered numerous briefings to friendly out-of-town reporters, while ignoring the regular White House press or burying them with press releases about trivial subjects. In part because of fears that Reagan might misspeak, the president's handlers rarely made him available to the media. He held fewer press conferences than any predecessor since Calvin Coolidge, and Reagan was happy to be seen mostly through rehearsed speeches and through "pseudo-events" and photo ops—staged events that attracted news photographers who were told where to stand. Reagan announced during his first term that he would not answer questions during photo opportunities, prompting one journalism scholar to note that the White House photo op had turned into "nothing short of press agentry, no different from the Hollywood publicity stunt that Reagan mastered so many years before."[30] Like John F. Kennedy, he let cameramen follow him on vacation, where they shot photos of the president riding horses and chopping wood.[31] (George W. Bush would later pursue an almost identical vacation strategy on a Texas ranch that he had purchased while campaigning for president, though his ride of choice was a pickup truck or mountain bike, and he preferred a chain saw to an ax. Bush's activities prompted one liberal commentator to write: "In the 1980s, America watched a B-movie actor become a President. Today, it seems things are reversed: We are watching our President become a B-movie actor."[32])

Perhaps the best example, and the best sign of things to come, came with Reagan's first inauguration. For the first time, the inaugural ceremony was held at the scenic West Front of the Capitol building, looking out on the mall, where Reagan could point out various monuments. But simply pointing out the monuments to illustrate his patriotic themes was not enough for a television age. Reagan's people also "helped" the news media by providing an advance script so that prearranged camera shots could be called forth to illustrate his mentions of the Washington Monument, the Jefferson Memorial, the Lincoln Memorial, and so on. Reagan and his aides knew what local television news had discovered a few years earlier: "talking heads" are boring, while the right pictures can say more than words—even if the pictures say something entirely different. An example of that point came when a CBS program criticized Reagan for some of his policies, but the story was illustrated by pictures that portrayed the president in a flattering light. The Reagan camp appreciated the story.[33] "Putting spin on the day's news, particularly the evening network television news, was the administration's top priority," one historian writes. "The White House obsession with influencing daily stories, especially television reports, combined with the already skeptical post-Watergate press attitude to create constant press-administration tension."[34] The degree of that tension varied. Journalists complained that the administration simply ignored legitimate requests for information and instituted various measures to eviscerate press freedom, including lie-detector tests for federal employees suspected of leaking information, cuts in the release of statistical information, and "attempts to gut the FOIA [Freedom of Information Act]."[35] A 2000 American Society of Newspaper Editors timeline notes that the Reporters Committee for Freedom of the Press documented more than three hundred attempts under Ronald Reagan and George H. W. Bush to limit press and public access to information.[36] Though at least one study found that the first-year television coverage of Reagan and each of his successors was negative by a nearly two-to-one ratio, some critics complained that Reagan received the gentlest press treatment of any modern president. For example, Mark Hertsgaard interviewed members of the Reagan administration and the media and reviewed every evening newscast from the three major networks during most of Reagan's two terms, concluding that the press went easy on the president. He argued that the press had become too much a part of, and too beholden to, the structure of power and privilege in the United States, saying that reporters trying to protect and promote their own careers feared countering Reagan's popularity.[37]

In essence the so-called liberal media became boosters for the hero of the conservative resurgence. Though the *New York Times,* the *Washington Post,* and a few other newspapers regularly criticized Reagan, in general he received the most gentle press treatment of any president after Kennedy. Most journalists liked the president, even if many thought he lacked curiosity or intellectual depth. "He doesn't tax our intellect," one *Washington Post* journalist wrote. "So we—and I am talking here about my own profession as well as the president's political opponents—tend not to challenge his."[38] Soon after Reagan took office, journalists began routinely to refer to him as "the Great Communicator" and to regularly cite the president's popularity with the American people. In fact, polls suggest that Reagan was somewhat unpopular, except with die-hard conservatives, early in his presidency—though the press may have boosted his popularity by repeating their own mistaken impressions. Two journalism scholars write, "The media took Reagan's popularity for granted and tried to explain away low polls—Reagan was popular but the economy was on the downturn; Reagan was popular but his policies were not well liked; Reagan was popular but . . ."[39]

The president's popularity rose somewhat among journalists and other Americans when he and three other men were shot less than three months after he took office. At first, most Americans had little indication of how seriously Reagan was injured, as the

White House issued misleading positive statements and the media reported rumors. The Associated Press, CBS, and ABC wrongly reported that press secretary James Brady had been killed, as news organizations battled to be first with various tidbits of news—harming their own credibility in the process. "No one outside a small group of broadcasters cared whether ABC was four minutes ahead of NBC," one historian complained. "The pressure of the moment was to get it right, and the networks failed, because it was not clear to them why being first was not the priority in such a grievous situation."[40] For his part, Reagan handled the situation with aplomb, quipping to his wife in the hospital, "Honey, I forgot to duck," and telling doctors, "I hope you're all Republicans."[41] The quotes were consistent with the cowboy image that the president and the news media created. One result of the shooting, however, was that Reagan ended up dismaying some of his conservative supporters by signing tougher gun control legislation.

Reagan had another opportunity to look tough later that same year. In August 1981, more than eleven thousand members of the Professional Air Traffic Controllers Organization (PATCO) went on strike, demanding higher wages and a shorter work week. PATCO was one of few unions that endorsed the former Screen Actors Guild president a year earlier, but the walkout violated a federal law prohibiting strikes by federal workers. Reagan quickly announced that he would fire all controllers who did not return to work within forty-eight hours. When they refused to return, four PATCO leaders were jailed and all the strikers were fired. Supervisors, union members who decided not to strike, and military air-traffic controllers filled in, and most planes flew as scheduled. Perhaps in part because the strike came at the height of the summer vacation season, the public generally supported the president. For all practical purposes, Reagan's action also marked the end of organized labor—a longtime Democratic ally—as a significant force in politics and to some degree even in business. "By carrying out his threat to fire the controllers if they did not return to work Reagan not only set limits for public employee unions, but also signaled that it was OK for businesses to play hardball with private sector unions," a one reporter later wrote.[42] Experts disagree about whether the PATCO strike and its aftermath prompted or merely accelerated a nationwide decline in union membership and relevance.[43] Regardless, PATCO disintegrated. In what some airline workers considered an added insult, Washington National Airport was renamed Ronald Reagan Washington National Airport in 1998.

After economic problems and embarrassment on the world stage during the Carter years, Americans were in a mood to feel good about themselves. Jingoistic appeals happened to be Reagan's forte. He enjoyed a visible role in two major patriotism-invoking events on America's opposite coasts during his time in office. The Los Angeles Memorial Coliseum rang with chants of "U-S-A, U-S-A . . ." during the 1984 Olympics. Because the Soviet Union and other nations boycotted the Olympics in retaliation for the U.S. Olympic boycott of 1980, the United States was assured of claiming more gold medals than any other country. Two years later all of the major networks covered the Statue of Liberty centennial celebration, highlighted by a July Fourth unveiling of the newly refurbished statue.[44]

Of course, the act that most stirs patriotism is war, and Reagan loved war stories. He enjoyed them so much, in fact, that he sometimes made them up. He regularly told a story about a B-17 captain who was unable to rescue a wounded crewman; instead of parachuting to safety the captain took the young man's hand and said, "Never mind son, we'll ride it down together." Reagan even told the story to the Congressional Medal of Honor Society, noting that the captain had posthumously been awarded the Medal of Honor. In fact, no known such incident occurred outside of the movies, and one might wonder how anyone not on the plane at the time would know if it had. An even more blatant fabrication—though some have suggested that Reagan believed his own stories, so they were not actually lies—came when Reagan told the Israeli prime minister that as a signal corp photographer he had filmed the Nazi death camps. In fact, Reagan's World War II service consisted of making military training films, and he never left the states during the war.[45]

Reagan did get to oversee his own war as commander in chief. As with any good Hollywood movie war, "the good guys" on the U.S. side were guaranteed of winning. American troops invaded Grenada, the smallest independent nation in the Western Hemisphere, to rescue American medical students from a new Cuban-backed Communist government (conservative magazines went so far as to call the new government a Soviet operation). Titled Operation Urgent Fury—like television networks, presidential administrations come up with names for all their most noteworthy actions—the 1983 war ended quickly. The Americans left least satisfied by the war were those in the news media.

A Reagan-ordered press blackout of the invasion kept journalists off the island until the third day of fighting. U.S. Marines arrested two journalists who reached Grenada on their own. When other reporters tried to reach the island with a chartered speedboat, a fighter plane fired warning shots across its bow to force it to turn back. With no media on hand to verify claims, American officials exaggerated the size of the enemy Grenadian and Cuban forces and lied about civilian casualties, claiming there were none (there were at least fourteen). Yet the Cuban news media "accurately reported that the Cuban contingent numbered 750 and that there had been civilian casualties," a *Washington Post* columnist later wrote. "It is another irony of this anti-communist administration that Oct. 27 was one of the few times in history when citizens of a communist country knew more about what was going on than Americans did."[46] Later figures put the number of enemy combatants lower yet, perhaps at no more than one hundred. Americans at home saw no battle scenes but two weeks later did see in newspapers around the country a staged photo of Reagan saluting a marine who had served in Grenada. Even pro-Reagan news media protested the administration's "private war," and a Reagan press aide resigned over the incident. Afterward, journalists and the administration worked out details for a media pool in which a few pool members would accompany soldiers to future conflicts, with stories and photos to be shared by all media.[47]

Some questioned the timing and need for the 1983 Grenada invasion, in part because it came just two days after an American military disaster thousands of miles away in Lebanon. A year earlier, Reagan sent 1,800 marines to Beirut as peacekeepers between warring Christian and Muslim factions, an action that came under increasing criticism. Even the secretary of defense urged removal of the troops, but before the withdrawal a suicide bomber drove a truckload of explosives into U.S. barracks and killed 241 marines. After the Grenada invasion most media attention turned away from Beirut to the new war—and to complaints about the treatment of the press. Those complaints were not shared by the public, however, prompting one columnist to complain, "Reagan's advisers are convinced that the media are virtually devoid of public support in their protests of both the news blackout of the invasion and the misleading statements made about it."[48] Fewer than twenty years after Watergate, if Americans had to choose between the press and government, the government came out on top—"a jolting revelation to many people in the news media," noted the *Chicago Tribune*.[49] Much of the criticism cited concerns for military safety and effectiveness, but many Americans urged censorship simply because they viewed the press as too antigovernment. The news media obviously had done a typically poor job of explaining their role as a government watchdog to most Americans.

As demonstrated by the Grenada invasion, the fight against global communism continued to be an ongoing theme for the Reagan administration. That focus met with approval from many of his supporters, who tended to agree with the *National Review* writer who argued shortly after Reagan's election, "Few things can be more certain than that the most salient political issue for the remainder of the century will be the worldwide confrontation between Western democracy, which means especially the United States, and Communism, which means especially the Soviet Union."[50] Though the Vietnam War had proven to be a costly and deadly embarrassment, other fronts remained on which to battle worldwide communism. The Reagan Doctrine called for U.S. intervention to resist communism wherever it arose, including through aiding anti-Communist insurgencies. Reagan authorized the CIA to train and assist anti-Communist groups in various parts of the world, including aiding the Nicaraguan rebels, or Contras, in 1981. That part of the battle provided the biggest problem of the Reagan administration and became known as the Iran-Contra scandal.

Though Reagan called the rebels "the moral equivalent of our Founding Fathers," Congress prohibited the use of government funds to help overthrow the elected leftist Nicaraguan government. Marine Major Oliver North then helped devise a plan to ignore an embargo by illegally selling American weapons to Iran and then diverting the profits to the Contras. Under the plan, Iran also agreed to arrange the release of seven American hostages held in Lebanon. Three were released, but three more were captured, while more than 1,500 missiles went to the same nation that had helped cripple Carter's presidency. When the plan was revealed in 1986 by a small Lebanese magazine, Reagan told a national television audience that he had never authorized the sale. He was forced to retract that statement a week later. Congress slated hearings about the illegal activities, and North lied to Congress. He and National Security Adviser John Poindexter were briefly convicted of various charges (later overturned on appeal). Called to testify in congressional hearings, which failed to determine whether the president had approved of the plan, Reagan repeatedly said he had forgotten various details. One critic wrote: "Reagan's frequent memory lapses during the testimony were embarrassing to watch . . . but he did look like a man with nothing to hide. Or at least like a man who has forgotten if he has anything to hide."[51] The president changed details of his testimony, probably less a reflection of dishonesty than a reflection of his disinterest in day-to-day details of governing. "Unhappily, it may be concluded either that Reagan was not capable of checking for accuracy . . . the texts of his Iran-Contra speeches, or that he preferred not to know what he was really saying," one rhetorician noted.[52]

Reagan's Iran-Contra testimony was not his first bout with memory loss under oath. In 1961, the Justice Department conducted an investigation to try to determine whether the Music Corporation of America (MCA) had violated antitrust laws through a deal with the Screen Actors Guild. By then, MCA employed the former SAG president on a television show and served as his agent. Called to testify before a grand jury, Reagan said he could recall only two things about the deal. Unfortunately, both of the things he "remembered" were false. "When evidence was produced to show that both contentions were untrue, he retreated further into forgetfulness and contradicted himself on the reason for his memory lapses," one historian notes.[53]

The *Miami Herald* won a Pulitzer Prize for its Iran–Contra coverage, but few in the press looked very deeply into the issue. "The media, in a country priding itself on its level of education and information, kept the public informed only on the most superficial level," one liberal historian complained. "The whole Iran-contra affair became a perfect example of the double line of defense for the American Establishment. The first defense is to deny the truth. If exposed, the second defense is to investigate, but not too much; the press will publicize, but they will not get to the heart of the matter."[54] Vice President George H. W. Bush's involvement remained (and remains) largely a mystery, though independent prosecutor Lawrence Walsh finally concluded in 1993—months after Bush's own term as president ended—that Bush had withheld evidence and had been "fully aware" of the arms deal. "The criminal investigation of Bush was regrettably incomplete," Walsh wrote, noting, "Bush refused to be interviewed for a final time in light of evidence developed in the latter stages of [the] investigation, leaving unresolved a clear picture of his Iran/contra involvement."[55] In one of the few mainstream media attempts to explore the issue, CBS news anchor Dan Rather had brought it up during a live 1988 interview with Bush. But Bush, then a sitting vice president who was campaigning for the presidency, dodged the issue. He attacked Rather's professionalism, bringing up an incident in which the anchor had walked off the news set a few months earlier. What *Time* called "the ambush that failed" actually made Bush look tough, while bolstering conservative arguments about the "liberal media" being out to get him.[56] Shortly after he became president in 1989, Bush pardoned former defense secretary Caspar Weinberger and five others involved in the scandal. "The Weinberger pardon marked the first time a President ever pardoned someone in whose trial he might have been called as a witness, because the President was knowledgeable of factual events underlying the case," independent prosecutor Walsh later reported.[57] Reagan suffered no serious damage to his reputation from the Iran-Contra incident, demonstrating why he had come to be widely known as the "Teflon president" (after Democratic representative Patricia Schroeder referred, in a 1984 speech, to a "Teflon-coated presidency"). Interesting in part because of its parallel to George W. Bush's fight against terrorism, one scholar for a libertarian think tank said at the end of Reagan's second term that the Iran-Contra affair was no aberration:

> It was a scandal waiting to happen because the Reagan Doctrine's underlying ideological ethos led its adherents to believe they had a monopoly on defining the "true" national interest. . . . A policy of ultimate ends justified the use of any means, and the doctrine's architects believed they were justified in arrogating to themselves the right to ignore political and legal norms in pursuit of what were for them morally transcendent objectives. The crusade against communism was deemed to be too vital to be constrained by such abstract notions as the popular will or constitutional propriety.[58]

The independent prosecutor reached a similar conclusion, noting that while "the investigation found no credible evidence that President Reagan violated any criminal statute . . . he set the stage for the illegal activities of others by encouraging and, in general terms, ordering support of the contras." Furthermore, the report concluded, "The President's disregard for civil laws enacted to limit presidential actions abroad . . . created a climate in which some of the Government officers assigned to implement his policies felt emboldened to circumvent such laws."[59]

Less noticed but perhaps more interesting and even more important from a historical perspective than the Iran-Contra issue is another Persian Gulf–region story tied to the Reagan administration. Before dealing weapons to Iran, the administration had supported Iraq during the Iran-Iraq war (which began when Iraq attacked Iran in 1980). Donald Rumsfeld, who as secretary of defense two decades later would lead the U.S. war against Iraq and Saddam Hussein, served as Reagan's special envoy to Iraq in 1983. His meeting with Hussein helped pave the way for normalization of relations between the two nations. "The United States, in a shift of policy, has informed friendly Persian Gulf nations that the defeat of Iraq in the 3-year-old war with Iran would be 'contrary to U.S. interests' and has made several moves to prevent that result," the *Washington Post* reported after Rumsfeld met with Hussein. "The U.S. statements during an unannounced mission by officials of the State and Defense departments to the Persian Gulf in early December moved the administration closer to the Iraqi side in the war and further from its original 'neutral' position."[60]

About a month later, the *New York Times* reported that the war had taken "a new, more ominous turn" because for the first time Iraq had deliberately bombed Iranian citizens.[61] Iraq still was permitted to buy military hardware from U.S. sellers, and the Reagan administration essentially ignored Hussein's use of poison gas against Iran in 1984 and then four years later against Kurdish Iraqis. In response to the later incident, the U.S. House of Representatives and Senate overwhelmingly approved sanctions that would have denied Iraq access to some U.S. technology, but Reagan refused to approve the sanctions. Reagan did call for a worldwide ban on chemical and gas warfare—an interesting and somewhat hypocritical perspective considering that he had, since the beginning of his presidency, promoted renewed U.S. production of chemical weapons. That production finally began in 1987 after an eighteen-year moratorium.

Stories and photos from the 1988 Iraq gas attacks gained widespread circulation fourteen years later, helping provide support for George W. Bush's claims that Hussein posed a threat to the United States because Iraq possessed "weapons of mass destruction." The mainstream press did little to investigate or correct Bush's claims before the Iraq War began, to remind Americans of the date or circumstances of Hussein's earlier gas attacks, or to point out administration members' earlier efforts to help Hussein gain and keep power. Instead, journalists generally acted as cheerleaders in support of the pending war effort.[62]

Reagan's most important political issue continued to be anticommunism, and his relationship with the Soviet Union defined his presidency more than anything else. Perhaps more appropriate to his movie background than to 1980s world politics, he referred to the Soviet Union as an "Evil Empire" and proposed a "Star Wars" defense that would put a "missile shield" in space.[63] He angered some critics with an off-the-cuff remark into a microphone before a speech that he had outlawed the Soviet Union and would "begin bombing in five minutes." He warned repeatedly about the spread of Communist influence, yet, like Richard Nixon, he also angered some die-hard anti-Communists by making overtures to the Soviet Union. He and Soviet Premier Mikhail Gorbachev met several times, seemed genuinely to like one another, and signed a 1987 missile treaty. What now probably is Reagan's best-remembered presidential speech came that same year in Berlin, when he demanded, "Mr. Gorbachev, tear down this wall."

Two years later, the Berlin Wall came down. Built in 1963 and separating East Berlin from West Berlin, the wall symbolized the "Iron Curtain" between Soviet-bloc countries and the West. Television cameras around the world captured images of young East Germans battering the wall with sledgehammers as guards stood by and watched. American networks replayed Reagan's speech and showed images of the wall coming down, and all three anchors for the major networks broadcast from Germany for a few days. The Soviet Union itself broke apart in 1991, and conservatives credited Reagan's foreign policy for the downfall of the world's leading Communist threat.[64] Others have largely disagreed, however, saying that the Soviet Union was doomed by more bureaucratic factors and that most Americans no longer believed it posed much of a threat, anyway. "Anticommunism had successfully mobilized public support during the cold war years," one scholar writes. "By the 1980s, however, Americans had a more realistic understanding of the world and saw international politics in shades of gray rather than black and white."[65] That statement may be true, but it is also true that many Americans went back to black-and-white thinking after 9/11. The news media are partly to blame, because they had contributed to a decline in understanding about international affairs. Besides, subtleties often fade during periods of societal fear and uncertainty—which is largely why many conservatives have worked so hard to promote fear, as discussed further in the next chapter.

Aside from Reagan's possible influence on negating a Communist threat to the United States, his presidency produced few tangible accomplishments other than increased optimism among Americans. Perhaps most important from a political perspective, Reagan managed to meld disparate groups—fiscal conservatives, neoconservatives, and the Religious Right—under the GOP banner, even though he actually achieved little for those groups. Some key economic factors improved, but some critics said they had bottomed out under Carter, anyway, and had nowhere to go but up. Employment rates increased during the Reagan administration, but most of the gains came in relatively low-paying retail and service sectors: "Higher-paying jobs in manufacturing disappeared at a rate unmatched since the Great Depression," two Pulitzer Prize–winning journalists found.[66] The highest-bracket tax rate was slashed from 70 percent to 28 percent, though taxation overall actually increased under Reagan. He complained throughout most of his political life about bureaucracy and the size of government, but the federal government expanded considerably under Reagan (just as California's government had grown when he was governor of the state). He promised to eliminate the Department of Education and then expanded it. He professed to hate big government spending, but such spending boomed under Reagan. He and his supporters sometimes blamed Congress for the increased spending, but in fact the budgets submitted by the president were larger than those Congress ultimately approved. Reagan complained about the federal deficit during his first inaugural address, but under his administration the deficit exploded to historic highs (surpassed later by those of both Bush administrations). That boom probably was predictable, considering that California's deficit also ballooned during his time as governor. In Reagan's second year as president, the U.S. deficit surpassed one hundred billion dollars for the first time. A year later, it surpassed two hundred billion dollars.[67] Incidentally, high deficits trouble neoconservatives much less than they do traditional fiscal conservatives, especially when much of the increased funding goes to the military, as it did under Reagan.

Reagan encouraged corporate America by overseeing the deregulation of some industries, most disastrously the savings and loan industry. The *New York Times* warned in 1984 that risky lending practices threatened the nation's 3,400 savings and loan institutions and nearly five hundred banks.[68] A year later, the *Washington Post* warned that 431 savings and loan institutions were insolvent and that the cost of shutting them down would be "well over twice the $6 billion in the federal S&L deposit insurance fund."[69] At the end of Reagan's second term, the *New York Times* reported that nearly a third of the nation's savings and loan institutions were "insolvent or nearly so," primarily because of deregulation.[70] High interest rates, bad investments, greed, and fraud by savings and loan managers eventually led to the collapse of several institutions and the government seizure of others before a government bailout cost taxpayers billions of dollars.

On the social values front, Reagan appointed more than half of the federal judiciary during his time in office, and similar conservative nominations by George H. W. Bush and George W. Bush would seem to guarantee an increasingly conservative judiciary. Such trends are difficult to predict, however, and help to illustrate some of the contradictions in modern conservatism. For example, some conservatives loathe government interference in such matters as education and personal privacy, while other conservatives promote it. Reagan supported a constitutional amendment to allow prayer in classrooms, though such an amendment seems unlikely. He managed to make "welfare queens" a part of the vernacular, cutting social programs that included school lunches, subsidized housing, and Aid to Families with Dependent Children (though Democratic president Bill Clinton oversaw even more sweeping welfare reform) while apparently believing that he was increasing opportunities for the poor. By the time Reagan left office, the gap between rich and poor was at an all-time high.[71]

Social conservatives liked Reagan in part because he opposed abortion, once writing: "Every legislator, every doctor, and every citizen needs to recognize that the real issue is whether to affirm and protect the sanctity of all human life, or to embrace a social ethic where some human lives are valued and others are not. As a nation, we must choose between the sanctity of life ethic and the 'quality of life' ethic."[72] He also opposed the Equal Rights Amendment, though he appointed the first woman Supreme Court justice, Sandra Day O'Connor. She and another Reagan appointee, Anthony Kennedy, disappointed social conservatives by twice voting in 5–4 decisions to uphold *Roe v. Wade*. Kennedy also has supported gay rights.

Even more interesting is the fact that Kennedy became a justice because Reagan's most important Supreme Court nomination may have been the one that failed. Robert Bork—already somewhat famous as the acting attorney general who carried out Richard Nixon's order to fire Watergate special prosecutor Archibald Cox—likely would have been the most conservative member of the court. His 1987 nomination drew immediate fire from those who feared he would help roll back previous court decisions. After a significant public-relations campaign by Bork opponents, the Senate refused to confirm the nomination. "Bork" became a verb describing efforts to politically undermine court appointments.

Had he been appointed, Bork might have been the weapon Reagan needed to implement what many conservatives hoped would be the most important part of his legacy. "For a President not to insist on some assurance of ideological congeniality in a prospective federal judge would be inconsistent with the true nature of federal judicial power," one conservative legal educator wrote as Reagan was about to take office, adding: "Roe v.

Wade can someday be overturned. All it takes is five votes out of nine. Nothing about it is illegal, unpatriotic, ignorant, or insulting."[73] Another wrote, "I love the Bill of Rights, I cherish the independent judiciary, and I voted for Reagan in the hope that his appointments will radically and fundamentally improve the Supreme Court."[74]

Though one would not know it from newspaper obituaries or many books written by conservatives, in most respects Reagan achieved little of significance as president for his biggest supporters. He was a link in a conservative chain that began with supporters of Goldwater (who, notably, strenuously opposed Reagan's 1968 and 1976 presidential bids) and continued after he left office. "Ronald Reagan's conservative agenda was not new, it merely reflected the historical development of conservative ideas, many of which were rooted in the debates of Christian denominations during the 1960s and 1970s," two historians note.[75] Still, Reagan did provide the voice of those conservative ideas at a time when, for various reasons, America was ready to listen. Later presidents and other politicians would build on his successes and work to overcome his failures, adding to the Reagan mythology. His most important contribution may have been the bringing together of various branches of conservatism into a cohesive whole, accepted by a majority of voters, that only recently has showed signs of fracturing. As one Clinton aide later wrote:

> Conservatives had repeatedly attempted to fuse the various doctrinal creeds of the movement into a single force. But precisely because the movement was based on ideology it was rent apart; inconsistent logic could not be reconciled as consistent politics. What Reaganism represented was the effort to unify in politics the disparate strands of conservatism. He animated the intel-

lectuals' theories with a resonant symbolism—images of idyllic small-town life, enterprising entrepreneurs whose success derived from moral character, and failure induced only by federal bureaucrats. By translating a complex ideology into a soothing vernacular he made it accessible to Americans yearning for reassurance of their own special grace. Reagan's popular rendition of conservatism was in one sense a simplification, but in another sense an improvement. For he turned the movement outward by transforming a sectarian interpretation of the world into a political mythology, a civil religion. The point, he demonstrated, was to get people to participate in the myth-making.[76]

FIVE

---◇---

THE POLITICAL PROCESS
TRANSFORMED

Ronald Reagan's election may have heralded the official arrival of the conservative movement, but political factors beyond Reagan did more to help conservatives gain and maintain power. Yet the mainstream news media generally failed to recognize those factors when they arose and also failed to explain their significance, even as the press contributed notably to their effectiveness. A political structure built by conservatives made Reagan's election possible, and his appeal made him the perfect figurehead to provide a decorative capstone for that structure. By the time Reagan left office the conservative machine was nearly strong enough to elect most of the candidates it needed and to bend or break the politicians it opposed. Though Americans and their news media understood that conservative influence well enough to keep talking about Republican "appeals to the conservative base," most had little idea of its scope or its history.

In part because of how well Republicans used the media, the recognized "Republican revolution" came six years after Reagan left office, during Bill Clinton's presidency. Republicans gained control of both houses of Congress in 1994. In fact, despite his

Democratic Party affiliation, Clinton might justifiably be considered the best conservative president of the modern age. After all, both his successes and failures helped conservatives more often than they did liberals. By turning the federal deficit into a surplus (with substantial help from a Republican Congress, of course), overseeing sweeping welfare reform, and pushing through a North American Free Trade Agreement that corporations favored and most unions disliked, Clinton was truer to the policies of traditional conservatives than Reagan had been. "The entire context of American politics exists on a spectrum that is itself well to the Right of that in most industrialized democracies," one critic later pointed out. "Bill Clinton was probably further to the Right than most ruling western European conservatives, such as Germany's Helmut Kohl and France's Jacques Chirac. Indeed, virtually the entire axis of political conversation in the United States takes place on ideological ground that would be considered conservative in just about every nation in democratic western Europe."[1] Further evidence of Clinton's innate conservatism might be seen in the fact that many prominent neoconservatives turned their backs on Reagan's former vice president to align themselves with Clinton when he campaigned for the presidency.[2]

Before Clinton, of course, came President George H. W. Bush. Despite his involvement with the Iran-Contra scandal, Reagan's vice president won the presidency fairly easily. Democrats helped Bush by choosing Michael Dukakis as their candidate after front-runner Gary Hart became embroiled in a sexual scandal and Joseph Biden plagiarized a British Labor leader's speech. Like Dukakis, Bush was from the Northeast, but he benefited from his affiliation with Reagan and his part-time home in Texas. Aided by fear-mongering political ads, conservatives found it easy to demonize Dukakis, an admitted "card-carrying member of the

ACLU," as a Massachusetts liberal. (Conservatives also regularly demonize the American Civil Liberties Union, of course, though they likely have benefited as much from its activities as have liberals.) Dukakis drew criticism for vetoing a bill—which probably would have been overturned as unconstitutional, anyway—that would have required teachers to lead students in the Pledge of Allegiance. Conservatives also managed to classify him as weak on crime. In the most famous ad of the 1988 campaign, which came to be known as the "Willie Horton ad," television viewers saw the mug shot of a convicted African American murderer who escaped while on a weekend furlough and raped a woman while Dukakis was Massachusetts governor.

The ad and the resulting controversy illustrated three key points that would become common in later campaigns. First, the ad did not come from the Bush campaign; it was sponsored by an "independent" group called the National Security Political Action Committee (though even before the ad ran, Bush regularly cited Horton as an example of how Dukakis was "soft on crime"). Second, fewer people apparently saw the ad in its original context than on news programs discussing its controversial nature, so the news media shared the blame for its wide circulation. Third, the press oversimplified the issue, helping to perpetuate a number of misperceptions. For example, Dukakis inherited the program from a Republican governor and eventually ended it, and President Reagan had supported a similar program as governor of California.

The Horton case also provides a good example of how myth becomes accepted as reality, in part through the neglect of the press. The news media apparently did little to combat a lasting misperception that has become a common belief: that Senator Al Gore first used Horton to bash Dukakis during the 1988 primaries. Perhaps demonstrating that even conservatives were somewhat uncomfortable with the racist overtones of the ad, a number of conservative columnists and radio hosts have promoted the false claim that Gore first introduced Horton to the campaign. Demonstrating the vitriol and inattention to detail common to many talk radio hosts, Sean Hannity has repeated the claim numerous times throughout the years. On a rare occasion when he was contradicted by Gore campaign manager Donna Brazile, Hannity claimed, "I have the tape."[3] In one program in which he repeats the statement, Hannity said: "Thank God for Nexis-Lexis. We can go back and study the whole campaign."[4] In truth, the LexisNexis database is better at chronicling reports about campaigns than actual campaign activities. Still, a relatively simple search of the database finds several debate-related articles noting that Gore asked Dukakis about prison furloughs, claiming that eleven released prisoners had escaped and two had committed additional murders. But the articles say nothing about race or prisoners' names. Nor did Gore have the Horton mug shot as a visual hammer, of course, even if he wanted to make race an issue.

To blame or credit Gore for bringing public attention to Willie Horton is specious, anyway. After all, the Lawrence (Massachusetts) *Sunday Eagle-Tribune* won a 1988 Pulitzer Prize for its extensive, inflammatory, and frequently inaccurate coverage of the Horton case. Most of the newspaper's coverage came the previous year.[5] Three weeks before the debate in which Gore criticized the furlough program, an Associated Press article mentioned Horton and reported that Dukakis had "changed his stance" to take a tougher position of furloughs.[6] Two months before, a *Newsweek* article also highlighted Horton and the furloughs. Neither of those articles noted Horton's race.[7] In July, as Dukakis was about to formally win the nomination, PBS correspondent Judy Woodruff noted that Horton's escape and subsequent crimes had prompted "a loud reaction from the public and from law enforcement groups like the Massachusetts Police Association" two years earlier.[8] As for Bush, United Press International (UPI) and the Associated Press both reported in June that he had begun using Horton's name while attacking the Massachusetts prison furlough program.

The mainstream media contributed to the apparent myth through ignorance or carelessness. "He's no powder puff. . . . Gore was the first to taunt Michael Dukakis about Willie Horton," a *Philadelphia Daily News* columnist wrote in 1998, as Gore was starting his most recent presidential campaign.[9] "Gore's a mean, tough, political fighter," neoconservative editor Bill Kristol said on ABC's *This Week* a year later. "Gore is the one who introduced Willie Horton to American politics in the 1988 primary against Michael Dukakis."[10] Cokie Roberts, George Stephanopoulos (the former Clinton communications director who hosts *This Week*), and George Will all failed to challenge the statement. Worse, seven years earlier Will had managed to make the same claim twice and use Horton's name four times in the course of asking a single question as Gore campaigned to be Bill Clinton's vice president. In the often-tedious three-sentence style of question popular with national television interviewers, Will "asked" Gore: "Senator, it's an article of faith in your party and in much of the media that the use of Willie Horton by the Bush campaign was impliedly racist and certainly negative beyond propriety. The Republicans learned about Willie Horton because you used Willie Horton against Michael Dukakis in this city in April 1988, running against him in the primary. Given that you used Willie Horton, do you agree that it was racist and insupportably negative?"[11] Gore offered a "polite correction" to Will's premise, saying that not only had he not mentioned Horton, but, "I didn't know his name, much less what his race was. I raised the issue of crime."[12]

Will's questioning also highlights another problem for journalism. For the casual viewer, the Pulitzer Prize–winning columnist seems to act like a journalist, though he has professed not to be one. In 1980, Will apparently saw a debate briefing book stolen from Jimmy Carter's campaign, helped Ronald Reagan practice for the debate, and then, on *Nightline,* praised Reagan's debate performance. When Will's actions were revealed three years later the *New York Daily News* dropped his column, but he remained a popular columnist and television commentator. To explain his activity on behalf of Reagan he wrote that columnists were not expected to be impartial like reporters.[13] Given the confusion that such visibility might create, Will is among dozens of commentators who can say, "I'm not a journalist, but I play one on TV."

Four years after Bush defeated Dukakis, he lost to Clinton. One problem for Bush may have been the fact that Reagan's election and then a dozen years of Reagan and Bush "engendered a sense of complacency among rank-and-file New Rightists," one political historian argues: "Consequently, the flow of money into New Right coffers slowed considerably, and the organizational zeal that had been its hallmark since the late seventies could no longer be sustained."[14] Bush, who had enjoyed especially high popularity during the 1991 Persian Gulf War, may still have won had conservatives not split their vote. Clinton won a smaller percentage of the popular vote than Dukakis had won, claiming only 43 percent. Third-party candidate Ross Perot won almost 19 percent of the popular vote, most of it from Bush. Though Clinton's electoral victory over Bush looked large (370–168), he won 50 percent of the popular vote only in his home state of Arkansas and the District of Columbia.

Clinton won much more easily in 1996, but by then he had proven that he was not particularly liberal. Even before the 1994 election in which Republicans claimed control of Congress, two British observers noted: "Left-wing America was given the answer to all its prayers—the most talented politician in a generation, a long period of peace and prosperity, and a series of Republican blunders—and the agenda was still set by the right. Clinton's big achievements—welfare reform, a balanced budget, a booming stock market and cutting 350,000 people from the federal payroll—would have delighted Ronald Reagan. Whenever Clinton veered to the left—over gays in the military, over health care—he was slapped down."[15] On those latter two issues, Clinton's failures may have come because he tried to do too much too soon. He had campaigned for the presidency on both issues, promising to end discrimination against homosexuals in the military and to reform health care in the United States.

By the end of 1992, gays already legally served in the militaries of Japan, Israel, and most Western nations; Australia and Canada began allowing homosexuals to serve that year. While still a candidate, Clinton proposed an executive order to override a 1948 Department of Defense regulation that barred gays from service. After Clinton's election, conservatives and military officials immediately opposed the plan. General Colin Powell, chairman of the Joint Chiefs of Staff, said allowing gays into the military "would be detrimental to good order of discipline."[16] News stories typically focused on the conflicts and potential problems involved, with little historical context or comparison to the policies of other nations, though the *Washington Post* and the *Boston Globe* offered rare examples of the latter.[17] Clinton and Congress reached what the president called "an honorable compromise" that actually made the ban federal law, though it did make some changes in the military treatment of gays. The new law made it still illegal for an openly homosexual man or woman to serve, but asking whether someone is gay was prohibited. The Don't Ask, Don't Tell policy managed to offend both social conservatives because it went too far and gays because it fell short of Clinton's original promise.

Clinton made conservatives happier when he signed the Defense of Marriage Act, passed overwhelmingly by Congress less than two months before the 1996 elections. That law, which one columnist called "an excuse for gay bashing in a year when Republicans desperately need an issue, and so they're turning gay Americans into Willie Horton," allowed states to refuse to recognize same-sex marriages.[18] Clinton avoided some news coverage by signing the bill at 12:50 A.M. on a Saturday morning, but his campaign touted the signing in ads that ran on Christian radio stations.[19] Proposed state constitutional amendments banning gay marriage became a popular way of bringing out conservative voters during future elections.

Americans may have been reticent to grant homosexuals any new rights, but Clinton's proposal to reform health care was more popular. The United States had the world's highest health care costs yet was (and remains) the only major democracy in which a significant number of citizens lacked basic medical insurance. Even the American Medical Association and the Health Insurance Association of America—what one Clinton aide called "the two great, historic bastions of opposition to compulsory health insurance"—and the U.S. Chamber of Commerce all supported universal coverage.[20] With that kind of support for the idea, Clinton put his wife, Hillary, in charge of a task force assigned to devise a plan that would bring "universal health care" to Americans. Polls showed that most Americans liked the plan, and with a Democratic majority in Congress, it seemed likely to pass. Still, many conservatives disliked the proposal and Hillary Clinton's involvement with it, and the insurance industry waged a public-relations campaign to convince middle-class Americans who already had insurance that they would suffer under the plan. The plan died less than two months before the 1994 elections. "The Republicans enjoyed a double triumph, killing reform and then watching jurors find the president guilty," wrote one supporter. "It was the political equivalent of the perfect crime."[21]

The health care debate also demonstrated another issue that would create problems for Clinton or any successor who wanted to promote a significant policy shift. Congress had changed, in part because of changes in the media environment. One rhetorical scholar writes:

> The health care debate is in many ways an illustration of a process that is increasingly evident, albeit in less spectacular form, whenever legislation is proposed affecting large numbers of people. On such occasions, it is now common not merely to debate the issues in Congress but to engage the people directly in ways that resemble an election campaign. Members of Congress, of course, return to their districts as they have always done to talk with constituents. But Congressional leaders, along with the President, speak directly to the people through televised speeches and appearances on talk shows. Interest groups also participate more and more actively by televised ads, electronic messages, and other forms of modern technology to reach the public and urge them to communicate with their representatives in Congress. When one adds in media reporters, talk show hosts, Op-Ed writers and expert commentary of various kinds, a major piece of legislation, such as Clinton's health care plan, can set off a national debate of formidable proportions.[22]

As new Republicans gained office, they began to demand more power than their seniority normally would have permitted. Clinton's failures involving gays in the military and national health care contributed to the large influx of those new Republicans in 1994, when the GOP won control of both the House and the Senate for the first time in decades. "Something that hasn't happened in about 40 years happened last week on Capitol Hill," the *Washington Post* noted after the election. "House Republicans talked and everyone listened."[23] Republicans won 230 of the 435 House positions, gaining more than fifty seats. They also gained control of the Senate for the first time since the 1980s, giving them control of the entire legislative branch. House minority whip Newt Gingrich, credited as the primary architect of the "Republican revolution," became a powerful and controversial speaker of the house.

The scope of the sweep surprised most people in government and in the press, but the Republicans had waged a cohesive national campaign that linked their opponents with Clinton's weaknesses. Those weaknesses went beyond his failures on two key legislative goals. The president had dealt with media portrayals suggesting indecisiveness and a lack of character even before his presidency, when he fended off allegations of infidelity, marijuana use, and avoiding service in Vietnam. Personal issues were not what caused him the biggest problems in the first years of his presidency, though. "He has taken a beating on virtually all issues: 68 percent negative on health care, 60 percent negative on the economy, 64 percent negative on other domestic issues, 66 percent negative on foreign policy, and 56 percent negative on character questions," the *Washington Post* reported, based on a 1994 Center for Media and Public Affairs study.[24] From his inauguration day through late June 1994, Clinton drew more than 2,400 negative comments on the network evening newscasts, an average of almost five per night.[25]

One of the most obvious reasons for the Republican sweep in

1994 was the GOP success in nationalizing the election. Rather than asking voters to focus on their own members of Congress, Republicans worked to connect all Democrats to Clinton and to a "culture of corruption" that had ensnared some congressional Democrats. The strategy perpetuated a still-popular trend in which candidates commonly "run *for* Congress by campaigning *against* Congress."[26] In a flashy visual and rhetorical move, more than three hundred congressional candidates gathered on the steps of the U.S. Capitol to sign an eight-point "Contract with America." Democratic critics referred to the document as a "contract on America" and called the mass signing political showboating, but the contract gave candidates and voters a focus. "Republican members of Congress and would-be Republican members are not merely running against someone; they have united to say that they are running for something as well," argued a *Washington Times* editorial.[27] The document outlined ten bills Republicans promised to introduce during the first one hundred days of a GOP majority, calling for lower taxes and decreased government spending (though more spending for the military and for prisons). It stated that Congress would balance the budget and implement term limits. The first two tenets of the contract stated that "all laws that apply to the rest of the country also apply equally to the Congress" and called for "a comprehensive audit of Congress for waste, fraud or abuse." Candidates—and to a large extent the news media—left voters to assume for themselves that congressional lawbreaking and waste were rampant.[28] In fact, the Contract with America had little legislative impact. The House passed nine of the ten proposed bills, but the Senate (which was also under GOP control, but traditionally less reactionary than the House) rejected some and Clinton vetoed another. The contract did help Republicans with their primary goal of gaining political power, though its electoral effect is debatable; some argue that most Americans knew little about it and had other reasons, among them general disgust with Congress, for voting as they did.

The new members of Congress wielded disproportionate power within the House itself. They pushed through reforms that made seniority less important in assigning and holding positions of power, a shift that had partially begun several years earlier under Democratic control. The newcomers also had a less reverent view of the institution. "Congress has been something more than the sum of its parts," one conservative writer noted in 1980. "I have a growing sense that Congress now is something *less* than the sum of its parts. There is certainly in the new members—many of them—a view that there are more important things in their lives, in their careers, than Congress and their work here."[29] The article also noted two other trends that may have been true two decades ago, but clearly are untrue today. First, party leaders had become concerned that congressional newcomers seemed to be less tied to their parties, but in recent years it has become obvious that party loyalties matter a great deal. Second, the writer worried about the rapid turnover in Congress, but modern gerrymandering by politicians has made it far more difficult for an incumbent to lose a seat than to win one.

Newspapers and television newscasters frequently lament low voter turnout while reminding citizens before every election that their vote matters. Few of those journalists honestly tell voters just how small their chances are of influencing a national election, or that for congressional elections, those chances have steadily decreased (making a shift such as that seen in the 2006 congressional elections particularly remarkable). Yet for weeks ahead of a modern national election, the news media focus heavily on a few races that might truly matter: the few states that for one reason or another can expect competitive elections. With fewer people to keep track of, Senate races are covered more heavily than House races. Unreported—yet perhaps innately understood by many of the stay-at-home electoral dropouts—is that such factors as redistricting to protect incumbency, the fundraising advantages of incumbents, and the conflict-driven coverage of the media themselves have determined the outcome of almost all congressional races long before election day. The exception is the candidate who commits a blunder that is too big and too close to the election to overcome. The news media report and repeatedly discuss such errors, meaning that much of modern election coverage has become what one political scientist calls "gaffe-driven news."[30]

With the new breed of legislators, public appeals via the press became an increasingly common means of influencing policy. Ironically, the shift came at a time when the press was decreasing its overall coverage of Congress and when more of that coverage was negative. The size and complexity of Congress, with its two houses, hundreds of committees, and 535 personalities, make it more difficult to understand than the White House. Reporters, though, tend to go to the same few legislators over and over again, and thanks to the choices made by television networks, almost every American can probably name a few members of Congress. Yet far fewer Americans can name their own senators or representatives.[31]

The news media focused heavily on the conflicts but less on the meaning of policy changes, continuing a dumbing down of policy discussions that had begun decades earlier. That focus on conflict did not always benefit the Republicans after they gained power. Clinton was personally popular with most Americans, nearly as adept as Reagan had been in using pseudo-events to promote policy and better than Reagan at speaking without a script. Clinton won reelection in 1996 partly because voters blamed House Speaker Newt Gingrich and his fellow Republicans for a budget impasse that led to a shutdown of the federal government. Still, the GOP maintained control of both houses of Congress throughout Clinton's term, which proved a boon for fiscal conservatives. Clinton's veto pen kept Republicans from spending recklessly, and he approved of welfare reform and other cuts that conservatives wanted and had not been able to get under Ronald Reagan.

While fiscal conservatives may have enjoyed life under Clinton, others in the conservative coalition found plenty to complain about. With the Soviet Union no longer a threat, Clinton cut military spending. He strengthened trade relations with China and approved the trade of high-tech equipment to the Communist nation, prompting one critic to write, "For the first time in our history, a U.S. administration has made diluting American power and strengthening her potential adversaries the centerpiece of its national-security policy."[32] Most damaging to Clinton and the Democrats, however, were actions by the president that inflamed social conservatives. Clinton was socially fairly liberal in his politics despite a personal ease in discussing religion and a mixed record on gay-rights issues. He drew criticism during his first campaign for avoiding the military draft during the Vietnam War. Most importantly, at least since revelations about Gary Hart's affair during the 1988 campaign had helped make politicians' sex lives part of the media picture, rumors of infidelity frequently swirled around Clinton. Then in January 1998, Internet tabloid–style "journalist" Matt Drudge broke the story that *Newsweek* had withheld a report about President Clinton's alleged affair with White House intern Monica Lewinsky. Prompted by the Drudge report, several mainstream media organizations soon reported the allegations. Already under investigation for alleged financial misdealing and being sued for alleged sexual harassment of Arkansas state employee Paula Jones while he was governor, Clinton denied wrongdoing in both criminal cases. Both eventually were dropped (Clinton settled out of court with Jones for $850,000 with no admission of guilt), but they led independent prosecutor Kenneth Starr to various other investigations, all of which also failed to turn up criminal wrongdoing by Clinton. Ironically, most conservatives had disagreed with the 1978 statute that permitted independent prosecutors, especially during Reagan's Iran-Contra problems, as noted by one neoconservative writer who disagreed with Starr's activities: "Of course, Democrats have grotesquely abused both the independent-council law and sexual harassment law. It is asking a lot to expect Republicans to forgo such a weapon themselves."[33] Regardless, after four years of investigation and more than thirty million dollars, Starr turned up evidence of the affair with Lewinsky.

Clinton at first denied knowing Jones or having a sexual relationship with Lewinsky, and Hillary Clinton blamed the accusations and investigations on a "right-wing conspiracy." As the investigation revealed more details, Clinton finally admitted lying about the Lewinsky affair but said he had violated no laws. The media and public flocked to a leaked 445-page report of the Clinton-Lewinsky investigation, in which Starr told Congress that the president had committed eleven impeachable acts, including perjury and obstruction of justice. Many newspapers and Internet Web sites carried the full "Starr report," which included statements that Lewinsky performed oral sex on the president at least nine times, that she and Clinton had repeatedly engaged in phone sex, and that a semen stain on an infamous blue dress contained Clinton's DNA. News sources quoted liberally from the report, though some toned down or bypassed the most graphic sexual material. Some cable stations repeatedly ran a videotape of

Clinton's grand jury testimony. Much of the coverage was sensationalistic in tone and relied heavily on unidentified sources. One study found that less than 20 percent of sourcing "offered even the slightest hint of the source's allegiances" and that the mainstream news media's use of anonymous sources varied little from that of the tabloid press.[34]

Despite the investigations and a steady stream of negative coverage, the public liked Clinton more than critics could understand or explain—or at least Americans were willing to overlook many of his personal flaws. "Americans think Mr. Clinton is doing a good job and that he is a sleazeball," a *Washington Times* columnist lamented.[35] Noted conservative William F. Buckley Jr. wrote: "It is not inconceivable that, at some point ahead, we will be asking ourselves: What is the matter with the general public? Why does it not understand the gravity of what is happening?"[36] Other conservative columnists and radio hosts became increasingly shrill in their criticism as the scandal dragged on. Some blamed Clinton for degrading American culture. Others said he merely reflected its degradation. "The news has been unfit for children since the 1970s," one critic wrote. "No one accused John Kennedy of vulgarizing American culture, because he didn't. Nor did Bill Clinton. It was vulgar when he got to it—and putting oral sex on the network news was the networks' doing, not the President's."[37] Voters' lack of concern about Clinton's actions could not prevent him from becoming the second U.S. president to be impeached by the House of Representatives. The impeachment proceedings, along with Clinton's supporters and detractors, took to the airwaves. Journalists and others began investigating the extramarital sexual activities of various members of Congress, exposing the infidelities of some of those members. With voting split largely along party lines, the House impeached Clinton on two charges.

Most Americans thought Clinton should be punished but not removed from office, and his job approval ratings and personal popularity remained generally high (despite predictions by ABC newsman Sam Donaldson and others that the scandal would force the president's resignation). "There's only one way Bill Clinton could get more popular right now, only one way the president could get more scorchingly HOT!—and that's if the U.S. Senate votes to convict him and remove him from office. Because impeachment is proving a great political tonic for the president's health," the *Washington Post* noted.[38] With a two-thirds Senate vote required to remove him, Clinton stood little chance of being forced out of office, and, as it turned out, the prosecution failed to win even a simple majority on either count. But the combination of Clinton's fiscal conservatism, which left Americans relatively unconcerned about economic issues, and Clinton's apparent moral shortcomings helped social conservatives gain unprecedented influence with George W. Bush's 2000 election as president.

That Bush could even be a candidate for president would once have been surprising, especially in the television age. He did not boast an impressive record in military service, business, or politics. He could not compare to Reagan or Clinton as a politician. Not particularly media savvy, he frequently misspoke during public appearances. Even early in his presidency, stiff movements and too-rapid speech accompanied a wide-eyed "deer-in-the-headlights" expression when Bush faced television cameras. After he became more comfortable on camera, he still had a tendency to lecture listeners, even though handlers rarely let him face unfriendly audiences. Thanks to his father, George H. W. Bush, he did have important family connections to both politics and corporate America, yet those dynamics alone could not make him the most politically powerful individual in the world. Other factors, however, almost assured that someone much like Bush would end up as president, supported by a Congress that then exercised almost no legislative oversight over his administration—and which he typically ignored on the rare occasions when it tried.

Many of the key factors culminating in a Bush presidency have already been discussed, yet perhaps most important is something that most Americans (and perhaps most of the news media) may know the least about. Conservative intellectuals frequently boast that ideas matter. But when it comes to electoral politics, organization matters more. In reviewing a book about the rise of conservatism George Will agreed with the British authors that "conservative power derives from two sources—its congruence with American values, especially the nation's anomalous religiosity, and the elaborate infrastructure of think tanks and other institutions that stresses that congruence."[39] The names of those institutions sometimes show up in newspaper articles and on television screens along with the faces of sources, but most Americans know little about the organizations or the multitude of proconservative activities in which they have engaged.

Like-minded people always have formed groups through which they could support one another and promote their ideas. Liberals and conservatives both have done so throughout American history. Most such organizations are local in nature. Regardless of their scope, they typically last about as long as the enthusiasm of their founders. One book lists several grassroots and educational conservative organizations that "would flourish for a while, then wither away when their overworked founders were no longer able to keep them afloat."[40] Those groups include For America, Pro-America, the Committee for Constitutional Government, the American Good Government Society, We the People!, the Manion Forum, Facts Forum, and America's Future.[41]

Few of those organizations managed to be as successful—and yet remain so relatively invisible—as the conservative groups of the past four decades or so.

One influential organization from an educational perspective was the Intercollegiate Society of Individualists, later renamed the Intercollegiate Studies Institute. While "not activist," the ISI "gave hundreds of future activists a firm grounding in conservative and libertarian philosophy."[42] Its members went on to serve in various government positions, including in the Reagan administration, and helped establish other conservative organizations such as the Heritage Foundation, the Philadelphia Society, the Claremont Institute, the Federalist Society, and Thomas Aquinas College.[43] Of a more activist bent were the members of the National Student Committee for the Loyalty Oath, formed in 1959 to urge Congress to keep a loyalty oath requirement for National Defense Education Act loans. A year later, Youth for Goldwater for Vice President demonstrated at the 1960 Republican Convention. Members of that group then founded Young Americans for Freedom, which staged a rally of more than eighteen thousand conservatives in New York in 1962 and remained active throughout the 1960s and 1970s. The 1962 rally "took the liberals completely by surprise," two conservative authors later wrote. "All this young conservative activity . . . had taken place below their radar, and now they could ignore it no more." Noting that the *New York Times* gave the rally front-page, above-the-fold coverage, the authors argue, "If you're looking for a birth date when the conservative movement emerged out of the womb and announced itself to the public, no other event would qualify better than YAF's Madison Square Garden rally."[44]

One liberal historian agreed that organized groups had little influence on conservative politics: "Until the 1960s, there had been almost no relevant right-wing organization in America; rightists could be found in nonideological groups such as the Republican Party or the National Association of Manufacturers, with the exception of the Americans for Constitutional Action, a Capitol Hill–based organization that issued ratings of senators and congressmen, and stood 'against collective morality and a socialized economy through centralization of power.'"[45] A decade later, many conservative organizations had been formed, prompted by a variety of concerns and promoters. Two of the larger, more inclusive groups were the American Conservative Union and the Conservative Caucus.

Early conservative stalwarts such as William F. Buckley and M. Stanton Evans formed the American Conservative Union in 1964. The ACU now calls itself "the nation's oldest and largest grassroots conservative lobbying organization."[46] Since 1971 it has issued an annual rating of every member of Congress, ranking each according to adherence to selected conservative principles. It began hosting the annual Conservative Political Action Conference in 1974, bringing together thousands of conservatives to hear speakers and exchange ideas.[47] One of its strongest efforts came in the 1970s, when it tried to prevent ratification of a treaty giving up the Panama Canal. "In its first year of lobbying, the union spent more than $1.4 million, purchasing antiratification commercials on several hundred radio and television stations across the country, publishing ads in major newspapers, and mailing more than 2.4 million letters to mobilize sentiment against what they called the surrender of American property," one critic noted.[48]

Howard Phillips, who had been a founding board member of the Young Americans for Freedom before going to work in the Richard Nixon administration, founded the Conservative Caucus in 1974 "in the belief that conservatives could win in Washington only by mobilizing conservative strength at the state and Congressional district level."[49] The organization focused heavily on telling members and others how to use letters to the editor and calls to radio programs to voice conservative views and to pressure their congressional representatives. As with most conservative organizations at the time, anti-communism was a major theme when the Conservative Caucus began, though communism is no longer listed among the ten items on its Statement of Principle.[50] Phillips has been called one of six men at "the heart of the New Right leadership." The other five were direct-mail expert Richard Viguerie (discussed further in chapter 6), Edwin Feulner, Paul Weyrich, John T. Dolan, and Morton Blackwell. The men worked together in various ways, and each was primarily responsible for establishing one or more organizations that contributed significantly to conservatives' future success.[51] Other key individuals in the resurgence included Phyllis Schlafly, founder of Eagle Forum and Stop ERA (discussed in more detail in chapter 2), and Reed Larson, cofounder and longtime president of the antiunion National Right to Work Committee.

With financial backing from Colorado beer tycoon Joseph Coors, Paul Weyrich and Edwin Feulner founded the now-powerful Heritage Foundation in 1973. Feulner has served as chairman of the board of the Intercollegiate Studies Institute and as a trustee for the International Republican Institute, among numerous other conservative affiliations. He became president of the Heritage Foundation, a think tank with the mission "to formulate and promote conservative public policies based on the principles of free enterprise, limited government, individual freedom, traditional American values, and a strong national defense."[52] Called by one critic "the mother of all think tanks in its single-minded focus on co-opting the media," the organization spends millions of dollars annually on media and government relations.[53] It offers numerous experts to media outlets and boasts its own syndicated columnists and radio hosts. It also publishes books, has its own television and radio studios, and in 2000 began offering Computer-Assisted Research and Reporting Boot Camps for conservative journalists and bloggers.[54] The foundation also conducts and publicizes research on numerous issues, including agriculture, foreign affairs, health care, labor, national defense, political thought, religion, taxes, and welfare.

Also in 1973, Weyrich helped found the American Legislative Exchange Council "to advance the Jeffersonian principles of free markets, limited government, federalism, and individual liberty, through a non-partisan, public-private partnership between America's state legislators and concerned members of the private sector, the federal government and the general public."[55] The following year, again with support from Coors, Weyrich founded the Committee for the Survival of a Free Congress, an organization to recruit and train conservative activists and candidates and raise funds for conservative causes. In 1981, along with conservative religious leader Tim LaHaye and others, Weyrich helped establish the Council for National Policy—called by ABC News "the most powerful conservative group you've never heard of."[56] In a relatively rare exploration of a political organization, ABC noted, "The council has deservedly attained the reputation for conceiving and promoting the ideas of many who in fact do want to control everything in the world."[57] Leading conservatives frequently address gatherings of the secretive organization. George W. Bush spoke to the group while running for president in 1999: "Depending on whose account you believe, Bush promised to appoint only anti-abortion-rights judges to the Supreme Court, or he stuck to his campaign 'strict constructionist' phrase. Or he took a tough stance against gays and lesbians, or maybe he didn't."[58]

Reforms passed after Watergate made it more difficult for individuals to donate large amounts of money to individual campaigns. Compiling smaller donations required more effort and more organization, leading to an explosion of political-action committees, or PACs. Formed by both liberals and conservatives, those organizations often focused on single issues. But the National Conservative Political Action Committee was broader. It was formed in 1975 as a conservative version of the American Federation of Labor and Congress of Industrial Organizations' (AFL-CIO) Committee on Political Education.[59] John "Terry" Dolan, who had become politically active with Youth for Freedom, chaired the organization during its early years and was primarily responsible for the fact that it apparently raised more money than any other conservative group in 1976. Four years later it helped defeat incumbent Democratic senators Birch Bayh, Frank Church, John Culver, and George McGovern and to elect Ronald Reagan president.[60] Dolan took pride in the viciousness of the group's attacks and in its conflicts with the Federal Elections Commission over negative campaign ads. In a 1980 interview, he seemed to predict the state of things to come:

> Groups like ours are potentially very dangerous to the political process. We could be a menace, yes. Ten independent expenditure groups, for example, could amass this great amount of money and defeat the point of accountability in politics. We could say whatever we want about an opponent of a Senator Smith and the senator wouldn't have to say anything. A group like ours could lie through its teeth and the candidate it helps stays clean.[61]

Among other complaints, the organization's ads supported the claims of social conservatives that the "nation's moral fiber is weakened by the growing homosexual movement."[62] Dolan, a closeted homosexual, began voicing support for gay rights in the early 1980s. He denied that he was gay, however, or that he had AIDS before he died of the disease in 1986.[63]

Former Reagan staffer and longtime Republican activist Morton Blackwell has served on the boards of directors of the American Conservative Union and the National Right to Work Committee and as the executive director of the Council for National Policy. Blackwell started the Leadership Institute in 1979. As a nonprofit corporation the institute cannot endorse specific parties or candidates and accepts liberal and conservative students, but it is funded mostly by conservatives and makes no pretense of its antiliberal slant. According to its mission statement, its mission is "to identify, recruit, train, and place conservatives in politics, government, and media."[64] The institute offers dozens of workshops and seminars and boasts that fifty-three thousand students have enrolled in its programs. Many of those programs are media related.[65] "At the Institute, there is no clear demarcation between media success and public policy success—each exists to serve the other," one supportive book notes.[66] The institute calls its two-day Broadcast Journalism School a "one-stop, full-service seminar for conservatives who want a career in journalism." It promised to teach students how to find good internships, gain networking skills, develop their resumes, and effectively hunt for jobs. The Broadcast Placement Service also offers a somewhat ironically titled Balance in Media Fellowship to help graduates "land unpaid broadcast internships." Besides the Broadcast Journalism School, other programs include workshops in campaign leadership and development, public speaking, "effective TV techniques," public relations, and "grassroots" activism. One of the most interesting programs from a media perspective is a two-day Student Publica-

tions School, designed to help participants "start your own independent, conservative campus publication or give your existing
paper a boost."[67] According to one source, the program helped
launch twenty-one new publications in 2003 alone, and approximately one hundred graduates of the Leadership Institute were
"working professionally in TV news."[68]

Incidentally, if the Leadership Institute's Bi-Partisan Congressional Advisory Board is an example, media organizations might
be well advised to examine the ethics of what the institute teach-
es before hiring its graduates. Though the document neglected
to identify members by party affiliation, as of late 2006 the "bi-
partisan" board was comprised of 102 Republicans, all living, and
one long-dead Democrat—ultraconservative Georgian Larry Mc-
Donald, who had been killed in a bizarre incident twenty-three
years earlier.[69] McDonald was so conservative that at the time of
his death he served as the second-ever national chairman of the
John Birch Society, which had long since been rejected even by
most conservatives as an extremist organization. McDonald and
268 other people died when a Soviet jet shot down a South Korean airliner that accidentally flew into Soviet airspace, prompting
some of McDonald's political allies to suspect a Communist plot.
"There is a real question in my mind that the Soviets may have actually murdered 269 passengers and crew on the Korean Air Lines
Flight 007 in order to kill Larry McDonald," said Jerry Falwell,
head of the Moral Majority.[70]

Falwell's comments provide a reminder that groups affiliated
with the Religious Right have been more visible than most of
the conservative organizations already cited. The power of Christian conservatism has been a popular news media topic for almost thirty years, but nonreligious organizations—perhaps ultimately more influential—such as those discussed in this chapter

have received much less attention from journalists. In fact, many of the most influential conservatives even in recent years have not been particularly religious, a fact seldom pointed out by either the mainstream media or the Religious Right. The relative lack of fervor in their own religious faith, of course, has not prevented those conservatives from accepting the support of conservative Christians in dealing with a host of issues on which the two simply happen to agree.

Many of the organizations discussed here have spawned other groups, some of which devote much of their effort to attacking the news media for its supposedly liberal nature. Spin-off organizations also help wealthy donors legally circumvent normal spending limits, because donors can then donate the legal maximum to each group. Legally the groups are separate; philosophically they may be identical. Their power since the 1970s has been immense, yet few in the media noticed them until after conservatives gained power. For example, two months after Reagan's election as president, the *Washington Post* told readers about a landscape of conservative organizations that aided Reagan: "This landscape, much of it overlooked by liberals until their November election debacle, is made up of an extensive and well-financed network of think tanks in Washington and New York, national magazines, organizations that crank out research on dozens of public policy issues or spread the conservative message on campuses, and activist legal groups that help corporations fight government regulation."[71] The article failed to mention that the mainstream media also had "overlooked" much of the landscape.

Sometimes news media use sources from organizations such as the Cato Institute, a libertarian think tank that has promoted privatization of Social Security and disputed scientific claims about global warming, without specifically identifying the conservative nature of the organizations. Some stories discuss individual political activities involving the organizations. Yet journalists almost never connect the organizations to one another or to a larger conservative movement. A rare exception came with a 1977 article in *U.S. News and World Report,* a somewhat conservative newsmagazine that may have looked at the time like it was engaging in wishful thinking: "While Democrats and Republicans stripe away at each other from entrenched positions, a third force is quietly building a political apparatus that pointedly disregards party labels. The newcomers: conservatives of widely varying backgrounds, linked by a common devotion to limited government, free enterprise and a strong national defense."[72] The article also noted that several new conservative groups had been established within the previous year, "and most get their money from small donors through direct-mail solicitation."[73] Direct mail had become one of the most important of several new conservative forms of media.

SIX

THE RISE OF THE RIGHT-WING MEDIA

Several conservative publications—and later, talk radio—deserve credit for helping bolster the conservative resurgence. Yet part of the reason that the growing movement escaped notice for so long was because of the medium primarily responsible for promoting that growth. Media scholars often look to newspapers, magazines, and even broadcast transcripts to explain historical events, but those mass media showed little of the uprising when it was under way. In fact, direct mail, which for conservatives became anything but "junk mail," did more than any other medium to build the movement. Direct mail also made Richard Viguerie one of the godfathers of modern conservatism. Viguerie and coauthor David Franke have written that after Barry Goldwater was soundly defeated in 1964, conservatives "stripped of any delusions that we could get a fair shake from the establishment's mass media" decided they had to concentrate on "guerrilla warfare."[1]

Viguerie did not invent direct mail. A few political campaigns had used it during the 1950s. Businesses had been doing so for years before Viguerie became involved in fund-raising for conservative causes in the 1960s. While working on behalf of Young

Americans for Freedom, however, Viguerie found that he disliked asking people for money over the phone or face to face, and he discovered that he had a knack for writing letters. He left YAF to found his own direct-mail company, focusing on ways that he might promote conservatism and draw conservative clients to his new venture:

> Plenty of young conservatives were boning up on conservative philosophy, and many others were studying the techniques of political organization. Nobody, as far as I could tell, was studying how to *sell* conservatism to the American people. I knew I was never going to be a conservative intellectual, so for a period of a few years I didn't read the growing number of conservative books that were being published, and I barely looked at *National Review* or *Human Events*. . . . I decided to spend every spare moment intensively studying commercial direct mail, so I could apply those techniques to political nonprofit groups.[2]

One early Viguerie idea involved the clerk of the House of Representatives, who kept a list of the names and addresses of anyone who had donated at least fifty dollars to a federal political campaign. Viguerie and his employees copied down the names and addresses of approximately 12,500 Goldwater donors and then had them compiled in a computer database. Viguerie later bought other lists, building a total list of more than 150,000 names by the mid-1960s. By 1980, the number was about ten times that, or fifteen million potential donors.[3] In addition to constantly adding names to his own list, perhaps Viguerie's most important service was managing to persuade various conservative organizations to rent their mailing lists to him and to other organizations and to pay fees to rent lists from him and from other groups. That consolidation of effort helped conservatism become a movement, not just a collection of entities. Though they now use the same techniques, neither liberals nor the Democratic Party have ever caught up.

The use of direct mail helped Viguerie and others reach conservatives who did not typically read conservative magazines or books, or even pay attention to the news media (which conservatives felt were biased against them, anyway). In that way, direct mail created new conservative voters and activists. Direct mail helped recipients feel connected to the political process, as they learned about and gave money to causes in which they believed. In addition, mailings typically focused on single issues such as abortion, gun control, or school prayer. That focus attracted donors who were unlikely to contribute to individual candidates or parties and helped make some candidates increasingly viable. Stirred up in part by direct mail, single-issue voters helped sway even national elections. For example, anti–gay marriage proposals that appeared on the ballots of several states, including the key state of Ohio, helped George W. Bush win the presidency in 2004.

Particularly important from a media standpoint, direct mail gave sponsoring organizations a means to get out their message in an unfiltered, emotional, one-sided way—without drawing the attention of the mainstream media or political opponents. One especially notable aspect of a great deal of conservative direct mail has always been its reliance on scare tactics, the same kinds of anger-and-fear-based appeals later found useful by talk radio hosts. That focus is not surprising, considering how much the uncertainties brought by social turmoil had influenced conservatism. The politics of anger that later became common to talk radio and Fox News programming punctuated what became a key element of the movement—that what one opposed often mattered more than what one supported. But direct mail focused on anger and fear as political tools long before the broadcast media did. Critics complained profusely that the tactics often were dishonest and unfair. One political writer maintains that since the 1960s conservatives have specialized in "the Great Backlash," that instead of focusing on reasoned discourse, conservatives use social issues to provoke outrage that is then channeled to promote probusiness economic policies: "Cultural anger is marshaled to achieve economic ends."[4] The professed solution to the outrage then becomes obvious for those marshaling conservative support: "Because some artist decides to shock the hicks by dunking Jesus in urine, the entire planet must remake itself along the lines preferred by the Republican Party, U.S.A."[5]

One critic described Viguerie's customary mailing as a formula involving three elements: raising an alarm, identifying the perpetrator at fault for the perceived problem, and then offering some means of action—typically joining the organization or just sending a donation—to defeat the perpetrator.[6] Liberal groups may use some of the same techniques, though some argue that angry appeals may work better for conservatives than they do for liberals anyway. "There are twice as many angry conservatives in this country as there are angry liberals," a direct mailer for Democratic causes is quoted as saying. "Liberals, by their very nature, don't get as angry as conservatives do, and that puts the Democratic Party at a great disadvantage."[7] Anger and frustration bring conservatives into politics, he added: "There's almost a certain level of irritation about a conservative coming to politics. A conservative is coming to politics because there's something they have to stop. Democrats come to politics because there's something they want to create."[8] The 2006 congressional elections may suggest otherwise, of course, as many political activists expressed their efforts as a means to "stop Bush" or "stop the war." Regardless, others suggest that anger, fear, and other negative emotions also have a wider purpose, usually seen with campaign advertising but which may also apply to other media use. The idea is not to improve democracy by getting more voters to turn out. Instead, the goal is to get the *right* voters to turn out, while helping prompt less predictable voters—turned off by the negativity of politics—to decide to stay home. "You're going to see more of this sensational, off-the-wall stuff," one scholar said during the buildup to a recent election. "If you get people disgusted, they might withdraw from politics, and that's the real goal these days."[9] Of course, one drawback to such appeals may be the relative difficulty of maintaining emotional intensity (and eventually political power) if the appeals achieve their purpose. For example, the election and presidency of Ronald Reagan, the darling of conservatives, forced Viguerie to lay off hundreds of staffers in his direct-mail operation.[10]

In addition to the impressive impact of direct mail, some more traditional mass media did contribute significantly to the conservative resurgence. Starting in 1955, a number of publications arose to help define and promote conservatism's growth. *Human Events* (at first a newsletter, later a magazine) began that year, as did the *Freeman,* a more libertarian magazine. By far the most important 1955 arrival, however, was William F. Buckley's *National Review.* Combining traditional conservatism, libertarian economics, and especially anti-communism, the magazine gave conservatism both a focus and a voice—most notably the caustically witty and erudite voice of Buckley himself. "We offer, besides ourselves, a position that has not grown old under the weight of a gigantic, parasitic bureaucracy, a position untempered by the doctoral dissertations of a generation of Ph.D.'s in social architecture, unattenuated by a thousand vulgar promises to a thousand different pressure groups, uncorroded by a cynical attempt for human freedom," Buckley wrote in his opening publisher's statement. "And that, ladies and gentlemen, leaves us just about the hottest thing in town."[11] The first issue offered seven of the publisher's convictions, including, "The profound crisis of our era is, in essence, the conflict between the Social Engineers, who seek to adjust mankind to conform with scientific utopias, and the disciples of Truth, who defend the organic moral order."[12] Buckley called communism "the century's most blatant force of satanic utopianism," while issuing warnings about intellectual conformity, "Big Brother government," labor unions, the United Nations, and a lack of a "traditional two-party system that fights its feuds in public and honestly."[13]

Buckley's skillful use of language failed to impress every reader. An early issue of *National Review* carried thirty-nine letters to the editor, almost all complimentary. One reader, however, suggested "that you *not* make it too erudite for the average reader."[14] Another wrote, "Please ask your writers to use plain simple language, and not to hide their meaning under sarcastic double-talk."[15] The publication's tone irritated even some conservatives. Irving Kristol wrote that he would have preferred a conservative magazine "that would help refine and elevate public discourse," but his early impression was that "*National Review* was certainly not that. It was brash, even vulgar in its antiliberal polemics. There was something collegiate—sophomoric to be blunt—about its high-spiritedness, and its general tone was anti-intellectual."[16] Buckley's was not the only strong conservative voice in the magazine. "No other journal in American history comes so close to constituting a conservative who's who," one historian noted.[17] The "unstable compound of traditionalists, libertarians, and ex-communists" that comprised the long list of writers and editors included L. Brent Bozell, Whittaker Chambers, Frank Chodorov, Frank S. Meyer, M. Stanton Evans, and Russell Kirk.[18]

The early subscription price for the *National Review* was seven dollars for one year, five dollars for each additional year. The newsstand price was twenty cents. The first issue carried only two full-page advertisements, one an anti-Communist message from an office machine manufacturer. The publication lost millions of dollars in its early years. William Rusher, the magazine's second publisher, reported after a decade that while circulation had climbed to ninety thousand, the publication had yet to break even: "Advertising has been slow in coming—heartbreakingly slow. American business, in general, seems pathetically eager to play Follow the Leader provided somebody else is the leader. . . . Never, certainly, in the field of conservative journalism has so much been owed to so few."[19] He said the magazine might never be profitable but predicted that change would come as conservatism continued to grow: "Once the *fact* of the new conservatism is accepted in our society rather than resisted blindly like some sort of foreign object, the NATIONAL REVIEW, as the premier spokesman of the conservative movement, will be hailed and made much of for the very qualities that render it suspect today."[20] In fact, *National Review* was able to hang on and maintain message consistency because the popular Buckley remained heavily involved throughout its early years, because he had enough money and friends to keep the publication afloat even as it lost millions of dollars, and because he controlled the majority of the voting stock. "It's amazing how many fights are avoided when you have total control," he once said.[21] In its efforts to keep itself and the conservative movement on track, the publication sometimes harshly criticized other forms of conservatism. One complimentary history of the publication notes:

In the context of the new conservative movement, Objectivists—followers of the anti-religious Ayn Rand—were "left" deviationists, and in its early years *National Review* turned all its big guns on the Randians with a fury usually reserved for liberal targets. A couple of years later, it was the "right" deviationists of the John Birch Society who were accused of overly conspiratorial thinking and expelled from the movement by the *National Review.* The purpose of these purges was to keep the new movement on the path to power, without giving liberals handy targets for scaring the American people about a threat from the right. They also served to keep the *National Review* type of anti-communist conservatives in firm control of the growing movement.[22]

Irving Kristol later called his early dismissal of the magazine "the kind of mistake that intellectuals are especially prone to make in politics"—a failure to recognize that while complicated ideas matter, "simple ideas, allied to passion and organization, also have consequences."[23] The readers of *National Review* did more than perhaps anyone else to make Barry Goldwater the 1964 Republican candidate over Nelson Rockefeller, dealing a crippling blow to the more liberal republicanism of the party's eastern wing.[24] Buckley also increased attention for himself and the conservative cause by hosting a long-running public-affairs television show, *Firing Line.* Started in 1966 as an hour-long syndicated program that ran on various commercial stations, five years later the show moved to public television, where it ran until 1999 (having been shortened to a half hour in 1988). Buckley's conservative perspective was obvious on the program, though that perspective was countered and moderated by guests and other panelists.[25]

Republican conservatism has changed in recent decades, and publications other than *National Review* contributed both to those changes and to the continued growth of conservatism. In 1957, just two years after the birth of *National Review,* Russell Kirk founded *Modern Age* as "a dignified forum for reflective, traditionalist conservatism."[26] Kirk also started the *University Bookman,* a small quarterly devoted to reviewing textbooks and criticizing higher education from a decidedly conservative and usually negative perspective. First appearing in 1960, the *Bookman* had its own distribution list but also was distributed free to all *National Review* subscribers.[27] In 1965, the libertarian Intercollegiate Society of Individualists began publishing the *Intercollegiate Review,* which throughout its history has offered articles from various strands of conservatism.[28]

A more important 1965 arrival came when Irving Kristol helped found *Public Interest,* a quarterly publication that promised to be "as lively, as readable, and as controversial as possible," while making room "for the occasional 'dull' article that merely reports the truth about a matter under public discussion."[29] Much of the magazine's concern focused on social issues, especially skepticism about the social programs incorporated into Lyndon Johnson's war on poverty. Kristol served as coeditor for its entire history. It folded in 2005, but by then, as one conservative columnist noted, the publication's neoconservative perspective had "quietly shaped, and then came to dominate, political discourse in America."[30] Helping illustrate the differences between neoconservatives and more traditional conservatives, one historian notes, "Libertarians especially would find little in the *Public Interest* that would please them."[31]

Other magazines contributed to the conservative resurgence. Another publication with a neoconservative bent arrived in 1977, courtesy of a conservative think tank, the Heritage Foundation. *Policy Review* argued in its first issue that "the large-scale social programs of the 60's and early 70's" needed closer scrutiny and suggested that it also would focus heavily on foreign policy (the focus of five of the nine articles in that issue). "And if, now and then, a Congressman sees some good in a proposal in Policy Review, or an assistant secretary in some department takes to heart a critique of a governmental program, we will all be better off," the magazine's introductory column stated.[32] Norman Podhoretz cofounded *Commentary* in 1945. Like Podhoretz himself, the publication started out liberal and concerned with Jewish thought, then in the 1970s became a neoconservative voice.[33] Richard Viguerie began publishing *Conservative Digest* in 1975, also with a neoconservative focus but aimed at, in the words of one historian, "the lower-middle-class Americans intimidated by the intellectual style of the *National Review* and *Human Events.*"[34]

Providing a reminder that objectivity is every bit as fleeting among historians as among journalists, *Continuity,* aimed primarily at conservative professional historians and those interested in conservative historical themes, began in 1980. The publication claims to adamantly oppose determinism, presentism, and didacticism—political or moral messages such as those often found in Marxist, feminist, or labor histories.[35] Of course, good liberal professional historians also oppose the first two of those "isms," while pointing out that the third is far more difficult and perhaps impossible to avoid. Those who write meaningful histories must choose relevant sources and interpret data that are never entirely complete, then use those sources and data to tell stories. How successfully and fairly they do so is one measure of their professionalism.

Conservative opinion publications also thrived during the Clinton presidency, among them the *American Spectator.* Originally founded on a college campus in 1967, it proudly slammed feminists and homosexuals in the strident tone one might expect of college students or right-wing radio talk show hosts. Before legal problems, financial issues, and internal struggles considerably weakened it, the *Spectator* briefly became the most-read U.S. opinion journal by bashing the Clintons and other perceived liberals in power. In 1995, boosted by a three-million-dollar annual subsidy from media magnate Rupert Murdoch, William Kristol (the son of Irving Kristol) started the *Weekly Standard* as the new voice of neoconservatism. The magazine heavily pushed the neoconservative call for exporting American-style democracy and for the Iraq War. "While it has never achieved a large circulation it probably is the most influential ideological magazine in Bush-era Washington," one conservative book argued in 2004.[36] By then neoconservatives also comprised most of the editorial staff of the *National Review,* still by far the leader among conservative journals in terms of circulation. The Clinton presidency helped that magazine's circulation peak at more than two hundred thousand, though it later lost almost a fourth of that readership. As the authors of one study note, "The journals supporting the political party or point of view that is out of power often do better than the ones supporting those in power."[37] Further evidence is provided by the fact that in recent years a left-leaning magazine, *The Nation,* passed *National Review* in circulation.[38]

Unlike magazines, few contemporary American newspapers profess strong conservative or liberal political views. Conservative columnists such as William F. Buckley, George Will, Patrick Buchanan, James J. Kilpatrick, Cal Thomas, Robert Novak, and Mona Charen have been syndicated in hundreds of newspapers, but typically those same newspapers also carry more liberal columnists. In addition, columns tend to be more reactive, responding to events, than consistently intellectual in nature. As a result, newspapers were far less influential than their print cousins in explaining or helping develop conservative thought. Still, the 1982 arrival of the *Washington Times* warrants attention not just because it countered a longtime decline in the number of cities with competing newspapers but because of its obvious conservatism, its location in the nation's capital, and its owner. Sun Myung Moon, the Korean billionaire and founder of the Unification Church, founded the newspaper. Commonly viewed as a cult leader whose followers were known as "Moonies," Moon had drawn considerable media attention through mass "marriages" involving thousands of couples, and he also served a brief prison term after a tax-fraud conviction in the same year as the newspaper began publication.

Conservative Christians undoubtedly could identify with Moon's anti-communism, his professed belief in Jesus Christ, his disdain for mainstream media, and his commitment to "restoring the family as the building block of the community, society, nation, and the world."[39] He founded a "pro-family" organization, the American Family Coalition, with professed concerns virtually identical to those of organizations founded by evangelical Christians.[40] More problematic to American evangelicals, however, might be Moon's claims to be "the second messiah," or that he and his third wife are "True Parents . . . the first couple to have the complete blessing of God, and to be able to bring forth children with no original sin."[41]

The *Times* calls itself "America's Newspaper" and continues to provide Washington with a conservative alternative to the *Washington Post*. Though not of the same quality or influence as the *Post*, the *Times* has made Washington a rare example of a city with daily newspapers that compete ideologically in their editorials—and in the tone of their headlines, for that matter. *Columbia Journalism Review* has noted that the *Times'* alternative voice "forces stories into the mainstream that might not otherwise get there."[42] The *Washington Post* reported that by the newspaper's twentieth anniversary it had become "a must-read for conservatives in town," and "even many liberals have come to respect it for aggressive reporting and provocative editorials."[43] Others have been more critical, with one former employee saying that at least in its early years, "Nobody paid much attention to it. . . . Considering that the paper was governed by a calculatedly unfair political bias and that its journalistic ethics were close to nil, this was a good thing."[44]

At an anniversary celebration featuring conservative radio personality Laura Schlessinger as a paid speaker, Moon declared, "The *Washington Times* will become the instrument in spreading the truth about God to the world." That statement and others, the *Washington Post* reported, "tossed gasoline on the long-smoldering embers that some *Times* staffers have spent two decades trying to extinguish: the accusation that their paper is a mouthpiece for Moon's religious movement, the Unification Church. Or, at best, a public relations outlet for conservative values and the Republican Party."[45] Despite the fact that it apparently has never been profitable, the *Times* expanded its influence somewhat in 2000 by buying United Press International, the struggling wire service that once had been the primary competitor of the Associated Press.

The most obvious conservative mass media in recent years—coming along after conservative organizations, direct mail, magazines, and Ronald Reagan had already helped establish conservative politics as the status quo in America—have been broadcast media, especially talk radio. In a media shift that helped revive AM radio, talk radio exploded in popularity largely because of four factors spread over two decades. First, the liberal Pacifica Radio Network began experimenting during the 1960s with various types of call-in and talk programs. Second, National Public Radio, also typically considered more liberal than the mainstream, began syndicated talk-oriented programming via satellite in 1978.[46] Third, the Federal Communications Commission (FCC) under Ronald Reagan repealed the Fairness Doctrine in 1987, meaning broadcasters could air opinions without having to air opposing viewpoints. (Congress attempted to reinstate the Fairness Doctrine, but Reagan vetoed the bill.) Fourth, a year later, Rush Limbaugh's radio program was syndicated nationally and found a large audience with a bombastic conservative message. Bitingly witty and boasting that he dispensed wisdom through "talent on loan from God," Limbaugh called himself a news commentator, but his program actually became a leading source of news for some listeners. Many regular listeners proudly called themselves "dittoheads" because they agreed so completely with Limbaugh.[47]

Despite his "Excellence in Broadcasting" slogan, Limbaugh often exaggerates or distorts facts to better support his arguments while lambasting liberal politicians. He frequently attacks the *New York Times* and the *Washington Post* for their supposed liberalism, but he regularly cites articles from both newspapers, sometimes taken out of context, to support his own claims. Critics sometimes accuse him of racism and sexism, while supporters praise his lack of political correctness. Many conservatives now watch Fox News and tune in to other conservative radio programs. Yet despite a widely publicized battle with drug addiction and other setbacks, Limbaugh remains popular with millions of listeners, and hundreds of radio stations around the country carry his program. Other fans listen (and sometimes watch) via the Internet. He was most popular during Bill Clinton's presidency, though the election of a conservative Congress and then George W. Bush gave Limbaugh less to rail against. His success spawned numerous imitators, and conservative talk radio has become the most noteworthy kind of programming on AM radio.

In terms of television, though all of the main U.S. television networks except perhaps PBS tend to be primarily conservative by nature—pro-America, pro-capitalism, pro–status quo—one network has done more than any other to actively promote conservative ideology. Rupert Murdoch's Fox News first aired October 7, 1996, a month before Clinton was elected to his second term as president. The network drew immediate attention and an audience with its criticism of other media and its obvious support of conservatives. Liberal organizations waged a 2004 Internet campaign to try to persuade the Federal Trade Commission to prohibit Fox from using its ironic slogan of "fair and balanced news," calling it misleading advertising, but the network continued to grow and now battles CNN for supremacy among cable news stations.[48] Though Fox executives consistently deny a conservative bias, a national survey finds, "The single news channel that strikes most journalists as taking a particular ideological stance—either liberal or conservative—is Fox News Channel."[49] Apparently that stance has helped Republicans, as one study finds that GOP voting increases after Fox News is introduced to an area. Though not large, the vote shift may have been decisive in the 2000 elections.[50]

Helped by the ineptitude of other networks, Fox News also affected the 2000 presidential election by contributing to the resulting chaos. With the election extremely close, it became clear on election night that Al Gore would win the popular vote, but whichever candidate won Florida would claim enough electoral votes to win the election. Fox News first declared Bush the winner of the state and the election, followed by the other networks. All declarations were far too early, and the Fox News staffer behind the first projection turned out to be a Bush first cousin. The staffer had spoken to both Bush and his brother, Florida governor Jeb Bush, shortly before making his recommendation to project Bush as the winner. "Even as he was leading the Fox decision desk that night, John Ellis was also on the phone with his cousins—'Jebbie,' the governor of Florida, and the presidential candidate himself—giving them updated assessments of the vote count," the *Washington Post* later reported. "Ellis's projection was crucial because Fox News Channel put Florida in the *W.* column at 2:16 A.M. followed by NBC, CBS, CNN, and ABC within four minutes. That decision, which turned out to be wrong and was retracted by the embarrassed networks less than two hours later, created the impression that Bush had 'won' the White House."[51] Before joining Fox, Ellis had resigned as a political columnist for the *Boston Globe,* writing at the time that he could not continue to write about the 2000 campaign because: "I am loyal to my cousin, Governor George Bush of Texas. I put that loyalty ahead of my loyalty to anyone else outside my immediate family. . . . There is no way for you to know if I am telling you the truth about George W. Bush's presidential campaign because in his case, my loyalty goes to him and not to you."[52] The U.S. Supreme Court handed down a decision a month after the 2000 election that essentially declared the election over, with Bush the winner. On election night four years later, when the 2004 presidential election came down to how Ohio would vote, Fox called that state in favor of Bush twenty minutes before any other network.[53] Fox proved less speedy in giving conservatives bad electoral news, however. When Democrats gained control of Congress in 2006, ABC, CBS, NBC, and CNN all projected the shift before Fox.

Even farther outside of the mainstream than Fox News are Christian media. As the Religious Right became increasingly involved in politics, religious media also contributed to the growth of conservatism. In fact, evangelical Christians often have been better at using both mainstream news media and their own media sources than other conservatives, Christians, and religions. "Although evangelical and fundamentalist theology and cultural norms are definitely antimodern, religious conservatives have adeptly used modern communications technologies to spread their version of the gospel," one scholar notes. "Aggressively traditionalist in its explicit message, the Christian right avidly embraces change and sophistication in its media."[54] Besides a number of magazines and highly visible cable networks, those media—many of which have become overtly political—now include professional Internet sites, electronic newsletters or Listservs, and more than 1,200 Christian radio stations. For example, the American Family Association, a Bible-based organization that professes to stand "for traditional family values, focusing primarily on the influence of television and other media," owns more than one hundred stations, putting it in the top five companies in terms of number of stations owned. The professionalism and effectiveness of those media should not be surprising, however, considering how long Christian media producers have been practicing their craft.[55]

Like every other significant aspect of everyday American life, religion has always been a part of the American news media, including the first newspaper, the one-issue *Publick Occurrences Both Forreign and Domestick*. While religion was not a specific topic, it was embedded in stories as a reflection of printer Benjamin Harris's beliefs. Early Americans typically saw no separation between their era's mainstream media and religion. Christian faith was an inherent part of most early American newspapers, and one historian has noted that religious news was more common in colonial newspapers than news about any other subject. Editors gave God the credit for good news and blamed him for misfortune. Newspapers recorded baptisms and other religious activities, and they sometimes printed hymns, scriptures, prayers, or sermons. More than two centuries before evangelist Pat Robertson made similar claims, American newspapers blamed God's wrath for events ranging from miscarriages to high taxes to earthquakes.[56]

Those conservative Christians who promote the premise that the United States was founded as a Christian nation might be equally inclined to suggest that the free press promoted by the nation's founders was—and was intended to be—a Christian press. Even early on, however, most newspapers did little to proselytize or promote Christianity (or deism, or any other belief system). Religion typically served more as a moral foundation for editors' claims and actions than as a subject considered newsworthy in itself. Religious activities were covered because they were *activities*—common events that involved readers—not because they were religious. And as the potential readership grew, bringing an increasing number and range of interests, newspapers devoted less space to religion. Of course, over time the same has been true of a number of nonreligious topics ranging from international affairs to society news.[57] When a number of religious newspapers appeared in the early 1800s, many looked similar to other publications. They generally were nonsectarian so as not to limit the potential audience, and because some publishers wanted their publications to become community newspapers. Some religious newspapers did take strong political positions that corresponded with their faith, particularly over issues such as the abolition of slavery.[58]

At least one respected religious newspaper was started in self-defense. Mary Baker Eddy founded the *Christian Science Monitor* largely to counter criticism of Christian Science by other publications, especially *McClure's* and Joseph Pulitzer's *New York World*. The *Monitor* became one of the most trusted newspapers in America, undoubtedly in large part because it reflected its religious tenets through morality and ethical practices rather than through proselytizing.[59] It remains a very good newspaper, particularly in terms of international news coverage—a beat, like religion, that most news media tend not to cover consistently or well. But even the *Monitor* has seen its circulation drop considerably, from an apparent high of more than 191,500 in 1988 to less than 71,500 just before the 9/11 attacks on the World Trade Center boosted interest in international news and the circulation of the newspaper (by about nine thousand). By then, of course, many readers were reading the *Monitor* and other publications via the Internet.[60]

Aside from the occasional excesses of yellow journalists or others, and despite the claims of some religious conservatives, rarely has the mainstream American press been particularly unfriendly or unfair toward the faithful. After all, most journalists also identify themselves as Christians, and few publishers or news directors want to alienate a significant part of the potential audience. Admittedly, journalists often have been somewhat inept at covering social institutions, including religion. As with other subjects, journalists typically downplayed or ignored the everyday religious aspects of American life simply because those religious activities did not provide the immediacy or conflict of subjects considered newsworthy. Space limitations sometimes also dictate formal or informal "quotas" for various types of news. Occasional exceptions have come with conflict-oriented stories about issues such as school prayer or abortion, scandals involving church leaders, or discussions of how a political candidate's faith might influence the electorate. Other religious stories tended to be about religious conflict in the Middle East or about those viewed as religious extremists, ranging from Islamic militants to Baptist television evangelist Jerry Falwell's conservative Moral Majority. The more dramatic but atypical depictions of religion may have given a distorted picture of Christianity—and, for many Christians, of the news media.[61] Giving advice to new reporters on the religion beat, a *Newark Star-Ledger* reporter wrote: "Does your editor care about religion coverage? The short answer is: No." Still, he notes, it "is not that your editor—or any editor—is irreligious, unreligious, non-religious, whatever. . . . Editors, like most reporters, gravitate toward coverage of politics and crime. These are topics on which everyone is an expert, and they are stories that don't require a lot of interpretation or debate. A corpse is a corpse is a corpse."[62]

Largely shut out of the mainstream news media, the answer for many Christians was to start their own media. Numerous religious publications have had varying and sometimes unknowable degrees of influence. Two of the earliest and politically most important periodicals were the *Sword of the Lord,* founded by fundamentalist evangelist John R. Rice in 1934, and *Christian Beacon,* founded by defrocked Presbyterian minister Carl McIntire in 1936. The *Sword*'s contributors made up "a who's who in extreme fundamentalism, including Dr. Bob Jones, Sr., and Dr. Bob Jones, Jr., the founder and president of Bob Jones University, respectively . . . Dr. Carl McIntire, founder of the fundamentalist American Council of Christian Churches; and the Reverend Jerry Falwell, leader of the Moral Majority," one historian notes.[63] Rice and McIntire had similar political philosophies and sometimes exchanged articles. Both eventually considered noted evangelist Billy Graham to be too liberal. For example, a *Beacon* headline about a Graham trip to the Soviet Union stated, "Graham's Moscow Speech Reveals His Betrayal of Christianity and His Union with Buddhists, Muslims, Hindus, Jews, Pagan Religions."[64] Even Moral Majority leader Jerry Falwell drew criticism from the *Beacon* for "his alliances with Mormons, Roman Catholics, and Liberals."[65] Both publishers urged their readers to be politically active, and

both devoted much of their editorial effort to fighting communism. The *Sword* was strongly anti-Catholic until Catholic Joseph
McCarthy's anti-communism campaign (then again when John F.
Kennedy ran for president), regarded the Panama Canal treaty as
a violation of the biblical commandment against theft, and used
the Bible to justify capitalism, oppose taxes, and call for government regulations against television profanity, pornography, homosexuality, abortion, and smoking.[66] More widely read than either
of those publications was *Christianity Today,* founded by Graham
in 1956 as a more conservative alternative to a popular magazine
called the *Christian Century.* Though anti-Communist, promilitary, and procapitalism, *Christianity Today* has never been as strident
as the *Sword of the Lord* or the *Christian Beacon,* and it publishes a
much wider range of viewpoints.[67]

Those involved with conservative Christian radio probably had
more justification than evangelical printers or other conservatives
for distrust and anger toward the government. Christians have
been involved with radio almost since its beginning, but the relationship has not always been smooth, even though the earliest Christian broadcasters did little to promote political activism.
Broadcast sermons soon became fairly common. Two important
Christian radio pioneers were Walter A. Maier, whose *Lutheran
Hour* began in 1930, and Charles E. Fuller, who created the *Old-
Fashioned Revival Hour* in 1935. Maier's original focus would look
familiar to the conservative Christian of today: "To him, as to
many Americans, the twenties and thirties were decades of marked
decline, rising sinfulness, and the breakdown of traditional societal moorings. . . . Most of his sermons introduced some terrible
current evil, such as birth control, immorality, dishonesty, greed,
or decline of family values, and then discussed the cure: a return to Christ and His church."[68] Unlike many later broadcasters,

however, Maier apparently did not suggest that Christians try to fix society's problems through political means. The *Lutheran Hour* reached an estimated twenty million listeners around the world by 1948 (a year later, it also began airing on television). "By 1942, Maier was receiving more mail than *Amos 'n' Andy,* and Fuller was the biggest name on the Mutual Broadcasting Network, spending nearly thirty thousand dollars a week and purchasing 50 percent more airtime than the next largest secular broadcaster," marveled one Christian historian.[69]

The success of Maier and Fuller is particularly notable when considering the difficulty many religious leaders had in getting their programming on the air at all. Of course, some Christians considered broadcasting to be an inappropriate way to spread the word of God. But Maier began his radio ministry in 1924 with a part-time Christian station in a St. Louis seminary attic, and more than 10 percent of the six hundred stations operating in 1925 apparently were licensed to religious organizations. Still, Maier's station was one of the few church-owned stations to survive new regulations brought by the Radio Act of 1927. The Federal Regulatory Commission (FRC) typically classified religious stations as "propaganda" stations, shunting them to less desirable frequencies and/or hours, often causing them to share time with secular commercial stations. The agency also decreed that no new licenses would be assigned to religious stations because they did not offer enough diversity of opinion.[70]

Faced with few other options, many religious broadcasters had to seek airtime on commercial stations. Those stations often were happy to give time, in part because the FRC (and then its successor, the FCC) identified religious programs as one of the ways stations could meet required public-service obligations, and also because in the early years of radio, many stations had more airtime to fill than content to fill it. Not all of the time was offered free of charge, however, and stations tended to favor some denominations over others. Conservative evangelicals were among those frequently discriminated against. Sometimes that discrimination proved to be a long-term advantage because it forced conservative broadcasters to learn to produce programming that would attract attention, build audiences, and raise money. In some cases, however, some would-be Christian broadcasters could not even buy time. NBC, the first radio network, decided not to sell airtime to religious broadcasters, instead giving time to Catholic, Jewish, and Protestant groups. In the case of Protestants, the network turned to the Federal Council of Churches of Christ in America, which did not represent most conservative churches. One eventual result was the formation of the National Association of Evangelicals for United Action, formed in 1942 to promote and protect the rights of evangelical broadcasters. Two years later many of its members formed the National Religious Broadcasters, which lobbied on behalf of evangelical broadcasters.[71]

For much of radio history most conservative evangelical broadcasters were like Maier and other conservative believers, eschewing political involvement and focusing on their primary mission. "Broadcasters of the religious right never wavered in their commitment to a single, overriding goal: the conversion of the unsaved American public through the powerful—yet personal—reach of the medium of radio," one historian notes. "The drama embedded in revivalism—the enacting of a conversion or reliving of one's own past conversion—became another kind of American entertainment form."[72] Revivalism also proved profitable, as money contributed by the faithful helped keep those broadcasters on the air. Then in 1960, when the FCC changed its guidelines to let stations count even paid religious messages as public service programming, the incentive for stations to give time to religious broadcasters disappeared. Those best equipped to deal with the new system of having to pay were those who were already paying. In addition, when the FCC eased licensing restrictions after World War II, a number of religious organizations started new stations that appealed to radio preachers.

Activist religious broadcasters sometimes did have to worry about the FCC's Fairness Doctrine, which required broadcasters to air opposing political views. *Christian Beacon* publisher Carl McIntire lost his radio license for violating the Fairness Doctrine, drawing further media attention for his unsuccessful efforts to get around the FCC by broadcasting from an old minesweeper off the New Jersey coast in 1973. Still, from 1972 to 1982—a period corresponding to much of the political activism of Christian conservatives—Christian broadcasting boomed, with more than a thousand religious organizations producing programs that reached a weekly audience of millions. Because of the ratings measures used for religious programs and the obvious self-interest programmers have for making the numbers look as large as possible, just how many millions were listening is impossible to determine. But the number of religious radio stations more than doubled during that period, to almost nine hundred, and the number of religious television stations more than tripled, to seventy-nine. By the end of the Reagan presidency in 1988, those numbers had climbed to more than 1,100 radio stations and more than three hundred television stations, and those stations no longer had to worry about the Fairness Doctrine. They covered a broad range of perspectives, though one scholar notes that a defining factor of the "electronic church" is a reliance on charismatic leaders. And there is little doubt that for at least the past thirty-five years most of those leaders have been charismatic conservatives.[73] Three major religious organizations noted for their political influence during the conservative resurgence all were associated television evangelists: Jerry Falwell's Moral Majority, James Robinson's Religious Roundtable, and Pat Robertson's Christian Coalition.[74]

From a media standpoint, the most interesting of those religious leaders probably is Marion "Pat" Robertson. The son of a conservative Democratic U.S. senator from Virginia, Robertson applied to the FCC in 1960 for a license to operate the first television station devoted primarily to religious broadcasts. His Christian Broadcasting Network began broadcasting on WYAH in Portsmouth, Virginia, a year later. It struggled financially until Robertson took to the air to ask for seven hundred people—a "700 Club"—who would each pledge ten dollars per month to keep the station running. *The 700 Club* also became the name for the first daily Christian talk show, beginning in 1962. The flagship program of Robertson's Christian Broadcasting Network, the show offered prayer, news, and commentary from a conservative Christian perspective. It grew dramatically during the 1970s and 1980s and became increasingly political. Robertson, who founded Regent University in 1978, became popular enough to run for the U.S. presidency in 1988. He started the politically oriented Christian Coalition in 1989 and the American Center for Law and Justice, a nonprofit law firm that handles cases on behalf the Religious Right, in 1990.

Some viewers apparently now consider Robertson to be more journalist than entertainer and as much a journalist as a spiritual leader. He also has been a frequent political lightning rod. He has claimed that his prayers steered hurricanes away from his Virginia headquarters. He argued against an equal rights initiative in a fund-raising letter before the 1992 elections: "The feminist agenda is not about equal rights for women. It is about a socialist, anti-family political movement that encourages women to leave their husbands, destroy their children, practice witchcraft, destroy capitalism and become lesbians."[75] When Orlando, Florida, permitted gays to fly rainbow flags as a sign of diversity, Robertson told the city: "I don't think I'd be waving those flags in God's face if I were you. . . . A condition like this will bring about the destruction of your nation. It'll bring about terrorist bombs; it'll bring earthquakes, tornadoes and possibly a meteor."[76] He drew widespread criticism by advocating the assassination of Venezuelan president Hugo Chavez, telling voters of a Pennsylvanian town that they had rejected God by electing school board members who opposed the teaching of "intelligent design," and saying that God told him a U.S. terrorist attack would lead to "mass killings" in late 2007. "The Lord didn't say nuclear," Robertson said. "But I do believe it will be something like that."[77] Concerns about terrorism apparently prompted Robertson to confuse many Americans when in 2007 he endorsed former New York mayor Rudy Giuliani as the Republican nominee for president—after Giuliani had expressed support for both abortion and gay rights and had been married three times (living with his second wife while still married to his first and publicly dating his third wife while still married to his second). Despite Robertson's inconsistencies and sometimes extreme views, he still has thousands of viewers and supporters around the country whom he encourages to be politically involved. He also still is regularly given a forum for his views through interviews by mainstream news organizations—prompting conservative columnist David Brooks to say, "Some evangelicals say Pat Robertson has three main constituencies, ABC, CBS, and NBC."[78]

SEVEN

ECONOMIC AND REGULATORY CONSIDERATIONS

As mentioned in chapter 1, those who argue that the news media are more liberal than conservative typically point first to the fact that most journalists identify themselves as more liberal than most other Americans on selected survey questions. Yet aside from the fact that critics ignore other parts of the same surveys (which suggest that journalists have attitudes pretty much like those shared by most other Americans), no studies have shown that journalistic beliefs lead to liberal approaches to news. On the other hand, those who argue that the news media are more conservative than liberal typically point first to the business aspects of modern media and the fact that most media owners are conservatives—and numerous studies have shown that ownership issues do influence news content.

A 2000 Pew Research Center poll found that more than a third of reporters and news executives reported that news damaging to the news organization had gone unreported, while 29 percent said they had avoided stories that might prove harmful to advertisers.[1] The local media, from which most Americans get most of their news, often serve as boosters of their communities, not just of the nation as a whole. Newspapers have campaigned to keep military bases in their communities or have promoted other projects as good for business, and news organizations sometimes produce content they think their communities expect, even while downplaying or ignoring potential problems.[2] Sources opposed to the projects have trouble making their voices heard, not only because they may be viewed as less positive but also because those outside of the mainstream can be perceived as less credible. For example, one former journalist said about ignoring early environmentalists, "At the time, we considered it fair because they were nuts. They were regarded as a fringe group."[3] Even when many in the press and the country were becoming more liberal and more conscious of environmental issues during the 1960s, the publisher of the *Tri-City Herald* in Washington actively worked to promote his community as a center for nuclear power.[4] Though coverage of various topics including the poor and foreign affairs has decreased, coverage of business that appeals primarily to middle-class and upper-class audiences has steadily increased. Several television programs now focus almost entirely on news about business. "When PBS launched *Wall Street Week* with Louis Rukeyser in 1970, the program was conspicuous," one media critic notes. "Now there are dozens of national TV shows—most of them daily—devoted to the quest for high returns."[5] Network news programs and newspapers update the latest stock market numbers daily as if they were baseball scores, with little explanation of what the numbers may mean for most Americans. As one liberal critic has pointed out, a *New York Times* headline stating "Markets Surge as Labor Costs Stay in Check" might as well read, "Great News: Your Wages Aren't Going Up."[6]

Business aspects have become increasingly important to the news media, and not just as a subject of news. Of course, not all of the focus is new. Major publishers such as William Randolph Hearst, Joseph Patterson, Frank Gannett, and Robert McCormick used their newspapers to oppose Franklin D. Roosevelt's New Deal policies because of corporate concerns.[7] The American broadcast media might not exist without the initial investments and research of major corporations. General Electric, American Telegraph and Telephone, United Fruit, and Westinghouse joined to form the Radio Corporation of America (RCA). The consolidation may have violated antitrust laws, but it met with approval from both the government and the public.[8] Today a small number of corporate entities control most of the media content produced. Media organizations must meet the fiscal expectations of their corporate bosses and, increasingly, of stockholders. "The news has always been a commodity in America, and its behavior has followed the dictates of business and technology," the *Gannett Center Journal* noted in 1987. "One of the central ideas of capitalism is that commodities work most efficiently when produced, bought and sold in bulk and mass."[9] "The profit motive should be no surprise," one media historian points out. "America has always had both a capitalistic economy and culture, and few individuals who have started mass media companies were independently wealthy first."[10] Of course, in recent decades most of those companies have since been bought by corporations headed by individuals who were already wealthy.

Visible bias on the part of an individual news organization often reflects a desire to act in the best interests of the organization itself, such as to increase ratings or to undercut competitors.[11] For example, drug companies often sponsor news segments about health. "It seems unlikely that Bristol-Myers would be particularly happy to see CNN do a hard-hitting investigation of the drug industry," the *Washington Post* noted shortly after the network debuted such sponsorships in 1980. "And with so much at stake, it also seems unlikely that CNN would undertake such an endeavor."[12] A 1990 *Today* story about consumer boycotts neglected to mention that the nation's largest boycott targeted NBC parent company General Electric. ABC killed a newsmagazine story about Disney World, owned by ABC's parent company. CBS refused to run a *60 Minutes* story about corporate tobacco at a time when the network was for sale, until leaked details of the incident embarrassed the company. Even public broadcasting relies heavily on corporate underwriting that may influence what types of programs end up on the air.

When the conservative resurgence began in the decade after World War II, television had yet to achieve news dominance. Until the 1960s the majority of Americans received most of their news from newspapers. By then many cities already had only one daily newspaper, but probably few readers realized how much their print choices had begun to diminish. War hero Dwight D. Eisenhower's defeat of Robert Taft in the 1952 Republican convention dismayed conservatives, but those concerned about democracy in general had more reason for consternation that year: the number of American daily newspapers peaked in 1952. The number of dailies then fell for a few years, increased from 1958 until the mid-1960s, and then declined (except for one brief surge a decade later) for the rest of the century. By 1965 the *Los Angeles Times* led the nation in advertising and amount of editorial matter, largely because two other Los Angeles papers, the *Evening Mirror* and the *Examiner,* folded in 1962.[13]

Joint operating agreements (JOAs), in which two newspapers essentially merged all except editorial functions, also reduced competition. A dozen American cities saw new JOAs, during the 1950s and 1960s.[14] Concerned by the number of similar agreements, the

Justice Department briefly thwarted a Tucson JOA in 1969, calling it an infringement on free trade. But a year later Congress
passed the Newspaper Preservation Act, intended to help "save"
second dailies by allowing JOAs. Some argued that the act actually
hastened the deaths of some publications. "While JOAs probably
have 'preserved' some papers, it's likely that they kill more competition, and more papers, than they save," one legal scholar argued.
"Further, it's increasingly clear that JOAs perversely produce the
single-paper monopolies they are supposed to prevent."[15] Nine
JOA newspapers folded between 1970, the year the law was enacted, and 1994. The number of American cities with competing
dailies fell to nine. The *Pittsburgh Press,* which won Pulitzer Prizes for reporting in 1986 and 1987, folded in 1992 after an eight-
month strike against Pittsburgh's two dailies. During the strike
the *Pittsburgh Post-Gazette,* supposedly the weaker of the two papers, bought the *Press* and then promptly closed it when the strike
ended.[16]

Most daily newspapers belong to chains, reducing editorial diversity even further. More than one hundred chains existed
even before 1960. Their number would increase, but their influence would grow even more. By 1986 chains controlled 75 percent
of American newspaper circulation. The number of newspapers
controlled by chains more than doubled from 1960 to 1986, from
560 to 1,158, while the average number of dailies per chain jumped
from 5.1 to 9.1. The number of independent newspapers plunged
from 1,203 to 499—from more than two-thirds of newspapers to
fewer than a third. That year the American Society of Newspaper
Editors addressed the "mergers and acquisitions frenzy" with a
panel at its annual convention, asking, "Where will it end?"[17] Yet
concerns about decreasing editorial diversity were far from new,
even among supposed competitors. Two decades earlier, an NBC

board chairman warned that to adequately provide the depth that television news lacked, "The newspaper must find a way to check the decline of big city dailies."[18] Business owners who advertised in newspapers also had cause for concern as large chains took advantage of their power to demand significantly higher advertising rates.[19]

Media mergers increasingly became news. "The business of news, usually just an internal industry concern, looms large on the public agenda," stated the preface of the first issue of the new *Gannett Center Journal* in 1987.[20] That first issue focused entirely on business issues related to news production. By then, several large media properties had changed ownership. Australian media magnate Rupert Murdoch's News Corporation owned the *New York Post,* the *Boston Herald,* the *Chicago Sun-Times,* newspapers and television holdings in Australia and England, and six American television stations. And it had added the Fox network to the existing broadcast lineup of ABC, CBS, and NBC. To win approval for Fox, Murdoch agreed to become a U.S. citizen and to sell his Chicago and New York newspapers.[21] The FCC cited a desire for increased competition among media and the number of networks continued to rise, but in most respects competition did not increase. One thing that did increase was the ownership of media organizations by large, widely diversified corporations. For many corporate owners media organizations represented a small part of their overall holdings, and media scholar and former journalist Ben Bagdikian warned in 1965 that large corporations were making journalism a "byproduct" of their other business activities.[22]

All three of the major broadcast networks were sold in 1986: Capital Cities Communications bought ABC, General Electric picked up NBC as part of its purchase of RCA, and Laurence Tisch's Loews Corporation purchased CBS. Before the CBS sale the network fended off a takeover bid by Ted Turner, whose own network avoided bankruptcy a year later through a merger with Time Warner and TCI. News divisions found themselves increasingly answering to executives who specialized in entertainment and who expected each corporate division to contribute to the company's bottom line. Just a few years earlier, Bagdikian famously warned about potential conflicts of interest and diminishing perspectives that might result from the fact that by the beginning of the 1980s, fifty corporations controlled most major American media. In fact, the trend was just beginning. By the end of the twentieth century the number of controlling corporations had dropped to just six.[23] Supreme Court Justice Louis Brandeis is widely credited with saying in 1941, "We can have democracy in this country, or we can have great wealth concentrated in the hands of a few, but we can't have both." The same might be said of the "wealth" that provides the means to distribute political information.

Perhaps the most striking evidence of the effect of corporate ownership of network news came with the passage of the Telecommunications Act of 1996. Media corporations lobbied heavily for the legislation (and benefited heavily from it), while network news programs largely ignored it. The new law allowed corporations to own more media outlets and more types of media. It significantly relaxed other ownership rules (which later were eased even further). A flurry of new media mergers followed. The Walt Disney Company bought Cap Cities/ABC. Viacom bought CBS, which previously had been purchased by Westinghouse. Time Warner bought Turner Broadcasting and then merged with America Online.[24] A potential problem for consumers caused by such conglomeration became obvious in 2000, when as a result of a contract dispute Time Warner Cable briefly cut ABC stations from its cable offerings in New York, Los Angeles, and other cities.

That same year the Tribune Company, which owned the *Chicago Tribune,* purchased the family-controlled *Los Angeles Times* and its other media holdings, including several other newspapers and television and radio stations. Reactions to the merger from other newspapers offered hints about the new owner's priorities. "Tribune Co. has traditionally been one of the country's most profitable newspaper groups. Last year, its profit margin was 29.2 percent, the highest in the country, while the average for publicly held newspapers was 22.2 percent," noted a *Washington Post* article.[25] "The Tribune Co., which has made *Fortune's* list of 'most admired companies,' is a centrally managed operation known for its corporate efficiencies," the *Boston Globe* stated.[26] "Tribune Co. has a cost-cutting, profit-maximizing reputation," offered *USA Today.*[27] The *Christian Science Monitor* also noted the company's "wide reputation for stringent cost controls and annual profits that far exceed the industry average" but added that efficiency did not necessarily harm quality: "Its flagship newspaper, the *Chicago Tribune,* is widely recognized as one of the country's top five."[28] At least the new owner was another media company, unlike with many of the other corporate takeovers. Even the *Los Angeles Times,* though owned by a family that had controlled the newspaper for more than a century, at the time of the sale had a chief operating officer who had made his mark at General Mills. His newsroom cuts had led to him being nicknamed "the cereal killer."

Incidentally, a shift to chain ownership does not necessarily mean the quality of an individual newspaper will decrease. Besides the financial advantages that a larger corporate structure may offer, chain newspapers may have fewer divided loyalties. Family-owned newspapers were often led by men with political ambitions of their own who used their newspapers to openly promote those interests. "Many owners worried more about their friends at the country club—the other pillars of the community—than about service to readers, and many such owners stifled aggressive coverage of local institutions," two *Washington Post* critics note.[29]

One controversial part of the 1996 Telecommunications Act involved allocation of the digital spectrum, used to broadcast high-definition television. A few senators and public watchdog organizations maintained that the spectrum was public property worth tens of billions of dollars, but Congress voted to award future spectrum licenses—free of charge—to existing broadcasters. Though newspapers gained nothing from the Telecommunications Act, they did not do much better than television networks at covering its effects on ownership and consolidation provisions.[30] For one thing, the bill was both complicated and legislative— two factors that tend to turn off readers and reporters. Of course, many corporate owners of newspapers, including the *New York Times* and the *Los Angeles Times,* also boasted television holdings and had since the earliest days of television. "Publishers who own stations can tell you about profit," one editor complained in the 1940s. "They enjoy 100 per cent (and up) return on their electronic capital investment as compared to 5 to 10 per cent from their newspapers."[31]

Under Ronald Reagan, the FCC relaxed station ownership rules a dozen years before the Telecommunications Act, increasing the number of TV stations a company could hold from seven to twelve (fourteen, if at least two were minority-controlled). Many companies quickly expanded their holdings. The FCC kept rules that generally prevented ownership of more than one TV station in a community or the formation of new newspaper-TV combinations within a community, but the number of TV stations affiliated with newspapers from outside their own markets jumped more. ABC/Capital Communications, Gannett, Times Mirror, and

Scripps Howard were among the large media companies contributing to the growth. Corporate raiders who put profits ahead of public service found media companies to be perfect for leveraged buyouts, the companies typically having little outstanding debt, valuable assets that could be sold off, and healthy profit margins.[32] In a leveraged buyout, a buyer often financed the deal through high-risk bonds and then paid off the bonds by selling off company assets and slashing the work force. News staffers typically were the first employees cut loose to help corporations reach desired profit margins. Those margins were high. "In recent decades media companies have typically returned double-digit profits, often five to ten times higher than profits for department stores, banks, pharmaceutical companies, and automobile manufacturers," one economist notes. "This profitability has changed perceptions of the media, turned media firms into highly successful vehicles for investments, and produced demands for even higher profits."[33]

The FCC reduced ownership restrictions even further under President George W. Bush. Despite hundreds of thousands of e-mails and letters from opponents, and after holding only one public hearing (at which most participants also opposed the changes), the FCC voted to allow a single company to own three television stations, eight radio stations, a cable system, and a daily newspaper within a single city, and to permit a corporation to own stations that reached 45 percent of Americans. The previous limit had been 35 percent, though Viacom and News Corporation (owners of CBS and Fox) already exceeded that legal limit. Critics warned that the changes could drown out many independent voices, and protests from consumer interest groups, some journalism organizations, and others helped prompt the House of Representatives to vote overwhelmingly to stop the 10 percent increase in a network's potential reach. Bush and House Republicans then agreed to a cap of 39 percent, or approximately what the owners of Fox and CBS already had. The compromise angered many, but Congress passed the new limits as part of a large spending bill.[34] The compromise did not necessarily mean the end of FCC attempts to let big companies get bigger either. Under new chairman Kevin Martin, the FCC held six 2007 public hearings to seek input on Martin's proposal to loosen ownership restrictions in the nation's twenty largest media markets.

Even before Reagan's FCC eased restrictions on broadcast ownership in the 1980s, the family-owned newspaper was fading fast. In addition to the growth of chains, several large newspapers had followed the lead of broadcast network owners and gone public. They offered shares of the companies while simultaneously creating a new level of bosses—stockholders—and creating new economic pressures. Publicly held newspapers did tend to boast higher profits and pay better, but they also relied on smaller news staffs; fewer people did more work, leaving less time for in-depth stories.[35] A graphic example can be seen with Philadelphia, where the number of newspaper reporters fell from 500 to 220 from 1980 to 2005.[36] "There is no obvious way to simultaneously shrink a newspaper and make it better," note two *Washington Post* editors. "On the contrary, the predictable consequence of such cost cutting is a diminished paper, less interesting and less important to its readers and its community."[37] At the national level, ABC, NBC, and CBS all laid people off during the Reagan years. CBS made the deepest cuts, releasing more than 350 news staffers in less than three years.[38]

News organizations consistently sought new ways to bolster profits, eventually prompting some to warn about problems that resulted when efforts to appease advertisers and stockholders took precedence over news values.[39] "By no means is it unpatriotic to make money in the news business," longtime journalist Bonnie Anderson wrote, while nonetheless pointing out that public service–minded network executives once willingly accepted financial losses among their news divisions. "But the value of a free media should never be measured in terms of dollars earned or in ratings achieved. . . . Neither dollars nor ratings are ways to judge the health and value of journalism or of our society."[40] The shift in priorities frustrated dedicated journalists. "The old paradigm was that we were part of the public service of broadcasting," an NBC correspondent lamented. "The new paradigm is that we're part of the profitmaking machinery. Being a news person used to be a calling. Now it's a business."[41] While describing its annual survey of the state of the news media in 2006, the Project for Excellence in Journalism noted the following as one of six major trends: "At many old-media companies, though not all, the decades-long battle at the top between idealists and accountants is now over. The idealists have lost. . . . At many new-media companies, it is not clear if advocates for the public interest are present at all."[42]

A newspaper journalist wrote that newspapers had become increasingly like the other businesses that reporters covered, and that journalists themselves had "become a bottom-line problem, which is quite a comedown from being members of the Fourth Estate."[43] Many newspapers and broadcast companies adopted incentive programs that tied journalists' salaries to profitability, which, in one critical view, "changes the journalist's allegiance. The company is explicitly saying that a good portion of your loyalty must be to the corporate parent and to shareholders—ahead of your readers, listeners, or viewers."[44] Prominent broadcast journalist Christiane Amanpour asked a meeting of news directors, "What is the point of having all this money and this fancy new technology and being able to go anywhere and broadcast everywhere if we are simply going to drive ourselves and our news operations into the ground?" She added: "It really makes you wonder about mega-mergers. Yes, you are running businesses, and yes, we understand and accept that. But surely there must be a level beyond which profit from news is simply indecent."[45]

Newspapers and broadcast stations hired consultants to teach them how to reach bigger audiences more efficiently, prompting some critics to complain that owners were willing to experiment with any number of "journalistic fashions" but "usually avoided one obvious avenue to improvement: spending more money on covering the news."[46] Two editors argued:

> Just spending money can't compensate for a paucity of talent or energy, but newspapers do improve when money is spent on them. Merely adding space for more news can make a mediocre paper better by making it more complete. Adding employees allows a paper's ambitions to rise and gives all staff members more time to do their job more carefully. Management that supports its journalists with resources will bring out their very best. Managements that cut and squeeze demoralize their people as they shortchange their readers.[47]

Tracing the recent history of the *San Jose Mercury News* provides a simple illustration of how the newspaper business has changed. Originally two separate newspapers, the *Mercury* bought the *News* in the 1940s, and the two merged into a single publication in the 1980s. The newspaper won two Pulitzer Prizes during that same decade but drew more negative attention within the industry in 2001 after publisher Jay T. Harris resigned in protest over the economic priorities of corporate owner Knight Ridder (formed in 1974 from the consolidation of two smaller newspaper

chains). Profits had taken too much precedence over public service, Harris told the American Society of Newspaper Editors: "I
had lived as long as I should or could with a slowly widening gap
between creed and deed."[48] Five years later, McClatchy Company
bought Knight Ridder, with holdings that included thirty-two
dailies and sixty-five other newspapers. The deal may have resulted because Knight Ridder's largest shareholder—who controlled
less than 20 percent of the company—demanded a sale "because
he was unhappy with the stock's lackluster performance," the *San
Francisco Chronicle* reported.[49] The same article noted, "Wall Street
has soured on newspaper stocks because of uncertainty about
the industry's future."[50] After buying Knight Ridder, McClatchy
then immediately sold the *Mercury News,* the *Philadelphia Inquirer,*
and twelve other newspapers that reportedly failed to meet the
company's "longstanding acquisition criteria" related to potential
growth of their markets.[51] The *Mercury News* went to MediaNews,
making that company the largest newspaper publisher in the San
Francisco Bay area. MediaNews, which also owned the *Denver
Post,* the *Salt Lake Tribune,* the *Detroit News,* and the *Oakland Tribune,* soon announced that it would lay off dozens of newsroom
employees at the *Mercury News.* The Newspaper Guild (the union
representing newspaper employees) apparently negotiated a smaller layoff than originally planned, though part of the new contract
allowed the paper "to coordinate news coverage and advertising
sales with other MediaNews papers and take content from those
publications."[52]

As business concerns increased, journalistic practices changed.
Paying sources for information, once considered ethically taboo,
became common for the pseudo-news media such as tabloid
television shows—important because those media increasingly
helped define the news agenda for the mainstream media. In ad-

dition, corporations found other ways to "pay" for sources who appeared on mainstream news programs. A sought-after source who agreed to be interviewed for one or more of the network's news programs might also be offered a movie deal, book contract, or concert.[53] Other journalistic structures also proved shaky, including the supposed wall between news and advertising. Perhaps the most significant collapse of that wall came in 1999 when the *Los Angeles Times,* under CEO Mark Willes, devoted an issue of its Sunday magazine to the new Staples Center. Other publications then revealed that the newspaper shared advertising revenues from the insert with Staples in exchange for gaining special advertising privileges in the arena. Neither readers nor embarrassed *Times* reporters who had written for the special issue knew about the arrangement until other news media revealed it.

A more common example of the advertising-news connection comes daily on television news programs across the nation via the video news release (VNR). Virtually every local station and national network uses VNRs, television versions of print press releases that often promote products or services. Often indistinguishable from segments aired by journalists, some of the releases include narrated voice-overs, while others include scripts to be read by a local newsperson, making the "coverage" seem more local. The George W. Bush administration came under criticism for using VNRs, complete with a phony "reporter," to promote its policies.[54] Some local stations went beyond the use of VNRs to sign contracts with advertisers such as the one between a Baltimore station and a local hospital. The hospital advertised on the station, and the station ran regular "news" segments featuring the staff and patients of the hospital.[55] Other stations and newspapers have had similar agreements, with automobile dealers and real-estate companies among the most common beneficiaries. Even if there is no formal agreement, journalists often know where to go when seeking a quote about an issue in the news. One journalism critique notes: "We have to talk to somebody. It might as well be someone who sponsors our shows."[56]

Media organizations were willing to spend money when it came to major news events such as the outbreak of war, but they followed any such spending spree with increased belt tightening. Market research helped determine who was watching or reading and how news might be tailored to better attract potential media consumers, especially the types of consumers who appealed most to advertisers. Various groups such as racial minorities, conservative Christians, homosexuals, middle-class white women, young adult males, undernourished teen girls, and so on, appeared to become less important because of their influence on society and politics than because of their potential as audiences, and therefore as targets for advertising. In other words, a group's news value was secondary to its perceived value as a demographic. Some traditional news sources, ranging from poor, local neighborhoods to international news, began receiving less attention.

The decreased coverage of the poor and of foreign affairs had noteworthy political ramifications. One of the biggest complaints of conservatives since the 1960s had been about the growth of the "welfare state." Critics commonly ridiculed the denizens of that "state" as lazy and ignorant, complaining about the costs inflicted on government and the taxpayers. Yet rarely did the news media compare those costs to other governmental expenses, such as military spending, or examine the reasons that abject poverty persists in an American land of plenty. Perhaps more important, decreased coverage of the poor increased the likelihood for misunderstanding and stereotypes, while giving readers and viewers fewer opportunities to see the poor as fellow human beings.

As networks cut their overseas bureaus they increasingly relied on freelance journalists and on pooling, whereby networks share the pictures taken by one camera. One career journalist writes that CNN's travel unit was prohibited from spending money on most travel-related expenses for months, leading to anchors filing stories about waterfront vacation destinations with the Chattahoochee River as a backdrop.[57] Networks began sharing their own national feeds with other networks' affiliates. Easier travel and better equipment made it more convenient for a reporter to cover a wider geographic area, perhaps multiple countries. A former CBS newsman reports that he was sent to Rwanda when trouble began between the Hutus and Tutsis, and then, after filing one story, he was sent seventy-two hours later to the Balkans: "Eight hundred thousand eventually died in that African genocide, but the media . . . turned a blind eye. The overwhelming coverage came, as usual, too late."[58] In addition, one media scholar notes that physical mobility was not "accompanied by sudden spurts in knowledge that would permit such 'parachute' reporters to cover a new area with insight."[59] Areas seen to have relatively little impact on the United States tended to be ignored, and naturally reporters were far more likely to be stationed in friendly locations than in hostile or neutral ones.

As mainstream media paid decreasing attention to international affairs, neoconservatives focused heavily on communism and then the exportation of American-style democracy. Uninformed and largely passive, Americans and their news media again relied on stereotypes and on government authority figures. Those figures were themselves becoming increasingly conservative. The Iraq War may have been the most dramatic result of the press's negligence. "The networks, instead of fulfilling the role of a free press to help set the national agenda, were at best just along for the ride," one former NBC journalist later wrote. "At worst, wrapped up in the flag, or blindfolded by it, they actively promoted the neoconservatives' flawed view of the world—while jacking up the ratings and their owners' share value."[60]

The slashing of foreign news reduced understanding of international affairs for the press and media consumers and may have led to tragic political errors. Some critics also suggest that shortsightedness by media companies ended up financially hurting those same corporations. After airliners slammed into the twin towers of the World Trade Center, former CBS journalist Tom Fenton wrote: "With the events of 9/11, the cutback of news output has proved costly to the very conglomerates that made those cutbacks in the first place—GE, Disney, Viacom, Time Warner, et al. Who knows but that, with the kind of foreknowledge (and loud drumbeat) that a real news operation would have provided, all of us, including those conglomerates, might have avoided the disaster of 9/11. Nobody has done a proper study of how badly 9/11 affected their bottom line."[61] Losses included tourism-related income, insurance payouts, decreased stock values, and sometimes assets lost in newly unstable countries. "Forget the national interest (as they did by news cutting): Surely their own bottom line requires them to be more informed about events abroad than they can possibly be today," Fenton argued. "They cut their own throats when they cut the news."[62]

Reduced geographic coverage, a decreasing number of newspapers, and an increasing number of journalism graduates combined to mean that news organizations could choose to pay new journalists less money (perhaps widening the political gap between reporters and management even further, since those who pursued careers in journalism had even less reason to do so for financial reasons). Further aggravating the situation for journalists, labor unions were losing power at the same time. While member-ship in the Newspaper Guild climbed slightly from 1961 to 1986, the number of newspapers with guild contracts dropped from 180 to 144 during the same period.[63] Incidentally, those who complain about the supposed political biases of newspapers might consider the labor history of the press.

Newspaper strikes have been as common as strikes in other industries, though the effects often are more visible. Not surpris-ingly, in such cases managers work for the owners' economic in-terests. More surprising—or at least it would be were the press truly liberal—is how readily other newspapers take the side of owners in opposition to workers. For much of the twentieth cen-tury, newspapers were more antagonistic than friendly toward labor and working-class issues in general; the same usually held true even when the laborers in question worked for other news-papers.[64]

Newspapers have a long union history, though less so in the newsroom. The International Typographical Union had repre-sented printers since 1852, making it the oldest labor union in America, and publishers started a trade association in 1887. But editorial workers did not form the American Newspaper Guild until 1933, when the American Newspaper Publishers Associa-tion proved unfriendly toward progressive labor policies.[65] De-spite its late start, the guild acted quickly. It waged twenty strikes in its first five years of existence and further irritated owners by approving a code of ethics that listed unethical practices com-mon to some newspapers. Interestingly, though American critics often have blamed strikes in various industries on Communist influences, and despite its generally liberal views on treatment of workers, one of the noteworthy aspects of the guild was its early anti-communism.[66]

Several major American cities experienced newspaper strikes during the turbulent 1960s and 1970s, early in the conservative resurgence. Most New York newspapers shut down for sixteen weeks in 1963 and for twenty-five days in 1965. The reaction from newspapers in other parts of the country was anything but supportive toward labor, however. One common structure of strike-related news stories was what one scholar called a "sincere bosses, underhanded unions" framework.[67] Another common frame pits "cheerful mediators" against "grim-faced unionists," while yet another—seen often in editorials as well as news stories—is that of the "public as victim."[68] One scholar suggests that the mainstream news media "have not only overseen and actively facilitated the deterioration of organized labor in general, but . . . have acted in like fashion to contain or eliminate such organization and activity among their own workers."[69] After the *Washington Post* put down a press workers strike in the 1970s, one critic said the result "contributed to 'maximizing profits' but surely did nothing to 'maximize the collective good'—unless we assume that busting unions, throwing people out of work, and holding down wages for remaining employees is beneficial for all concerned."[70]

In terms of the liberal versus conservative argument about the media, as one media scholar notes, "Of today's well-known names in publishing, most have been primarily interested in making money rather than achieving political, religious, or public service goals."[71] The same obviously is true of most broadcasters. And in recent decades, at least, conservatism has paid better than liberalism while posing fewer financial risks. More importantly, staying a bit to the right of the political middle pays the best, even though it has allowed conservatives to define most of the public agenda.

EIGHT

REDEFINING THE MAINSTREAM

The Cable News Network, the first twenty-four-hour all-news network, debuted in 1980. Though it was greeted with widespread skepticism, many of those who rooted for the network's success anticipated that more time for news would allow for more depth of coverage. After all, the major networks had only a half hour per night, minus commercials, to describe the key events of the day. In fact, CNN did treat the news seriously, including an exclusive interview with President Jimmy Carter about international affairs on its first broadcast day. The ongoing Iranian hostage crisis and presidential campaigns guaranteed events worthy of coverage. But unfortunately most of what the network offered varied little from that of the existing networks. With twenty-four hours of daily time to fill but a news budget considerably smaller than that of ABC, CBS, or NBC, news stories at CNN often were repeated, and many were trivial. "Just tune in, sit back, and get your fill of news, sports, fashions, gossip, financial and garden tips, and almost anything else you can think of," one critic wrote shortly after the network first aired.[1] Another complained after the debut: "Certainly keeping things brisk and brief had a higher priority than making them thorough or substantial. Often it seemed that, as with much of network TV news, the point of getting anything onto the screen was chiefly to get it off again and replace it with something else, lest viewers grow weary."[2]

CNN and the cable news networks that followed often focused heavily on spot news events with little relevance, though sometimes CNN covered events such as natural disasters and wars better than its broadcast brethren did.[3] It reached its high point in terms of credibility and value with the 1991 Persian Gulf War when reporters Peter Arnett, Bernard Shaw, and John Holliman described the bright flashes and explosive sounds of American bombing outside their hotel windows. Iraqi dictator Saddam Hussein let CNN stay in Baghdad during the war, and even some journalists criticized the network's reports. Each of Arnett's stories had to be cleared by an Iraqi censor, though he later said no official ever told him what to say.[4] Thanks to its coverage of the war, CNN's ratings jumped 500 percent, and it boosted its rate for thirty-second ads from $3,500 to $20,000.[5]

Twenty-four-hour-a-day news with around-the-clock deadlines created added pressure, perhaps increasing the number of errors and further threatening journalists' credibility. And like the other mainstream news media that tried to demonstrate a lack of bias in their reporting, CNN naturally drew heavy fire from conservatives who complained that the network was too liberal. During the 1990s those critics regularly referred to CNN as the "Clinton News Network," and *National Review* once quipped, "First Dog Buddy has been obeying Bill Clinton with such slavish devotion, he should have been named CNN."[6] Such statements obscure Clinton's actual conservatism, but of course conservatives were attempting to run over CNN years before a car killed Buddy.

Despite increasing conservatism among the mainstream media, especially after the 1996 arrival of Rupert Murdoch's Fox News

Channel, conservative critics naturally continued the attack on networks' perceived politics. And despite its slogan of "fair and balanced news"—which liberal activists unsuccessfully attempted to persuade the Federal Trade Commission to forbid as misleading advertising—Fox brought an obvious conservative slant to the news. In addition, actual news coverage increasingly gave way to scheduled programs featuring commentary over journalism, with much of the talk coming from hosts who had achieved recognition on conservative talk radio.

As the new network gained popularity, eventually vying with CNN for the top spot in the ratings, competitors began to copy some Fox strategies.[7] In addition to bringing in their own commentary-centered programs, typically featuring more conservatives than liberals, cable networks also changed the look and tone of news coverage. Cable news programming in general, one journalism watchdog group found, "is thinly reported, suffers from a focus on the immediate, especially during the day, is prone to opinion mongering and is easily controlled by sources who want to filibuster."[8] A former CNN journalist noted:

> The shift toward Fox-like programming has also been very evident on the air. During the 1991 Gulf War, the network would never have used anything resembling an American flag in its onscreen graphics. That wasn't because CNN was anti-U.S.A. or anti-anything. It was to preserve impartiality, an ethically responsible decision for an international news organization. But during the 2003 war in Iraq, on-air patriotism was the order of the day. Red, white, and blue graphics were prominent, while anchors and reporters routinely referred to U.S. servicemen and women as "our" troops.[9]

Though CNN had been permitted to broadcast from Iraq during the Persian Gulf War, the Iraqis booted the network out of Baghdad before the 2003 Iraq War because they said "that CNN had become even more conservative than the Bush administration."[10]

The mainstream media boosted the war effort in ways other than on-screen flag waving (or flag wearing, as flag lapel pins became popular accessories for anchors). In fact, the war might never have occurred without the aid of the press, which had slipped into the habit of taking administrative claims at face value. Shortly after the 2001 attacks on the World Trade Center, Congress overwhelmingly passed the Patriot Act (officially, the USA PATRIOT, or Uniting and Strengthening America by Providing Appropriate Tools Required to Intercept and Obstruct Terrorism, Act of 2001) to help fight terrorism. One part of the law permitted indefinite imprisonment without trial of any noncitizen the attorney general declared to be a national security threat. The law also eased restrictions on federal law enforcement officials wanting to search a suspect's home or computer or to eavesdrop on communications. Bush also signed a directive to try suspected terrorists in secret military tribunals rather than in the courts. Before passage of the Patriot Act, however, neither Congress nor the news media paid much attention to what it contained.

Journalists also did little to examine the rationale for going to war in Iraq and helped the administration promote that rationale. In fact, CBS anchor Dan Rather may have been one of the first to publicly suggest a link between 9/11 and Iraq's leader, asking a former defense secretary the day after the tragedy: "True or untrue that if we are to defeat terrorism, that sooner or later we have to deal and have to deal strongly with Saddam Hussein?"[11] The following day MSNBC reported that Bush administration officials were "looking at the possibility that Iraq's Saddam Hussein may have lent some support to the terrorists, all potential targets now in this new war on terrorism, a war that will surely prove long and bloody."[12] Soon George Bush and other members of the administration were suggesting a link between Iraq and 9/11 and ties between Hussein and terrorism. In his January 2002, State of the Union address, Bush identified Iraq as part of an "axis of evil." He and others regularly maintained that Iraq posed a threat to the United States because it possessed "weapons of mass destruction." Conservative media had been making that claim even before 9/11: after coming under neoconservative editorial control the once-paleoconservative *National Review* maintained five months before the World Trade Center attacks that "Iraqi scientists defect regularly, and there can be no doubting their testimony that Saddam has chemical and biological weapons of mass destruction."[13] The same report implied that Iraq had obtained enriched uranium from South Africa and suggested that Hussein be replaced by members of the dissident Iraqi National Congress, then living outside of Iraq.[14]

In a 2002 speech at West Point, Bush introduced a new neoconservative defense doctrine, stating that the United States had a right to take "preemptive action" to prevent the growth of a potential threat. Trying to generate support from other nations, Secretary of State Colin Powell told the United Nations in a televised address that Iraq had dangerous weapons and links to al-Qaeda. "Powell cited 'irrefutable and undeniable' evidence yesterday that Iraq still conceals massive quantities of terror weapons," the *New York Daily News* reported.[15] Still, *Columbia Journalism Review* pointed out that Powell's UN presentation "was nothing if not selective," noting previous cases of misleading intelligence.[16]

Though some newspapers questioned a relationship between Iraq and the war on terrorism before the war began, few criticized the war effort or tried to check administration claims. Newspapers "all essentially pronounced Powell right, though they couldn't possibly know for sure that he was," one critic noted. "The country could have profited from a much more searching examination of the so-called preemption doctrine."[17] When no weapons of mass destruction were found, administration officials blamed "faulty intelligence." More than a year after the war began, the *New York Times* publicly acknowledged that it also had relied on faulty and biased information while writing erroneous reports about alleged Iraqi weapons programs and terrorist training camps. An editor's note admitted to "a number of instances of coverage that was not as rigorous as it should have been."[18] Still, the note prompted at least one reader to wonder "why the *NYT* buried its editors' note—full of apologies for burying stories on A10—on A10."[19] A few days after the editor's note appeared *Times* ombudsman Daniel Okrent was much more critical of the newspaper. Though reporter Judith Miller's stories were the most consistently flawed, Okrent found, "The failure was not individual, but institutional," tainted by "hunger for scoops," a dysfunctional editing process, and "anonymity-cloaked assertions of people with vested interests."[20] Long before the admission, other *Times* journalists covering Iraq apparently questioned some of Miller's stories, which, noted *Columbia Journalism Review,* suggested that "such weapons were just about to be found or had recently been destroyed."[21] Newspapers throughout the country carried those stories, distributed by the New York Times News Service. Of course, when the news media did question the war, they were portrayed as unpatriotic, claims that may have made journalists back away from asking tough questions.

After the war began, the Pentagon invited reporters to join the battle. Approximately six hundred national and local embedded reporters joined troops, signing contracts agreeing to the overview of military commanders. Many of the stories focused on the journalists themselves, with a former ABC executive writing that too many of the reports "were of the standing-in-front-of-the-camera, chest-thumping, look-where-I-am, and we're-ready-to-go-but-I-can't-tell-you-exactly-where-for-security-reasons variety, followed by the anchors back home warning the reporters to 'stay safe' and asking them to relay best wishes to the troops."[22] The "embeds" occasionally provided meaningful news, however, such as when a *Washington Post* reporter revealed that soldiers had killed ten members of an Iraqi family at a checkpoint.[23] One of the iconic images of the war demonstrated how the news media can casually support American interests even at the expense of truth. Even years after the war began, television broadcasts regularly illustrated Iraq War stories with footage of what seemed to be a large crowd of Iraqis pulling down a large statue of Saddam Hussein. Yet shortly after the statue fell, newspaper and Internet reports revealed that few Iraqis took part in the destruction, but news cameras "enlarged" the crowd by focusing tightly on the scene. After critics noted the availability of American equipment used to destroy the statue and suggested that the event, directly in front of a hotel occupied by journalists from around the world, may have been staged, an American military officer admitted coming up with the idea. Years later, however, news programs continued to use the film as if it depicted a spontaneous news event rather than a public-relations stunt to generate support for the war.

The growth of obviously conservative media apparently helped drag the mainstream news media further from liberalism, but almost no overtly liberal broadcast media exerted any pull in the opposite direction. Except for a few individual programs and two small radio networks—Pacifica and Air America, which started in 2004—those on the political left found themselves with relatively little meaningful representation. With the possible exception of

Keith Olbermann on MSNBC, the most notable liberal commentary came not from a news program but from Comedy Central, a network supposedly devoted to laughter. Two Comedy Central programs, *The Daily Show* and *The Colbert Report,* often feature political commentary and interviews, though the shows also subject viewers to sophomoric humor, gratuitous profanity, and singers or actors promoting their latest projects.

Not all of the prominent conservative "journalists" were relegated to cable networks. ABC named reporter John Stossel as coanchor of the newsmagazine program *20/20* in 2001—a position he continued to hold even after the publication of his book, *Give Me a Break: How I Exposed Hucksters, Cheats, and Scam Artists and Became the Scourge of the Liberal Media* (the back cover of which carries endorsements from Bill O'Reilly and Sean Hannity).[24] No similar avowedly liberal "scourge" holds a prominent news position for any of the three most-watched networks. In addition, network news programs regularly bring in entertaining but not particularly enlightening right-wing flamethrowers such as O'Reilly and Ann Coulter—whose primary television attributes seem to be short skirts, long legs, flowing blond hair, and an apparent willingness to say almost anything to make an antiliberal point—to discuss politics or public affairs, despite their primary jobs as conservative pundits and their total lack of experience as policymakers. CNN used Pat Robertson as its lead commentator about a 2002 Middle East policy speech, and Rush Limbaugh was an NBC election commentator the same year.[25] The quoting of those pundits is one part of a trend toward wider publication of even the most extreme conservative claims, even as the most liberal views go unpublished by mainstream media. "Because technological advances and the race for ratings and sales have made the wall between right-wing media and the rest of the media permeable, the American media as a whole has become a powerful conveyor belt for conservative-generated 'news,' commentary, story lines, jargon, and spin," one critic notes. "It is now possible to watch a lie move from a disreputable right-wing Web site onto the afternoon talk shows, to several cable chat shows throughout the evening, and into the next morning's *Washington Post*—all in twenty-four hours."[26]

After conservative critics complained that a Bill Moyers PBS program titled *Now* was too liberal, conservative Corporation for Public Broadcasting chairman Ken Tomlinson hired a consultant to monitor *Now* and other programs for bias. Apparently no network has hired an outside consultant to check the potential conservatism of its programming. Also boosting conservatives, television networks gave considerable legitimacy to an anti–John Kerry group calling themselves Swift Boat Veterans for Truth during the 2004 presidential campaign, while one relatively small network actually announced that it would require its stations to run a documentary produced by the Swift Boat group.[27] Shortly after the election, under fire from conservative critics, Dan Rather stepped down from his longtime position as CBS anchor when a preelection report critical of President Bush's military service was found to have been based on fraudulent documents.

Some complaints about news media bias stem from definitional problems. Too many critics fail to differentiate between news media and entertainment. Admittedly that differentiation is complicated by docudramas, newsmagazines, an explosion of pseudo-news such as that offered by MTV and *Entertainment Tonight,* and long-winded radio and television commentators who pose as journalists. As a result, far too many people end up lumping the myriad forms of media into some ill-defined singular "it."[28] Complicating the issue further, some critics conflate social issues with political issues in discussions of liberal versus conservative. For some, the brief exposure of singer Janet Jackson's breast during a Super Bowl halftime show reflected politically liberal sensibilities on the part of ABC, which carried the game.

A television incident in 2006—the same year in which morning-show personalities Katie Couric and Charles Gibson took over the nightly news anchor chairs at CBS and ABC—drew considerable news coverage while helping demonstrate the sometimes-confusing combination of news and entertainment. ABC aired a five-hour docudrama miniseries titled *The Path to 9/11*. Some media critics, former Clinton administration officials, and various liberal organizations slammed the program for its obvious distortions, but the program ran without commercial interruption, with the second segment running on the fifth anniversary of the 9/11 attacks. That segment was interrupted to air an Oval Office speech by Bush. Though a disclaimer noted that parts of the program had been fictionalized, the clear political perspective of the docudrama prompted the *New York Times* to editorialize about the temptations of trying to "improve on history," arguing that ABC "might have heard warning bells when Rush Limbaugh went on the air promoting the film and bragging that the writer was a friend of his."[29] Conservatives answered the complaints by pointing out that documentaries produced by Michael Moore and other liberal filmmakers had included similar distortions, though aside from the fact that Moore could not claim the support of a major television network that boasted "More Americans get their news from ABC news than from any other source," such arguments fail to address the reality that typically far more people see even a low-rated television program than are exposed to a popular film shown in theaters. The ABC controversy came three years after CBS scheduled and then cancelled a docudrama about Ronald

Reagan; after conservatives complained, that program was shifted from CBS to Showtime, a pay-cable affiliate.

The mainstream press needed little encouragement to be dragged to the right, but in fact much of its shift toward political conservatism came simply as a result of inattentive drift. Focused more on profits than on public service, the news media catered to viewers' tastes for the sensational and the trivial. Those aspects had virtually always been part of the news, but at most times in history they were supplemented by more of the hard news that helped concerned citizens contribute to running their political lives. In recent years, meaningful discussion of political policies has largely disappeared, especially as political figures increasingly faced the prospect that every misstatement would be repeatedly rebroadcast around the nation, amplified and distorted. The capability for constant exposure expanded further with the proliferation of home-video cameras, camera phones, and the Internet. Video-sharing software allowed YouTube to become a billion-dollar company just a year after its 2005 birth. A YouTube video featuring Virginia senator George Allen making what some perceived to be a racist statement may have cost Allen his U.S. Senate seat, and cost the Republicans a Senate majority.

Not surprisingly, as media exposure increased, evasion became an increasingly valuable skill. Politicians avoided potentially unfriendly journalists, and the networks—especially the cable networks with endless hours of airtime to fill—turned to often-pompous prattle from news pundits, think-tank experts, and spokesmen for the two major parties. Pseudo-debate programs contributed noise but little depth while managing to give conservative critics both a forum and yet another target. They also provided a reminder of what famed journalist A. J. Liebling said even before the dominance of television news about three kinds of writers: "the reporter, who writes what he sees"; "the interpretive reporter, who writes what he sees and what he construes to be its meaning"; and "the expert, who writes what he construes to be the meaning of what he hasn't seen."[30]

Commenting on the newsroom television sets that allow journalists "to keep track of what our competitors are doing," ABC newsman Ted Koppel once stated: "It is infrequent that all the networks are covering the same story at the same time. It is exceedingly rare that this happens for much of an entire day, especially when two different stories are involved."[31] Koppel's statement about content variety may once have been true, but not anymore. Whether the story is a natural disaster, the latest gaffe by a political candidate, or the gruesome death or disappearance of a pretty young woman, often a viewer can click through all of the news channels at the top of a given hour and find most or all of the networks covering the same story. The news personalities and the "experts"—often network regulars—chosen to comment about the incident often provide the only variation. In fact, the first major trend noted by the Project for Excellence in Journalism in describing its annual survey of the state of the news media in 2006 was, "The news paradox of journalism is more outlets covering fewer stories."[32]

The focus of stories also has changed, with journalists paying more attention to controversy and entertainment personalities. The press devotes less time and effort to digging for news, or even covering public affairs. As a result, politicians and pundits who do care about public affairs find it easier to define issues on their own terms. Contradiction may come from opposing pundits or politicians, but rarely from fact-based stories in the press. Increased reliance on public-relations sources and on set journalistic routines such as beats also reduces the likelihood that the actions of those in power—increasingly conservatives in recent decades—will be questioned.[33]

Critics have complained about the trivialization of news since before the arrival of television, but the new medium sharpened the criticism even as increasing numbers of viewers tuned in. By the mid-1960s most Americans relied on TV for much of their news, troubling serious newspaper journalists. "A picture may be worth a thousand words . . . but as least *we* write those words," one newspaper reporter complained.[34] Many complained about a lack of depth with TV news, especially as network documentaries, a staple of early 1960s network programming, began to disappear. In their place came TV newsmagazines, starting with *60 Minutes* in 1968. Even former news anchor Walter Cronkite, once considered the most trusted man in America, urged citizens to rely on more than the flitting images offered by television: "The problem is that we do such a good job, such a slick job in our presentation of the news that we have deluded the public into a belief that they are getting all they need to know from us."[35]

Newspapers could do more in terms of analysis and explanation, but they also became increasingly shallow.[36] Stories grew shorter and were shared among papers within chains. Design elements became more important, culminating with the 1982 arrival of a new Gannett newspaper designed to look much like television: *USA Today.* Numerous large, color photos and brightly colored graphics predominated, and stories rarely jumped from one page to another. Other publications made fun of the "McPaper," but as the *New York Times* noted a year later, *USA Today* was "loudly mocked and quietly mimicked."[37] Even before the arrival of *USA Today,* however, newspaper content was becoming less useful for the would-be informed citizen. Most newspaper leisure sections, containing elements such as restaurant reviews, entertainment listings, and travel features, arrived in the 1970s. Reporters and editors worried about features taking time and space away from more serious work, with a 1978 Associated Press Managing Editors Association report complaining that newspapers devoted too much space "to counter-culture and radical chic and other irrelevant nonsense."[38]

Concerns that newspapers catered too much to superficial audience whims deepened further with the arrival of what became known as *civic journalism* or *public journalism*. Implemented to varying degrees by many newspapers and television stations, civic journalism was intended to find out what readers or viewers wanted from news, politics, and society. The journalists then went even further, trying to meet those needs or tell news consumers how to meet them.[39] "At its heart is a belief that journalism has an obligation to public life—an obligation that goes beyond just telling the news or unloading lots of facts," argued the Pew Center for Civic Journalism, an organization devoted to promoting and expanding the movement.[40] Some argued that civic journalism might help save both journalism and democracy. "Civic journalism grew out of a sense that, as we in the press have dutifully reported for so long, our democracy actually *is* going to hell in a handbasket," one writer noted.[41]

The *Wichita Eagle* may have started civic journalism in 1990 when it initiated its "voter project" to help readers learn more about the candidates, issues, and process of the election. For three consecutive years, the *Eagle* asked readers to help determine which issues candidates and the newspaper should address, and then it ran regular election-related features. The *Eagle* later expanded the idea to issues such as education, family issues, and crime.[42] Other newspapers such as the *Charlotte Observer* and the Norfolk *Virginian-Pilot* also began engaging in civic journalism in the early 1990s, and within a few years newspapers and broadcast stations around the country began experimenting with new reader-centered forms, especially during election years. Still, civic journalism drew as many critics as converts among the press, and the Pew Center for Civic Journalism closed a decade after it began.[43]

While civic journalism attempted to involve citizens in the political process, the same could not be said of another trivializing trend in news: the increasing importance of entertainment values, especially with television. *Happy talk*—on-screen banter between coanchors or between an anchor and another news personality—came to local television in the late 1960s and quickly spread, eventually moving to national news programs. The general tone of local news coverage changed at the same time, with positive accounts of community events separated by blocks of fragmented stories about fires, crime, and car crashes, a trend that continues. "The range of topics that get full treatment is narrowing even more to crime and accidents, plus weather, traffic and sports," the Project for Excellence in Journalism found in 2005.[44] Often from other parts of the nation or world and typically of little relevance to local viewers' lives, such stories still raised viewers' anxiety. The phrase "If it bleeds, it leads" was tied to television news, though the availability of film footage mattered most. That focus bothered even the news people involved. "It was very annoying that I would have to do a live shot on a car wreck that affected basically nobody, just because we had pictures of it," one former Los Angeles reporter/anchor noted. "It happens 10 times a day, but if there's video of it, we would have to do a story on it."[45] As news directors tried to steer away from "talking heads" and policy-focused news decreased, sound and visuals helped hold the attention and stir the emotions of viewers. The spectacle progressed to the point where at any given time a viewer might have to try to

simultaneously process spoken words, music, and numerous separate visual elements: a waving and vaguely flag-like background,
a network logo in one corner of the screen, the name of the program pasted in another corner, a colored bar with a line or two
of bold text describing the news story, a moving one-line crawl
of brief, unrelated news headlines separated from one another by
another spinning or flashing network logo, and up to six separate
video or live-video images.[46]

A review of how various organizations ranked the top stories
of 2006 demonstrates some of the differences in news values between television and newspapers. According to Fox News, the top
ten national news stories for the year were two plane crashes that
killed a total of fifty-one people, seven crime stories, and, heading
the list, a deadly mine explosion. Failing to make the list were the
2006 elections, in which Democrats gained control of both houses
of Congress, the death of former president Gerald Ford, the resignation of Defense Secretary Donald Rumsfeld, and a variety of
political scandals involving Republican members of Congress and
major corporations.[47] The top two Fox News international stories
were the Iraq War and the hanging of Saddam Hussein. On the
other hand, the Associated Press annual poll of editors and news
directors combined international and national stories into a single
top ten. Respondents put the Iraq War first and the election results
second. The other two U.S. stories in the AP top ten were illegal
immigration and the congressional scandals.[48]

One of the year's top stories helped demonstrate the inade-
quacies of the news media in covering politics. Perhaps the most
important of various 2006 congressional scandals—particularly in
terms of how it may have affected the "values voters" who typically vote Republican—involved six-term Florida congressman
Mark Foley, who resigned after admitting that he had sent sexu-

ally suggestive e-mails to a former congressional page. Yet the information became public not because of a mainstream journalist, but because an anonymous liberal activist posted it on his Web log two months after sending it the *Los Angeles Times*. The *Times* apparently ignored the information and declined to investigate further, and other news organizations reportedly did the same. Three days after the e-mails were posted on the Internet, however, a Washington gossip site linked to the activist's site. An article about it appeared on the ABC Web site the following day, and a day later, confronted by ABC about the issue, Foley resigned. The activist who originally released the information then found himself sought by journalists who wanted to know more, including his identity. "If you were doing your job to begin with, Mark Foley would have been exposed a long time ago," he responded. "I'm nobody that anybody should care about. So, please, go about your day as if I don't exist."[49] Before the Foley incident, bloggers also helped uncover problems with documents used in a 2004 Dan Rather report critical of George W. Bush's National Guard service and were the first to report Senate Majority Leader Trent Lott's 2002 use of what some viewed as racist remarks in praising segregationist senator Strom Thurmond. Their credibility damaged by the political fallout, both Rather and Lott ended up resigning from their positions.

With an emphasis on entertainment values to draw audiences, good looks and personality became at least as important as news sense for reporters and anchors. Networks began training programs developed in part to find potential reporters with star power, considering characteristics such as perceived warmth and physical appeal. "Before anything else you have to be attractive and charismatic," a former CBS executive said.[50] In 1981, thirty-seven-year-old Kansas City anchorwoman Christine Craft was demoted for, as one executive put it, being "too old, too ugly and not deferential enough to men." After she sued the station owner and twice won judgments that were overturned, the Supreme Court refused to consider her appeal. Nationally, Dan Rather ridiculed the one-million-dollar salary given Barbara Walters in 1976, writing that no journalist was worth one million dollars, "no matter what or how many shows they do, unless they find a cure for cancer on the side." But within a few years Rather and several other newscasters also were drawing million-dollar salaries.[51] In 2006, Katie Couric signed a contract reportedly in excess of fifteen million dollars per year to assume Rather's former anchor position.[52] "Once *news* was the star; now the stars are the stars," complained one former reporter. "And what's worse, the stars are often the news. And more and more on-air journalists are collecting multimillion dollar paychecks and being treated like celebrities rather than as journalists."[53]

Some news figures were celebrities before becoming journalists. For example, Anderson Cooper had once hosted an ABC news program but was best known for hosting a reality game show before CNN hired him to host a prime-time newscast. Networks especially appreciated celebrity politicians who could become news personalities—"journalists" who might have no previous news experience other than as subjects or sources for political stories. (Although some of the new journalists and commentators did have prior journalism experience, it was rarely enough to justify their new positions.) That revolving door between political jobs and journalism increased the appearance, if not the likelihood, of bias. George Stephanopoulos went from serving as a Clinton staffer to ABC, where in 2002 he replaced longtime newsman David Brinkley as host of *This Week.* Diane Sawyer, coanchor of *60 Minutes,* once served as Richard Nixon's press aide. Joe Scarborough went from Republican congressman to MSNBC host. Bill Moyers served in the Lyndon Johnson White House before his career at PBS. CBS hired former Republican congresswoman Susan Molinari to host a Saturday morning news program. NBC's Tim Russert was Democratic senator Daniel Patrick Moynihan's chief of staff. David Gergen worked for Bill Clinton, three Republican presidents, and two networks. Pat Buchanan went back and forth between punditry and conservative politics. Other broadcast journalists or commentators who worked in national partisan politics at least briefly included Dotty Lynch at CBS, Pete Williams and Chris Matthews at NBC, Jeff Greenfield at CNN, and Jeff Gralnick, who worked for George McGovern, ABC, CBS, and NBC.[54]

Even as mainstream news increasingly turned toward celebrities and entertainment, political newsmakers turned to entertainment "news" programs to promote their messages. During the 1992 campaign, Bill Clinton and George H. W. Bush both answered audience questions on network morning shows, enjoying the fact that audience members typically asked softer questions than did trained journalists.[55] Clinton played his saxophone on *The Arsenio Hall Show*, and he and running mate Al Gore both appeared on MTV. Arnold Schwarzenegger later launched his campaign for governor on NBC's *Tonight Show with Jay Leno* and gave his last two interviews before polls opened to *Entertainment Tonight* and *Access Hollywood*.[56] John Edwards announced his 2004 presidential bid on *The Daily Show*, after which host Jon Stewart said, "I have to warn you that we are a fake show, so you might have to do this again somewhere."[57] Of course, even when they have the opportunity to explore issues, supposed professionals lob their fair share of softballs. CNN's *Inside Politics* anchor Judy Woodruff inaugurated a cooking segment in 2003, asking her first guest, Senator Barbara Mikulski of Maryland, only two political questions. Just before the Iraq War, Woodruff cooked Greek food with Senator Debbie Stabenow of Michigan, asking one question about the possibility of war with Iraq and one about health care.[58]

Several factors related to the production of news stories also contributed to the conservatism of the mainstream press. Use of sources, framing of stories, and reliance on public relations all effectively promoted conservative mainstream media. Policy makers quoted in news stories tend to be politically conservative, and the vast majority of those sources are white males. A reliance on expert commentators, referred to by one journalism scholar as *news shapers,* aggravates the situation.[59] Some of those experts are policy makers or university professors, but think tanks supposedly devoted to the study of public-policy issues also provide many of the "experts." Though stories often fail to identify the biases of think tanks, conservatives staff and fund most (and the best-funded) of those organizations. Thanks in large part to their effectiveness in working with the news media, the actions of the think tanks have, in the words of one award-winning former journalist, "given respectability to ideas and solutions that were considered impossible only a few years earlier."[60] The mainstream media continue to rely on conservative organizations such as the Heritage Foundation and the Cato Institute, even after their studies have been found to be biased and riddled with research flaws that would make the results unpublishable by any reputable academic journal.[61] Part of the problem may stem from the fact that too few journalists can effectively evaluate research methods or statistics.

Journalists also reinforce conservative policies through their routine reliance on what are known as *beats* and *framing.* Hundreds of academic studies devoted to the topic of agenda setting have discounted the common allegation that the media tell people what to think about issues, but those same studies have demonstrated that the news can influence what people think about.[62] The American news media provide a limited range of perspectives. Traditional beats include state and local government (sometimes combined, depending on the size of the news organization), law enforcement and courts (together or separately), and education, and much of every day's news justifiably stems from those areas. But the normal reporting practices of attending public meetings, talking to administrators, and reviewing routine public records produced by officials naturally produce a conservative pro–status quo bias. Journalists inevitably develop relationships with their regular sources and try to maintain those relationships so as not to be cut off from information. Except in cases of apparent scandal or fiscal wrongdoing, reporters rarely go beyond the usual sources to talk to activists who oppose the official sources. Even the perspectives of those most affected by the beats rarely appear in the press. Examples of those typically excluded include welfare recipients, the working poor, students, and accused criminals (though attorneys typically forbid their clients to talk to the media). The one source exception that gets more coverage is business owners, often those who advertise with the news organization, who tend to be political conservatives. Some news organizations that experimented with civic journalism tried focusing on issues instead of institutions, but most retained or went back to traditional beats.

A significant amount of recent research by journalism scholars has focused on the use of *media framing*—how journalists interpret or define events to explain them. "A news story would be a buzzing jumble of facts if journalists did not impose meaning on it," two scholars note. "At the same time, it is the frame, as much as the event or development itself, which affects how the citizen will interpret and respond to news events."[63] One common frame focuses on individuals involved in stories. That focus can help readers or viewers connect emotionally to the story, but it also typically fails to provide larger historical or political context—"to deny accountability to anyone but those directly involved."[64] As a result, it appears that the poor and the ignorant became that way solely because of their own choices, not because of institutional factors.

Another common news frame, which also lacks larger context, focuses on unusual circumstances. Levees collapse because of hurricanes, not because governments and corporations have for decades stripped away protective natural buffers while neglecting to inspect or maintain the levees. Houses burn because of freak wildfires, not because of choices made by government agencies or real-estate developers. Crimes occur solely because of individual cases of wrongdoing, uninfluenced by social or political factors. And despite the fact that more Americans die from automobile crashes than from almost any other cause, each accident is treated as a unique event—even though the less-common deaths from terrorism, a natural disaster, or a gun-wielding, disgruntled worker may be characterized as part of an ongoing and ominous trend.

One of the most common frames involves public policy. Journalists frame political news in terms of conflict, such as Democrats versus Republicans or the president versus Congress, rather than assuming the more difficult and more useful role of explaining policy. Readers and viewers consume political news as they would a sports story, with little understanding of how the policy being debated might affect them personally or how they might influence the course of action to be taken. Again the net effect is conservative, maintaining power among those who have it and reinforcing the status quo.

Even when not turning to entertainment media, politicians and others have figured out other ways to bypass or manipulate the mainstream news media. They send out their own video news releases in the hope that local stations will use them, or they turn to friendly media. For example, Clinton administration officials appeared on Fox News programs relatively rarely, but Fox quickly became the favorite network of the Bush administration. Vice President Dick Cheney and other administration officials appeared on Fox News more than on other networks, prompting one CNN commentator to quip, "That's a little like Bonnie interviewing Clyde, ain't it?"[65] Bush even chose Fox News commentator Tony Snow as his press secretary. Some critics suggested that Fox had become the unofficial house organ of the Bush administration and of the Republican Party. A writer for the neoconservative magazine *Policy Review* wrote, "Fox News is an old-fashioned nation-state network gaudied up by the latest technology."[66] Members of Congress from both parties use direct-satellite transmissions from a Washington congressional studio for interviews with local newscasters in their home districts. Those interviewers typically ask softer questions than do national political reporters, and tough questions might prompt the politician to turn to a competing station for future interview opportunities.[67] Almost all of Bush's 2004 presidential campaign appearances were restricted to audiences known to be friendly. Prescreened and coached members of the audience asked preapproved questions, and the president gave rehearsed answers. Nightly news programs then carried snippets of the rallies, frequently neglecting to mention that they were closed to anyone other than enthusiastic supporters of the president. Given the rare opportunity to cover a presidential visit, local television news programs frequently reported on a rally for days before and after it occurred.

The typical American might view public-relations professionals as more biased than either think tanks or traditional government sources but probably has little idea how much public relations shapes the news. Much of every day's "news" is generated by public-relations professionals—local television stations must be told where to send their cameras, and the available reporters could not come close to covering or writing enough stories to fill the open space. When journalists initiate their stories, they often must question public-relations professionals before talking to government or industry officials. The public-relations person may then tell the official how to appropriately respond. A presidential administration has hundreds of public-relations staffers, while the Pentagon has thousands. With other government agencies and industries also relying heavily on public relations to promote or filter messages, journalists often have little choice but to rely on public-information officers or press releases. The most obvious and troubling examples may be those involving war. In fact public-relations campaigns helped promote the Iraq War that began in 2003 and played a large role in initiating the 1991 Persian Gulf War.

Nine days after Iraq invaded Kuwait in 1990, a Kuwaiti group hired Hill and Knowlton, the world's largest public-relations firm and one of the first major companies to combine public relations and political lobbying efforts. The Hill and Knowlton effort became the largest foreign-funded public-relations campaign ever aimed at American public opinion, and despite one prewar *Washington Post* story, few Americans knew about the company's involvement, the extent of its campaign, or the effect that campaign had on the news.[68] The twelve-million-dollar operation involved more than a dozen other public-relations companies. Products included advertisements in the *Washington Post, New York Times,* and *USA Today,* dozens of video news releases that aired on news programs around the country (resulting in air time worth millions of dollars), and press kits containing a 154-page book titled *The*

Rape of Kuwait. The most successful public-relations move was the testimony of a sobbing fifteen-year-old Kuwaiti girl before the Congressional Human Rights Caucus, a group of politicians and witnesses pulled together by Hill and Knowlton for what resembled a congressional hearing. The girl told a heart-wrenching story about witnessing Iraqi soldiers grabbing babies from hospital incubators and leaving them on the floor to die, and then stealing the incubators. Hill and Knowlton sent a camera crew to the "hearing" and produced a video news release used by enough media (including *NBC Nightly News*) to make it the fourth-most successful VNR of 1990.[69]

As he tried to build support for the war during the following months, President George H. W. Bush freely used and embellished the incubator story, referring to "newborn babies thrown out of incubators" or "babies pulled from incubators and scattered like firewood across the floor."[70] Bush's details, including the number of babies supposedly killed and whether hospital employees also died, varied from one speech to another. The news media quoted some alleged details and largely ignored others, making little effort to explain the differences or to investigate the veracity of the statements.[71] Bush even referred to "babies heaved out of incubators" in a news conference a day *before* the Kuwaiti girl's testimony, noting, "I don't know how many of these tales can be authenticated."[72] The atrocity story was widely repeated by journalists in news stories, by members of Congress during hearings to consider whether the United States should go to war against Iraq, and in United Nations Security Council hearings held to build international support for the war effort. The *New York Times* and some human rights groups briefly questioned the story, but Bush managed to win Senate approval for the war by a scant five votes.[73] The press failed to seriously examine the supposed atrocities until after the war ended, when ABC and the *Washington Post* produced reports discrediting the story.[74] Other reports turned up financial ties between Hill and Knowlton and the cochairs of the so-called Congressional Human Rights Caucus.[75] The girl who testified turned out to be the daughter of the Kuwaiti ambassador to the United States, may not have been in Kuwait at the time of the supposed atrocities, and apparently was coached by Hill and Knowlton before she testified. The public-relations company "had done its job well," *Columbia Journalism Review* noted. "The same could not be said of the U.S. press."[76]

===========◇===========

NINE

PROBLEMS AND POSSIBILITIES

Some might be tempted to believe that the conservative political re-surgence has run its course, that American conservatism has peaked and is waning. Still, those who would view the results of the 2006 elections—coming after what one conservative leader called "the most disappointing political race in my political lifetime"—as a stumbling block for the conservative movement or as a sign of any sort of long-term shift back toward a more liberal political system should be circumspect.[1] Aside from the fact that after the election George W. Bush still could veto any legislation that congressional Democrats managed to pass, parties in power typically lose seats in off-year elections. The gains made by Democrats may simply have reflected dissatisfaction with Bush and the Iraq War. After all, Harry Truman's policies immediately after World War II prompted a 1946 congressional landslide for the Republicans. Yet two years lat-er Truman won reelection, and the Democrats reclaimed both the House and the Senate, in part because the Republican Congress accomplished so little. Though the 1946 election brought Richard Nixon and Joseph McCarthy (along with John F. Kennedy) to the Senate, one historian notes that for Republicans the election "was a turning point that did not turn."[2] The congressional gains of 2006 may have been the same kind of "turning point" for Democrats. Facing the likelihood of change, one neoconservative editor wrote just before the 2006 election:

> Sixth-year elections have a character and a pattern all their own. They are change elections. By year six, many voters have grown dissatisfied with the status quo. They've accumulated any number of grievances over the years. They are angry with the president and his administration for what's been done and what hasn't. They're tired and grumpy, even irate at times. Even some members of the president's party have lost faith in the president. And 2006 is no exception, as all the disagreeable aspects have come to pass—as usual.[3]

Of course the party in power automatically holds more seats that might be lost if people cast ballots more as an expression of dissatisfaction with Congress or the president than because they find individual candidates appealing. When Republicans won control of Congress in 1994, they were helped by the antigovernment unity signified by the Contract with America. But they failed to fulfill most of the contract and became viewed as every bit as corrupt and power-hungry as the Democrats they had replaced. When Democrats regained control of the House and Senate in 2006, their primary common theme was more like that of the 1946 Republicans: "Vote for us because we're not them." Such a message likely has little staying power.

In addition, many of the 2006 Democratic victors won with social and fiscal messages that in 1946 would have seemed too conservative even for most Republicans, indicating that conservatism still held political sway. One political journal even published a quiz that contained candidates' preelection stands, titled, "Which Candidate is the Republican?"[4] Of course, because approval ratings for both Congress and President George Bush were low before the election, many Republican candidates offered political rhetoric that emphasized their independence or centrism.[5] Such rhetoric failed to save the seats of some moderate Republicans, however, meaning that both parties in effect became more conservative than they had been before the election.

In fact, liberalism in American politics may be nearly as dead today as conservatism was in the 1940s, before the current resurgence began. Further evidence might be seen in the fact that even Democrats have lost or given up on the constituencies that gave them much of their power in the first place. Modern Democrats boast of their military toughness and their fiscal conservatism, speaking little of labor unions or the poor, while seeking campaign funding from the same corporations that fund Republicans. "The way to collect the votes and—more important—the money of these coveted constituencies, 'New Democrats' think, is to stand rock-solid on, say, the pro-choice position while making endless concessions on economic issues, on welfare, NAFTA, Social Security, labor law, privatization, deregulation, and the rest of it," one critic has noted. "Such Democrats explicitly rule out what they deride as 'class warfare' and take great pains to emphasize their friendliness to business interests."[6] Even before the Clinton presidency, political writer E. J. Dionne Jr. wrote that both major parties had become "vehicles for upper-middle-class interests."[7] Unfortunately, to a large degree the mainstream news media have done the same.

While both parties focused on people and institutions with money, the middle class in America diminished to the point that *Time* magazine called the shrinking of middle-class neighborhoods and "the resulting disparities between high- and low-income neighborhoods" one of the most underreported stories of 2006.[8] Progressive reformers once aided and politically relied upon those low-income neighborhoods. Those same neighborhoods now are filled with people who, attracted by the "values" of conservatives, vote for candidates who cut social programs, weaken regulations on corporations, and pass sweeping bankruptcy reforms that benefit the banking industry. While watching television those same hardworking Americans can switch from Fox News commentators complaining about liberal morality to raunchy reality television on the Fox entertainment channel, or perhaps catch a cable showing of a Fox studio production such as *Porky's* or the bloody slasher film, *The Hills Have Eyes.* Though corporate conglomeration has reduced citizens' choices in some respects, conservative free-market capitalism assures access to the popular media that social conservatives despise. And as social critic Thomas Frank has noted, "In an America where the chief sources about one's life possibilities are TV and the movies, it's not hard to be convinced that we inhabit a liberal-dominated world."[9] It also seems sadly unlikely that Americans will turn any time soon to the more realistic depictions of the world offered by the mainstream press, however much the press may improve.

Making predictions is as hazardous as it is tempting, yet based on history it seems likely that the United States will at some time become more politically liberal. It also seems likely that few of the mainstream news media will notice the shift until it is well under way. Most journalists will have—and therefore will be able to offer—relatively little understanding of how the shift took place. By nature and by training, journalists focus mostly on day-to-day events, learning to recognize and write catchy stories. Good reporters learn to use databases and interviews to provide valuable insights, but historical and political context too often go lacking.

Most press newcomers now have degrees in journalism or, increasingly, in communication, but technical skills classes have replaced much of their liberal arts education. As students they spend less time considering ideas, and as journalists they tend not to understand or investigate political philosophies or the origins or impact of those philosophies.

Perhaps the political shift toward liberalism already has begun. Despite the Clinton-Lewinski scandal, Al Gore won more votes than President George W. Bush in 2000. Four years later, John Kerry narrowly lost to Bush despite the fact that he was portrayed repeatedly by Republicans and the news media as a flip-flopping "Massachusetts liberal" who lacked personal warmth, while much of the Republican campaign stressed fears of terrorism and gay marriage. By 2006 most Americans believed the Iraq War was a mistake and that global warming existed (despite a Fox News story that same year that called global warming "the mother of all junk science controversies").[10] The coalition of various camps that had produced a conservative majority has shown signs of stress in recent years, with fiscal conservatives angry about burgeoning spending and the Iraq War calling into question the nation-building ideas of neoconservatives. "The conservative movement has been hijacked and turned into a globalist, interventionist, open borders ideology, which is not the conservative movement I grew up with," Pat Buchanan complained while helping found the *American Conservative* magazine.[11] Conservative Christians expressed unhappiness that Republicans had failed to end abortion, stop government corruption, or stem immorality, while more liberal Christian voices were drawing press attention and developing a significant Internet presence. In 2006, Democrats claimed both houses of Congress and, for the first time since the 1994 Republican revolution, won a majority of state governors' seats. Arizona voters, unlike those in several states in previous elections, rejected a constitutional ban on gay marriage. Missouri voters approved state funding of research involving embryonic stem cells. Also interesting was the state of Kansas, which previously had become the focus of a best-selling political book with the unflattering title of *What's the Matter with Kansas?* Kansas had garnered the attention because of its solid conservatism (along with a sometimes-radical streak).[12] In 2006, however, at least nine former Republicans ran for office in Kansas as Democrats, largely because they thought Republicans had become too preoccupied with divisive social issues such as abortion and homosexuality.[13] And in 2007, prominent social conservatives split their endorsements for a 2008 Republican presidential nominee. Pat Robertson endorsed former New York mayor Rudy Giuliani, who previously had supported gay rights and abortion rights. Paul Weyrich, cofounder of the Moral Majority and the Heritage Foundation, endorsed former Massachusetts governor Mitt Romney, who also once supported abortion rights and whose Mormon religion was considered a cult by some conservative Christians. Bob Jones III also endorsed Romney. After dropping his own short-lived presidential bid, conservative Kansas senator Sam Brownback endorsed fellow senator John McCain. The National Right to Life Committee endorsed former senator and *Law and Order* television actor Fred Thompson.

Democrats owed some of the credit for their 2006 gubernatorial and congressional success to former Vermont governor and presidential candidate Howard Dean, who, with help from the media, just two years earlier looked like he might have been consigned to political oblivion by a widely aired political gaffe. After an unprecedented Internet campaign and appeals to young voters and labor unions helped him gain ground in a 2004 presidential bid, Dean finished a disappointing third in the Iowa caucus. Shouting over the voices of supporters during his concession speech, he let loose a bellow of emotion that seemed especially loud because unidirectional microphones filtered out most of the crowd noise. News programs, talk shows, and late-night programs played the Dean scream hundreds of times during the following days, often for comic effect, and CNN and ABC later apologized for their role in distorting the message.[14] Dean did win the chairmanship of the Democratic National Committee in 2005, however, and pledged—against the opposition of some leading Democrats—to wage a "fifty-state strategy" to try to build local Democratic parties and win elections at every level in every state, rather than focusing on key swing elections. Dean's actions as DNC chair mirrored some of the early party-building by conservative Republicans.

Also reminiscent of conservative power building, a number of left-leaning think tanks and lobbying organizations such as MoveOn.org, ActforChange.com, and TrueMajority.org have sprung up in recent years. Noting how much influence similar conservative organizations had gained by the 1990s, columnist George Will wrote that liberals were "tardily trying to replicate that infrastructure."[15] Not surprisingly, Will also repeated familiar conservative claims that liberals controlled the major mainstream media, though he said those media had become less important, "marginalized by their insularity and by competitors born of new technologies."[16] A less conservative critic assessed the liberals' late start in equally harsh terms: "While leftists sit around congratulating themselves on their personal virtue, the right understands the central significance of movement-building, and they have taken to the task with admirable diligence."[17]

In trying to understand whether political change is indeed underway, hopeful liberals, pessimistic conservatives, and would-be political pundits might look for other parallels with the beginning of the conservative resurgence. For example, they might compare the 2004 Democratic Convention speech of Senator Barack Obama to Ronald Reagan's "A Time for Choosing" address of forty years earlier. Both speeches attracted positive national attention, and both men found themselves in demand as speakers inside and outside their parties. Though Reagan had a sharper wit, a folksier manner, and a more practiced delivery, both he and Obama spoke on behalf of their values in direct, positive, and personal ways that connected with listeners. In 2006 Obama was one of the most popular campaigners for Democratic candidates around the country. He also wrote a popular book that might be compared to conservative icon Barry Goldwater's *Conscience of a Conservative.* Obama's *Audacity of Hope* offered an image for the nation's political future, calling for, in one reviewer's words, "a mode of liberalism that sounds both highly pragmatic and deeply moral." Like a Reagan campaign speech, the book also was long on optimism and short on policy details.[18]

In this television age Obama has one distinct advantage and one disadvantage compared to Ronald Reagan. The advantage is that after the publication of his book, every national network devoted considerable coverage to the issue of whether Obama might run for president. Predictably, most of the coverage focused on whether in spite of his race and youth he was "electable," without discussing his political ideas (or even whether he had any). After months of free speculative publicity, Obama finally declared his candidacy for president. One disadvantage he faced was that even though he was relatively inexperienced as a politician, he had been in politics for most of his adult life. A sad fact of contemporary American politics is that many voters trust actors more than they do politicians, as perhaps demonstrated by the election of Arnold Schwarzenegger to the same governor's seat once held by Ronald Reagan. Two U.S. senators, Republican John McCain and Democrat Hillary Clinton, were viewed as very early front-runners for the 2008 presidential nominations of their parties, but the simple fact that they had voting records in a political body that sometimes requires compromise meant that opponents even in their own parties could attack them as wafflers and flip-floppers. It is no accident that almost every president since 1976 has been a governor, not a legislator (the single exception, George H. W. Bush, had been Reagan's vice president). As for candidates coming from Congress, one critic of the conservative movement made an observation decades ago that might now apply to Americans in general, and to their news media: "Compromise means cooperation . . . and a loss of integrity. By this logic, those who succeed in the political world and attain real influence are corrupt and can no longer be trusted to advance the true cause. Only the loners who refuse to play the game of the System are to be trusted."[19]

For Clinton or Obama to make a successful presidential run the candidate also would have to convince Americans to do something they have never done in electing a woman or an African American to the presidency. Race and gender still matter in American politics. Especially when a political ad seems to engage in race baiting, national journalists and commentators spend a lot of time asking other journalists and political figures whether the ad in question truly is racist (typically and not surprisingly drawing a "yes" from those on one side and a "no" from those on the other side) and the bigger question of whether the race of a candidate matters. A more useful (and admittedly more difficult) exercise would be to ask the voters themselves *why* and *how* it matters. Civil rights issues, busing, immigration, and crime and punishment all convincingly demonstrate that race-related factors influence society and politics, but the issues are far more complicated than black and white. Or even black, white, and brown. For example, some Latinos vote Republican; some vote Democratic. Yet rather than trying to figure out how most Hispanics will vote in a given election, journalists would perform a more valuable service by trying to determine which issues most affect those voters, and then explaining how individual politicians, not just parties, address those issues.

The question also remains whether any Democrat from outside of the South can win the White House. If so, the party's next-best option might seem to be still in the Sunbelt region but farther west. A logical choice might be a governor from a state such as Arizona, New Mexico, Texas, California, or even Colorado (though most of those now have Republican governors). Another reasonable possibility might be a political leader from a key swing state. Prominent among those is Ohio, which tipped the 2004 presidential election in George W. Bush's favor but which two years later replaced its Republican governor and a Republican senator with Democrats. Of course, Democratic does not necessarily mean liberal, especially in the South.

Regardless, political geography and television charisma might matter less if the news media did a better job of serving the electorate. John McCain and Hillary Clinton became early presidential front-runners for 2008 because the press identified them as such within days of the 2004 election. That identification helped both raise money for their 2006 senatorial campaigns. Clinton raised more money than any other Senate candidate, despite the fact that from the beginning of the campaign she was expected to win easily. Money not spent on one campaign could then be shifted to another. Yet neither Clinton nor McCain had even declared themselves as presidential candidates during the first two years of the press handicapping. The news media had slipped into familiar horse-race coverage, in this case with an election that was still four years away.

In another predictable media turn, during the last two weeks of the 2006 campaign every major network devoted airtime to the subject of negative campaign advertising. Virtually every individual program on CNN, MSNBC, and Fox News did the same. Those ads, all of which originally had run in individual state races, then received repeated national attention. The effect of that on a national electorate—for example, whether a negative ad run by either party in one state affects that party's electoral chances in another state—probably cannot be determined, though a dampening of enthusiasm for the entire electoral process seems likely. The questions asked of various experts and partisans were almost identical from program to program, almost identical to those asked during the election of two years before, and probably identical to those that would be asked in 2008. The answers were equally predictable. Question: "Do negative ads work?" Answer: "They can." After all, if such ads did not work, why would anyone run them? Question: "Are the ads more negative this year than in previous elections?" Answer: "They seem to be." Or, if the speaker has a sense of history: "Probably not, but they may get more attention from the media." Anyone who remembers Willie Horton or the 2000 Swift Boat ads probably should not have asked the question in the first place. Question: "Why does your side run negative ads?" Answer: "Our side just points out the facts about our opponent or answers attacks; the other side runs negative ads." Besides, as noted above, negative ads work. Question: "Do you think voters see through this negativity?" Answer: "Maybe they're beginning to." And maybe not, based on the continued popularity of those ads. Question: "Will voters get tired of these ads?" Answer: "They seem to be getting tired of them." The net result of that voter weariness, though—a depressed turnout of unpredictable, middle-of-the-road voters—and its ultimate effect on democracy may be the most important and one the most undercovered stories of every election season. Also essentially ignored is the amount of money networks and television stations rake in for premium-priced political ads during each election cycle and what ethical considerations, if any, television executives take into account when deciding to air vicious and misleading advertising.

The mainstream media obviously must be profitable, but if their corporate owners' only desire is for profit, then American democracy will undoubtedly suffer. One conservative columnist complained during the 2006 campaign that the television networks had abandoned any notion of civic responsibility in favor of profits: "One might just as well ask a chicken to fly as ask the cash-sucking networks to attempt shock therapy on the mostly brain-dead electorate, whose interest in politics they have helped diminish."[20] The tension between profits and democratic purpose is not new, of course. Reporter A. J. Liebling, most famous for noting, "Freedom of the press is guaranteed only to those who own one," wrote more than four decades ago:

> I take a grave view of the plight of the press. It is the weak slat under the bed of democracy. It is an anomaly that information, the one thing most necessary to our survival as choosers of our own way, should be a commodity subject to the same merchandising rules as chewing gum, while armament, a secondary instrument of liberty, is a Government concern. A man is not free if he cannot see where he is going, even if he has a gun to help him get there.[21]

Campaign ads illustrate another key point about mass media and their relationship to anything resembling self-government. Manipulation of media users is relatively easy—greeting-card commercials manage to generate a range of emotions in thirty seconds—but the ethics of that manipulation vary according to the intent involved. Making viewers laugh or cry or scream in fright during a movie may be justified. News content that angers or saddens viewers may be warranted, as well. But cuing up driving background music and patriotic graphics for the latest war footage raises more serious questions. For a public already skeptical of the news media, the use of technical tricks such as music, quick editing cuts, and dramatic lighting may contribute to cynicism among those who realize they've been manipulated into emotions that content alone would not have evoked. Media messages inundate Americans, but few users ever actively pursue media literacy. The news media could provide a valuable service, and perhaps strengthen their long-term prospects, by providing more literacy education.

Of course an educated public might then demand more from the news media, perhaps expecting the press to look more deeply at events in the news and rely less on polls, commentators, and public-relations practitioners. Rather than simply repeating a politician's stated goals to help middle-class Americans, journalists might be asked to examine how the politician had voted on legislation, what sorts of tax cuts he or she had approved (and who benefited most from those tax cuts), and actions actually taken regarding such issues as education and health care. The results for most candidates might be far more complicated than a conservative-liberal distinction, but few contemporary issues can sufficiently be framed in terms of black and white or red and blue. The news media helped create single-issue voters by too often focusing on simplistic, hot-button dualities. The press would have better served those voters by trying harder to investigate and help Americans through the true complexities involved with most issues and most candidates.

Obviously many in the press are trying. An encouraging sign during and between recent elections has been the added depth that some newspapers and broadcast stations provide via their Web sites. The *New York Times,* the *Washington Post,* the *Wall Street Journal,* the *Chicago Tribune,* the *Los Angeles Times,* the *Miami Herald,* and the *Boston Globe* all had political Web logs or *blogs* in 2006. The *Washington Post* maintained a database of incumbent congressional votes, and the *Los Angeles Times* updated statewide campaign spending on a daily basis.[22] Other newspapers referred readers to useful political sites such as those maintained by the League of Women Voters and Project Vote Smart.[23] Yet even those newspaper actions demonstrate how much easier it is for some groups than others to access meaningful political information. The political effects of this "digital divide" remain unknown, though some suggest its impact, and the impact of the Internet in general, is limited. The Internet helps political junkies follow issues and candidates, making it "easier for those people to be involved, and will therefore likely make them more so," one writer predicts. "For those people with little interest in politics, the Internet will make it easier for them to become more engaged in their own particular areas of interest, leaving them even less time for politics."[24]

Despite the perhaps-soothing words of this book's first chapter about how the news media have been through previous conservative and more liberal phases, the most recent conservative press resurgence differs from earlier versions. Today's conservative voices are louder and perhaps more widely respected than those of the past. They also cover a wide spectrum, from ranting right-wing Internet blogs to publications such as *Human Events* and *National Review,* from Rush Limbaugh–style talk radio to members of what many Americans consider part of the media mainstream such as Fox News, the *Washington Times,* and *U.S. News and World Report.* At the same time, the mainstream press has been under constant and consistent assault as never before. In addition to the obvious partisans who always have complained, a number of dedicated and well-funded organizations have joined the onslaught. They include two conservative media watchdogs: Accuracy in Media (AIM) and the Media Research Center.

Founded in 1969, Accuracy in Media calls itself "a non-profit, grassroots citizens watchdog of the news media that critiques botched and bungled news stories and sets the record straight on important issues that have received slanted coverage."[25] The site has links to the Web sites of numerous conservative think tanks and columnists, including William F. Buckley, Robert Novak, Phyllis Schlafly, Cal Thomas, and Matt Drudge. Despite contrary findings by investigator Kenneth Starr and the disagreement of three leading conservative magazines—*National Review, American Spectator,* and the *Weekly Standard*—AIM once gained some attention by claiming it had "overwhelming evidence that proves" that an attorney for Bill Clinton was murdered and demanding that the mainstream media investigate the "murder."[26] More recently, the organization sponsored an Internet campaign to try to keep the Al-Jazeera International network off of American cable systems.[27]

Conservative activist L. Brent Bozell III founded the Media Research Center in 1987. The MRC calls itself "the nation's largest and most sophisticated television and monitoring operation" and claims to have a sixty-person staff and a six-million-dollar annual budget.[28] Along with offering weekly updates of supposed liberal bias, the organization hosts an annual gala at which it presents " 'DisHonors Awards,' roasting the most outrageously biased liberal reporters as selected by a distinguished panel of leading media observers." Gala participants, according to the organization, "have featured a who's who of conservative opinion leaders, from Ann Coulter to Laura Ingraham to Sean Hannity."[29] In one MRC publication Bozell blamed the 2006 election results on a "left-wing [news media] onslaught unlike anything we'd ever seen before," adding, "They employed every dirty trick imaginable to advance their liberal agenda, and they succeeded."[30] He also has accused MSNBC commentator Keith Olbermann of using "hate speech" to "hatefully savage the President with personal smears," and he has called the Union of Concerned Scientists, an organization frequently cited in stories about global warming, "Nazi thought police . . . whose goal is to prevent the free debate of ideas on environmental issues."[31]

Conservative Christian organizations also devote much of their energy to attacking the "liberal media," though for those organizations "liberal" usually refers not to a political view but to the acceptance or promotion of activities deemed antibiblical and morally repugnant such as homosexuality, premarital sex, pornography, drug use, abortion, or violence. Those groups focus mainly on entertainment but sometimes include the news media (which, as discussed, have focused increasingly on entertainment themselves). Much of the focus for Christian groups centers on "protecting the traditional family," despite the fact that, as one religion professor points out, "this 'remembered family' is a fairly recent development, one that came about with the industrialization and concomitant urbanization of America. . . . Previously, women and men had been much more co-workers in the unified task of maintaining a home."[32] Examples of the profamily emphasis include James Dobson's Focus on the Family, Reverend Sun Myung Moon's American Family Coalition, and Donald Wildmon's American Family Association, which calls itself "America's largest pro-family action site."[33] Dobson also founded a think tank/lobbying organization called the Family Research Council, which has editorialized in favor of eliminating government funding of PBS, in part because viewers were "fed up with the liberal bias."[34] Morality in Media, a religious media watchdog that boasts the slogan "Promoting a Decent Society Through Law," has accused *60 Minutes* and the *New York Times* of promoting pornography.[35] More recently, with the help of a one-million-dollar Templeton Foundation grant, the Media Research Center spawned the Culture and Media Institute to "focus on the media's relentless assault on faith, traditional values and personal responsibility."[36]

In recent years the most conservative media have lost some of their relevance, and therefore some of their appeal. With their own kind in power, there is not as much to be angry about, though recent Democratic electoral gains may have helped sustain them. A few liberal political talk shows can now be heard, though mostly on the small and struggling Air America network, which in 2006 was forced into bankruptcy to restructure its finances. Still, if politically liberal shows can be shown to draw an audience—and therefore advertisers—they will appeal even to corporate media owners. A few liberal magazines continue to turn a profit, and some liberals are making good use of the Internet, which has provided a more scattered but tougher-to-control outlet for critics of all persuasions. Political balance may be improving among the alternative media, at least.

Obviously many complaints about the mainstream news media are warranted. They deserve criticism for their occasional ethical lapses (though such lapses are far less common than critics would suggest, especially considering the volume of news produced). The media's neglect of context leaves Americans less capable of dealing with a politically complicated world. The press focuses too much on the sensational and the fleeting and demonstrates an all-American preoccupation with celebrity and sex. Perhaps the biggest problem is that profit motives give the corporate-controlled mainstream news media little obvious incentive to overcome their current status as relatively passive, understaffed, and lacking in ambition.

At the same time, most journalists and journalism scholars re-main convinced that the profession matters for reasons other than corporate profit. The existence of many nonpartisan organizations devoted to improving the press demonstrates the persistence of the idea that journalism can be a potent and useful societal force. Along with trade associations and other interest groups, those or-ganizations include the Poynter Institute, the Project for Excel-lence in Journalism, the Committee of Concerned Journalists, the Association for Education in Journalism and Mass Communica-tion, the Dow Jones Newspaper Fund, the International Cen-ter for Journalists, and Investigative Reporters and Editors, Inc.[37] Throughout American history, a multitude of academics, media professionals, and disgruntled former journalists have debated the original role of the press while offering suggestions for improving the work of journalists and the news media as a whole, based on their own understanding of what the press should be. Some favor a watchdog press that serves, in the words of the 1960s *Chicago Tri-bune,* as "that check upon government which no constitution has ever been able to provide." Others favor an informational "mar-ketplace of ideas" role similar to that suggested by one Fox News slogan, "We report. You decide."[38] Critics believe the press should be less biased—or more biased in the right ways, with the critic's personal perspective determining those ways. Some believe the goal should be objectivity. For others the goal goes beyond journalism to some democratic ideal. Civic journalists advocate public involvement, even activism, on the part of the news media. Some Americans apparently believe that the press should be a national or local cheerleader. Some obviously turn to the news media at least in part for entertainment, while others bemoan the entertainment aspects that pervade journalism. One thing is clear: the press has done an inadequate job of defining its purpose, explaining the necessity of its mission, and convincing Americans that it can perform its chosen role. Seldom in American history has it tried very hard to do so.

If Americans see the news media as largely meaningless to their political lives—an increasingly understandable view, perhaps, considering press practices and general public apathy—then the press will be irrelevant. Still, one potentially positive aspect of conglomeration is that industry-wide change can happen more quickly. If even a small number of owners decide to alter their focus or methods, significant media transformation might occur. Among the many possibilities for press improvement suggested by groups both friendly and unfriendly to the media, one idea regularly stands out: public service. The problem, of course, is determining what kind of service the public needs most from the press.

Members of a democracy obviously cannot govern themselves without accurate and complete political information. The Internet and numerous public-service organizations have in many ways simplified the accumulation of information, but newspapers and cable channels could do a much better job of reporting public affairs. They need only look to the report produced annually for the past thirty years by Project Censored at Sonoma State University to find a lengthy list of issues worthy of deeper investigation.

The top story on the 2007 list was the debate about the possible control of the Internet by handful of major telecommunications corporations.[39]

Considering the fact that advertising pays the vast majority of the bills, and remembering the 1830s penny papers and 1900s Hearst-Pulitzer journalism aimed at the masses, newspapers might consider substantially reducing their newsstand prices to increase readership. The press should more consistently explain American politics and its potential problems, ranging from campaign financing to redistricting to party mechanics. Reporters also should cover the political actions of individual members of Congress in greater depth, explaining who benefits or suffers from each action, devoting less time to conflict and routine public appearances.

The press could become more useful to Americans by becoming unabashedly more liberal—not necessarily in the sense of opposing the policies of contemporary conservatives, but in the traditional sense of being reform-minded, helping to protect individual freedoms while promoting democracy. Recognizing that they will face criticism regardless of what they do, the news media might as well try to do good. They should not automatically oppose or favor either conservative or liberal ideas, but should reflexively question those who hold power. Members of the press also should learn to recognize criticism from the established order as an inevitable and even positive reflection of natural tension between forces, whether that established order happens to be as liberal as it was during the 1960s or as conservative as it is today. Considering recent elections, perhaps those in power also should appreciate more press oversight, which might help curb impulses that end up triggering feverish discontent. The history of the modern conservative resurgence aptly demonstrates that if discontent becomes feverish enough it can even prompt a resurrection of political philosophies widely believed to be dead.

A recent book dealt at length with the development, principles, and practices of the press, noting in the final pages, "Amid the many disagreements about the press, there is widespread concurrence on one thing: The media are in a moment of profound transition."[40] Though one might justifiably ask, "Aren't they always?" in fact the press may now face a defining moment in its history. Because of the success of the conservative resurgence, combined with Bush administration efforts to further secrecy and reduce the accountability of government, American democracy rarely has needed a watchdog press more than it does today.

In 2001 the Bush administration removed large amounts of information from official libraries and ordered federal agencies to tighten their restrictions on releasing information under Freedom of Information Act requests.[41] Many previously declassified reports were reclassified, including information that had already been published in newspapers. Shortly after taking office, Vice President Dick Cheney headed a committee to develop the administration's energy policy. The committee included energy company executives but excluded environmentalists, and the White House refused to release the minutes of the deliberations even to Congress. A congressional committee headed by Democrat Henry Waxman issued a 2004 report on laws regarding government transparency, calling the administration's actions "an unprecedented assault on the principle of open government."[42] The Republican-controlled Congress helped the administration by passing a bill that exempted many Pentagon files from Freedom of Information Act requests.[43] Not surprisingly, when it had to acknowledge bad news, the Bush administration typically followed the time-honored tradition of releasing such news on Friday afternoons to minimize media impact. "If you want to create a splash and dominate news coverage for a week, you make news on a Monday," a spokesman for the Center for Media and Public Affairs noted. "If you want it to drip quietly and go away, Friday afternoon is the ultimate media blind spot."[44]

During his first six years in office, Bush vetoed only one bill (for funding of embryonic stem-cell research, while surrounded by families in a made-for-television event). But he penned hundreds of signing statements—perhaps more than all previous presidents combined, attached to more than 10 percent of all the bills he signed—essentially stating that he retained the right to disregard the new laws under certain conditions.[45] "Among the laws Bush said he can ignore are military rules and regulations, affirmative-action provisions, requirements that Congress be told about immigration services problems, 'whistle-blower' protections for nuclear regulatory officials, and safeguards against political interference in federally funded research," the *Boston Globe* reported.[46] Administration officials regularly changed scientific reports or suppressed scientific findings in ways that favored corporate interests over environmental interests.[47] The Patriot Act and the 2003 Intelligence Authorization Act expanded officials' ability to search homes and businesses without warrants, to examine library records, and to track Internet surfing and phone company records. Bush ignored a law requiring warrants to tap the phones of Americans and later maintained that he also had a right to inspect individuals' mail.

An Associated Press report documents the inability of government to fully oversee itself, noting that some congressional Republicans tried in 2006 to eliminate the position of special prosecutor general for the ongoing Iraq War despite (or perhaps because of) the fact that the official had exposed waste amounting to billions of tax dollars. Much of the waste was blamed on Halliburton Corporation, which Vice President Dick Cheney once led. That same year, General Services Administration Director Lurita Doan compared her own inspector general to a terrorist and tried to trim his budget, apparently because of his zeal for tracking down misconduct, and directors of the federal legal aid program considered firing their own inspector general. With military spending at an all-time high, the Pentagon failed to fill its open inspector general position for well over a year. One nominee withdrew from consideration after telling Congress that the Pentagon, under Defense Secretary Donald Rumsfeld, required its inspector general to use lawyers picked by Rumsfeld rather than independent attorneys.[48] Federal agencies also reduced protections for whistle-blowers under Bush, decreasing the likelihood that abuses would be reported.[49]

Driven by party politics and fears of terrorism, the Bush administration and Congress acted together to strengthen the presidency and weaken congressional oversight. Wanting to increase its own power, and with the support of social conservatives who were convinced that activist judges threaten America's moral fabric (though most federal judges were appointed by conservatives), the administration also worked to weaken the judiciary. The diminishment of the legislative and judicial branches increases the prospects of the kind of government that other conservatives once feared most: a strong federal government headed by an imperial presidency. As *National Review* noted early in its history, while warning about the dangers of an overly robust executive branch, "With the arrogation of a large part of the judicial and legislative powers by that same Executive, the danger becomes a hundredfold more serious."[50] The same might be said of the danger resulting from the deterioration of a watchdog press.

Alternative media such as magazines and Internet blogs from various perspectives can perform some of the same oversight functions as the mainstream press, though obvious biases of such groups must prompt increased skepticism about their claims and actions. Even talk radio and cable television commentators occasionally "speak truth to power," though they more often spew half-truths to the relatively powerless.[51] Independent groups such as MoveOn.org and the Swift Boat Veterans for Truth also can provide added context, though the Federal Elections Commission (FEC) has ruled that many independent groups must register as political-action committees even if they do not coordinate their activities with those of candidates or political parties. The FEC decision limits the ability of such groups to accept large donations, which some fear could shut them down or dampen their effectiveness. In 2006, the agency also fined MoveOn.org and the Swift Boat Veterans for Truth for election activities—which consisted largely of using ads to criticize public officials—in which the groups had engaged two years earlier.[52]

In the same speech in which President Theodore Roosevelt famously gave muckraking journalists their name, he noted the possible good that a careful and concerned press could do: "The men who with stern sobriety and truth assail the many evils of our time, whether in the public press, or in magazines, or in books, are the leaders and allies of all engaged in the work for social and political betterment. But if they give good reason for distrust of what they say, if they chill the ardor of those who demand truth as a primary virtue, they thereby betray the good cause and play into the hands of the very men against whom they are nominally at war."[53] Though one might wonder how many inside or outside the media now "demand truth as a primary virtue," social and political betterment remain worthy goals. Of course, those goals would require the mainstream news media to look beyond profits to provide increased oversight—to act more like watchdogs than lapdogs. Unfortunately, even journalists have doubts about the possibility of change. "If you argue about the public trust today, you will be dismissed as an obstructionist and a romantic," the editor of one major paper said.[54] A poll also found that more than half of national journalists thought the news media had been "insufficiently critical" of the Bush administration during most of his time in office and that in recent years the press had become too timid.[55]

The news media could enhance their relevance (and perhaps even their profits, in the long run) by identifying and seriously exploring the issues that most impact Americans' lives. Journalists could educate readers and viewers through informative and investigative pieces. The media could call attention to social and political problems and keep attention focused on those issues, rather than letting others—whether conservative or liberal—set the agenda with focus group–tested sound bites, pseudo-events, and fear-based messages. Or the press could continue to become an increasingly irrelevant scapegoat for America's ills, belatedly following political shifts and pop culture while letting the politically adept and the charismatic lead a passive electorate toward its own destruction.

NOTES

CHAPTER ONE

1. Editorial, "Two Press Kidnapings," *Chicago Tribune,* February 22, 1974.

2. Editorial, "Left, Right Kidnapers," *Chicago Tribune,* February 26, 1974.

3. Editorial, "The Back-Patter," *Atlanta Constitution,* March 2, 1974.

4. Paul Ruschmann, *Point/Counterpoint: Media Bias* (Philadelphia: Chelsea House, 2006), 11–12.

5. Michael Sandel, "Introduction," in *Liberalism and Its Critics,* ed. Michael Sandel (New York: New York University Press, 1984), 1.

6. Francis Fukuyama, *America at the Crossroads: Democracy, Power, and the Neoconservative Legacy* (New Haven, Conn.: Yale University Press, 2006), 38.

7. Rodger Streitmatter, *Mightier Than the Sword: How the News Media Have Shaped American History* (Boulder, Colo.: Westview, 1997); James Brian McPherson, *Journalism at the End of the American Century, 1965– Present* (Westport, Conn.: Praeger, 2006).

8. Michael Savage, *Savage Nation,* MSNBC transcript, July 5, 2003.

9. Editorial, "New Guard, New York Times," *National Review,* November 7, 1986, 20. The editorial recognized the retirement of longtime *New York Times* editor A. M. Rosenthal, and said about him and two editors who would be assuming new duties: "Best wishes to them all. Goddammit."

10. Bernell E. Tripp, "The Media and Community Cohesiveness," in *The Significance of the Media in American History,* ed. James D. Startt and William David Sloan (Northport, Ala.: Vision, 1994), 147–64.

11. McPherson, *Journalism at the End of the American Century.*

12. David T. Z. Mindich, *Tuned Out: Why Americans Under 40 Don't Follow the News* (New York: Oxford University Press, 2005), 79.

13. James Brian McPherson, "Government Watchdogs: How Four Newspapers Expressed Their First Amendment Responsibilities in Editorials" (master's thesis, Washington State University, May 1993).

14. The *New York Times* endorsed Nixon's Democratic opponents in 1968 and 1972. The *Washington Post* did not endorse a presidential candidate in either election, but endorsed Democrats in every presidential election except one after 1972.

15. Steven Allen, "Introduction," in *And That's the Way It Is(n't): A Reference Guide to Media Bias,* ed. L. Brent Bozell III and Brent H. Baker (Alexandria, Va.: Media Research Center, 1990), 1. The quote refers to George H. W. Bush, not his son who later was elected president.

16. Mindich, *Tuned Out,* 98.

17. Project for Excellence in Journalism, "The State of the News Media 2006: An Annual Report on American Journalism," http://www.stateofthenewsmedia.org/2006/journalist_survey_prc.asp (accessed January 3, 2007).

18. Peter Novick, *That Noble Dream: The "Objectivity Question" and the American Historical Profession* (New York: Cambridge University Press, 1988), 522–72.

19. Martin A. Lee and Norman Solomon, *Unreliable Sources: A Guide to Detecting Bias in News Media* (New York: Carol, 1990), 104.

20. W. Lance Bennett, *News: The Politics of Illusion,* 2nd ed. (New York: Longman, 1988).

21. J. Herbert Altschull, *Agents of Power: The Role of the News Media in Human Affairs* (New York: Longman, 1984).

22. David Niven, *The Dissident Press: Alternative Journalism in American History* (Westport, Conn.: Praeger, 2002), 117–18.

23. Steven R. Knowlton, "The Media and Popular Sovereignty," in Startt and Sloan, *Significance of the Media in American History,* 17.

24. McPherson, *Journalism at the End of the American Century;* James Brian McPherson, "Crosses Before a Government Vampire: How Four Newspapers Addressed the First Amendment in Editorials, 1962–1991," *American Journalism* 13 (Summer 1996): 304–17; McPherson, "Government Watchdogs."

25. Herbert J. Gans, *Deciding What's News: A Study of CBS Evening News, NBC Nightly News, Newsweek and Time* (New York: Pantheon, 1979).

26. Pamela J. Shoemaker and Stephen D. Reese, *Mediating the Message: Theories of Influences on Mass Media Content,* 2nd ed. (White Plains, N.Y.: Longman, 1996), 222.

27. Stephen Ansolabehere, Rebecca Lessem, and James M. Snyder Jr., "The Orientation of Newspaper Endorsements in U.S. Elections, 1940–2002," *Quarterly Journal of Political Science* 1 (2006): 393–404.

28. Mitchell Stephens, *A History of News from the Drum to the Satellite* (New York: Viking, 1988), 267.

29. Bernard Goldberg, *Bias: A CBS Insider Exposes How the Media Distort the News* (Washington, D.C.: Regnery, 2001).

30. George E. Reedy, "Why Does Nobody Love the Press?" in *The Mass Media and Modern Democracy,* ed. Harry M. Clor (Chicago: Rand McNally, 1974), 20.

31. Ibid., 25.

32. Poll results can be seen at World Public Opinion, http://www.worldpublicopinion.org/pipa/articles/international_security_bt/102.php?nid=&id=&pnt=102&lb=brus (accessed September 11, 2006).

33. Lauren Kessler, *The Dissident Press: Alternative Journalism in American History* (Beverly Hills, Calif.: Sage, 1984), 155.

34. Walter M. Brasch, *Forerunners of Revolution: Muckrakers and the American Social Conscience* (Lanham, Md.: University Press of America, 1990), 154.

35. Rainer Mathes and Barbara Pfetsch, "The Role of the Alternative Press in the Agenda-Building Process: Spill-Over Effects and Media Opinion Leadership," *European Journal of Communication* 6 (March 1991): 33–62.

36. William David Sloan and Julie Hedgepeth Williams, *The Early American Press, 1690–1783* (Westport, Conn.: Greenwood, 1994), 1–10.

37. Ibid.; see also Julie Hedgepeth Williams, "The Purposes of Journalism," in *American Journalism: History, Principles, Practices,* ed. William David Sloan and Lisa Mullikin Parcell (Jefferson, N.C.: McFarland, 2002), 3–4.

38. Printed in various sources, including Sloan and Williams, *Early American Press,* 36.

39. Ibid.

40. Ibid., 19.

41. David Copeland, "The Colonial Press, 1690–1765," in *The Media*

in America: A History, 6th ed., ed. William David Sloan (Northport, Ala.: Vision, 2005), 40.

42. Sloan and Williams, *Early American Press,* 21.

43. Ibid.; see also Jeffery A. Smith, *Printers and Press Freedom: The Ideology of Early American Journalism* (New York: Oxford University Press, 1988).

44. Copeland, "Colonial Press," 40.

45. Sloan and Williams, *Early American Press,* 123.

46. Ibid., 141.

47. Michael S. Sweeney, *The Military and the Press: An Uneasy Truce* (Evanston, Ill.: Northwestern University Press, 2006), 9–10.

48. Sloan and Williams, *Early American Press,* 165.

49. Carol Sue Humphrey, "The Media and Wartime Morale," in Startt and Sloan, *Significance of the Media in American History,* 65.

50. William Prochnau, "The Military and the Media," in *The Press,* ed. Geneva Overholser and Kathleen Hall Jamieson (Oxford: Oxford University Press, 2005), 314.

51. *Porcupine's Gazette,* March 5, 1797.

52. William David Sloan, "The Party Press, 1783–1833," in Sloan, *Media in America,* 75.

53. *Statutes at Large,* 1:596–97.

54. Margaret A. Blanchard, "Freedom of the Press, 1690–1804," in Sloan, *Media in America,* 95–122; Margaret A. Blanchard, "Freedom of the Press," in Sloan and Parcell, *American Journalism,* 125–34.

55. William E. Huntzicker, *The Popular Press, 1833–1865* (Westport, Conn.: Greenwood, 1999); Michael Buchholz, "The Penny Press, 1833–1861," in Sloan, *Media in America,* 123–42.

56. Huntzicker, *Popular Press,* 12.

57. Ibid., 115.

58. Bruce J. Evensen, "Objectivity," in Sloan and Parcell, *American Journalism,* 262.

59. Sweeney, *The Military and the Press;* Manuel O. Torres, "War Coverage," in Sloan and Parcell, *American Journalism,* 236–47.

60. Debra Reddin van Tuyll, "The Media and National Crises, 1917–1945," in Sloan, *Media in America,* 319–42.

61. James Landers, "Specter of Stalemate: Vietnam War Perspectives

in *Newsweek, Time,* and *U.S. News and World Report,* 1965–1968," *Journalism History* 19 (Summer 2002): 13–38; "Anti-Viet Nam Rallies Go Off Front Page," *Editor and Publisher,* February 26, 1966, 59; Ray Erwin, "'The Green Berets' Land on Comics Page," *Editor and Publisher,* February 12, 1966, 75.

62. Liz Trotta, *Fighting for Air: In the Trenches with Television News* (New York: Simon and Schuster, 1991), 135.

63. Chris Mooney, "The Editorial Pages and the Case for War," *Columbia Journalism Review,* March/April 2004, 33.

64. John Burnett, "Embedded/Unembedded II," *Columbia Journalism Review,* May/June 2003, 43.

65. Roy Gutman, "Foreword," in Sweeney, *Military and the Press,* xiv.

66. McPherson, *Journalism at the End of the American Century,* 87. After the war began, NBC released a book on which the cover overleaf states: "From the initial 'target of opportunity' to the unforgettable images of liberation as Saddam Hussein's statue was toppled in central Baghdad, the war riveted the nation" (Marc Kusnetz and others, *Operation Iraqi Freedom* [Kansas City, Mo.: Andrews McMeel, 2003]).

67. Leonard Ray Teel, *The Public Press, 1900–1945* (Westport, Conn.: Praeger, 2006); Sandra Haarsager, "Choosing Silence: A Case of Reverse Agenda Setting in Depression Era News Coverage," *Journal of Mass Media Ethics* 6 (1991): 35–46; Maurine H. Beasley, "The Emergence of Modern Media, 1900–1945," in Sloan, *Media in America,* 283–302; van Tuyll, "Media and National Crises," in Sloan, *Media in America.*

68. Theodore Roosevelt, "The Man with the Muckrake," *New York Tribune,* April 15, 1906; reprinted in *The Muckrakers,* ed. Arthur Weinberg and Lila Weinberg (New York: Capricorn Books, 1964), 58.

69. Roosevelt, "Man with the Muckrake," in Weinberg and Weinberg, *The Muckrakers,* 59–60.

70. Williams, "Purposes of Journalism," in Sloan and Parcell, *American Journalism,* 10.

71. James Aucoin, "The Media and Reform, 1900–1917," in Sloan, *Media in America,* 303–18.

72. Upton Sinclair, *The Brass Check: A Study of American Journalism,* rev. ed. (Girard, Kan.: Haldeman Julius, 1919).

CHAPTER TWO

1. Lionel Trilling, *The Liberal Imagination: Essays on Literature and Society* (New York: Doubleday, 1950), ix.

2. Richard A. Viguerie and David Franke, *America's Right Turn: How Conservatives Used New and Alternative Media to Take Power* (Chicago: Bonus Books, 2004), 49–50.

3. Elliot Abrams, book review, "'McCarthyism' Reconsidered," *National Review,* February 26, 1996, 60.

4. Sidney Blumenthal, *The Rise of the Counter-Establishment: From Conservative Ideology to Political Power* (New York: Times Books, 1986), 4. Interestingly, Blumenthal chose a word that in a slightly different form—"counterculture"—had been more closely identified with liberals in the 1960s and 1970s.

5. David Halberstam, *The Fifties* (New York: Villard Books, 1993), 9.

6. Irving Kristol, "American Conservatism 1945–1996," *Public Interest,* Fall 1995, 84.

7. Russell Kirk, "Ten Conservative Principles," adapted from his book *The Politics of Prudence* and reprinted on the Russell Kirk Center for Cultural Renewal's Web site, http://www.kirkcenter.org/kirk/ten -principles.html (accessed October 4, 2006).

8. Paul Gottfried, *The Conservative Movement,* rev. ed. (New York: Twayne, 1993), 5. See also Gary Dorrien, *The Neoconservative Mind: Politics, Culture, and the War of Ideology* (Philadelphia: Temple University Press, 1993).

9. Jerome L. Himmelstein, *To the Right: The Transformation of American Conservatism* (Berkeley: University of California Press, 1990), 21.

10. B. Carroll Reese, quoted in Halberstam, *The Fifties,* 9–10.

11. Lee Edwards, *The Conservative Revolution: The Movement That Remade America* (New York: Free Press, 1999), 12.

12. Gregory L. Schneider, "Anticommunism," in *Conservatism in America Since 1930,* ed. Gregory L. Schneider (New York: New York University Press, 2003), 131.

13. Halberstam, *The Fifties;* Whittaker Chambers, "A Witness," in Schneider, *Conservatism in America,* 135–48. This is an excerpted version of Chambers's 1953 book of the same name.

14. Quoted in Francis P. Sempa, "Whittaker Chambers," *American Diplomacy,* 1991, http://www.unc.edu/depts/diplomat/archives_roll/2001 _07-09/sempa_chambers/sempa_chambers.html (accessed October 7, 2006).

15. Reagan's complete testimony can be found in numerous sources, including CNN, at http://www.cnn.com/SPECIALS/cold.war/ episodes/06/documents/huac/reagan.html (accessed October 7, 2006).

16. Frances Fitzgerald, *Way Out There in the Blue: Reagan, Star Wars and the End of the Cold War* (New York: Simon and Schuster, 2000).

17. Erik Barnouw, *Tube of Plenty: The Evolution of American Television,* 2nd rev. ed. (New York: Oxford University Press, 1990), 121–26.

18. Halberstam, *The Fifties,* 59.

19. Tom Engelhardt, *The End of Victory Culture: Cold War America and the Disillusioning of a Generation* (New York: Basic Books, 1995), 99.

20. "Preamble to the Constitution of the American Legion for God and Country," American Legion, http://www.legion.org/?section=our _legion&subsection=ol_who_we_are&content=ol_who_we_are (accessed October 7, 2006).

21. Peter L. de Rosa, "American Legion Firing Line," in *The Conservative Press in Twentieth-Century America,* ed. Ronald Lora and William Henry Longton (Westport, Conn.: Greenwood, 1999), 480.

22. Chambers, "A Witness," in Schneider, *Conservatism in America,* 141.

23. William Rusher, *The Rise of the Right* (New York: William Morrow, 1984), 24–25.

24. Paul L. Silver, "Christian Anti-Communism Crusade News Letter," in Lora and Longton, *Conservative Press in Twentieth-Century America,* 490.

25. Blumenthal, *Rise of the Counter-Establishment,* 15.

26. J. David Hoeveler Jr., *Watch on the Right: Conservatives in the Reagan Era* (Madison: University of Wisconsin Press, 1991), 82.

27. Ibid., 9.

28. Frank Ashburn, quoted in Rusher, *Rise of the Right,* 41.

29. Rusher, *Rise of the Right,* 161.

30. David R. Davies, *The Postwar Decline of American Newspapers, 1945– 1965* (Westport, Conn.: Praeger, 2006), 71–73.

31. Ibid. See also Streitmatter, *Mightier Than the Sword,* 173–76.

32. Blumenthal, *Rise of the Counter-Establishment,* 319.

33. Jean Hardisty, *Mobilizing Resentment: Conservative Resurgence from the John Birch Society to the Promise Keepers* (Boston: Beacon, 1999), 149.

34. Richard Brookhiser, "Son of the Emerging Republican Majority," *National Review,* December 31, 1980, 1590.

35. Alan Crawford, *Thunder on the Right: The "New Right" and the Politics of Resentment* (New York: Pantheon, 1980).

36. Edwards, *Conservative Revolution,* 125.

37. Crawford, *Thunder on the Right,* 182.

38. Kevin P. Phillips, *The Emerging Republican Majority* (New Rochelle, N.Y.: Arlington House, 1969).

39. M. Stanton Evans, *The Future of Conservatism: From Taft to Reagan and Beyond* (New York: Holt, Rinehart and Winston, 1968).

40. Quoted in Jim Wallis, *God's Politics: Why the Right Gets It Wrong and the Left Doesn't Get It* (San Francisco: HarperSanFrancisco, 2005), 312.

41. Patrick J. Buchanan, *Conservative Votes, Liberal Victories: Why the Right Has Failed* (New York: Quadrangle/New York Times Book Co., 1975), 66–67.

42. "Negro Riots Rage On; Death Toll 25: 21,000 Troops, Police Wage Guerrilla War; 8 p.m. Curfew Invoked," *Los Angeles Times,* August 15, 1965. See also the oral histories of California journalists from the Oral History Program of California State University-Fullerton, and the Southern California Journalism Oral History Project of California State University-Northridge; and see McPherson, *Journalism at the End of the American Century,* 8.

43. John Gregory Dunne, "TV's Riot Squad," *New Republic,* September 11, 1965, 26.

44. Carolyn Martindale, "Selected Newspaper Coverage of Causes of Black Protest," *Journalism Quarterly* 66 (Winter 1989): 920–23, 964; Earnest L. Perry, "Coverage of Crime," in Sloan and Parcell, *American Journalism,* 189–97; and McPherson, *Journalism at the End of the American Century.*

45. Charles W. Dunn and J. David Woodard, *American Conservatives from Burke to Bush: An Introduction* (Lanham, Md.: Madison Books, 1991), 10.

46. Several books have been written about the case and its participants. For a good overview of the trial, see Douglas O. Linder, "The

Scopes Trial: An Introduction," in the University of Missouri-Kansas City's "Famous Trials" Web site, http://www.law.umkc.edu/faculty/projects/FTrials/scopes/scopes.htm (accessed October 23, 2006).

47. C. Edward Caudill, "The Media and Ideas," in Startt and Sloan, *Significance of the Media in American History,* 220.

48. Many of the Ten Commandment displays went up during the 1950s because of the promotional efforts of Cecil B. DeMille, who wanted to promote his movie, *The Ten Commandments,* and worked with the Federal Order of Eagles, which funded granite monuments and gave them to communities.

49. Dunn and Woodard, *American Conservatives.*

50. Quoted in Himmelstein, *To the Right,* 118.

51. Ibid., 119.

52. Kenneth J. Heineman, *God Is a Conservative: Religion, Politics, and Morality in Contemporary America* (New York: New York University Press, 1998), 49. See also William Martin, *With God on Our Side: The Rise of the Religious Right in America,* paperback ed. (New York: Broadway, 1997).

53. Patrick Allitt, "Triumph," in Lora and Longton, *Conservative Press in Twentieth-Century America,* 206–7.

54. Heineman, *God Is a Conservative.*

55. George F. Will, "Looking Back to 1965," *Public Interest,* Fall 1995, 7.

56. Kristol, "American Conservatism 1945–1996," 89–90.

57. Amy Erdman Farrell, *Yours in Sisterhood: Ms. Magazine and the Promise of Popular Feminism* (Chapel Hill: University of North Carolina Press, 1998).

58. Classified advertising section, *Editor and Publisher,* January 2, 1965.

59. John B. Barron, "The Paper Dolls Are Paper Tigers But They're Crowding Journalism Schools," *Quill,* September 1965, 12–15.

60. "Women Pols" in table of contents, *National Review,* December 5, 1986, 4.

61. Farrell, *Yours in Sisterhood,* 16.

62. Equal Rights Amendment, http://www.equalrightsamendment.org/ (accessed October 10, 2006).

63. Eagle Forum, http://www.eagleforum.org/misc/bio.html (accessed October 10, 2006).

64. Blumenthal, *Rise of the Counter-Establishment,* 319.

65. Jerry Lisker, "Homo Nest Raided, Queen Bees Are Stinging Mad," *New York Daily News,* July 6, 1969.

66. "Four Policemen Hurt in 'Village' Raid," *New York Times,* June 29, 1969.

67. Lucian Truscott IV, "View from Outside: Gay Power Comes to Sheridan Square," *Village Voice,* July 3, 1969.

68. Jerry LeBlanc, "A Newsman's Assignment: I Picketed with 'Peaceniks,'" *Quill,* March 1966, 24–26.

69. Editorial, "Another Day of Mourning," *Chicago Tribune,* June 6, 1968; see also McPherson, *Journalism at the End of the American Century.*

CHAPTER THREE

1. Rusher, *Rise of the Right,* 176.

2. Theodore Peterson, "The Social Responsibility Theory," in *Four Theories of the Press,* ed. Fred S. Siebert, Theodore Peterson, and Wilbur Schram (Freeport, N.Y.: Books for Libraries reprint, 1973), 73–103.

3. McPherson, "Government Watchdogs," 39.

4. Ibid.

5. McPherson, "Crosses Before a Government Vampire," 304–17.

6. Editorial, "A Free Press," *Seattle Post-Intelligencer,* March 14, 1964.

7. James Aucoin, "Investigative Journalism," in Sloan and Parcell, *American Journalism,* 209–18.

8. Davies, *Postwar Decline of American Newspapers,* 18.

9. Ibid., 41.

10. Ibid.

11. Crawford, *Thunder on the Right,* 302–3.

12. Dorrien, *Neoconservative Mind,* 74. See also William F. Buckley and L. Brent Bozell Jr., *McCarthy and His Enemies: The Record and Its Meaning* (Washington, D.C.: Henry Regnery, 1954); several later editions of this book have also been produced.

13. Richard Dudman, *Men of the Far Right* (New York: Pyramid Books, 1962), 142.

14. McPherson, *Journalism at the End of the American Century.*

15. Tom Wolfe, *The New Journalism* (New York: Harper and Row, 1973). See also Norman Sims, ed., *The Literary Journalists* (New York: Ballantine, 1984); and John C. Hartsock, *A History of American Literary Journalism: The Emergence of a Modern Narrative Form* (Amherst: University of Massachusetts Press, 2000).

16. Wolfe, *The New Journalism;* Hartsock, *A History of American Literary Journalism.* See also Bruce J. Evensen, "Objectivity," in Sloan and Parcell, *American Journalism,* 258-66.

17. The exact number of such publications is unknown. Many lasted only one issue. See Abe Peck, *Uncovering the Sixties: The Life and Times of the Underground Press* (New York: Citadel Underground, 1991); Robert J. Glessing, *The Underground Press in America* (Bloomington, Ind.: Midland, 1971); Michael L. Johnson, *The New Journalism: The Underground Press, the Artists of Nonfiction, and Changes in the Established Media* (Lawrence: University Press of Kansas, 1971); and Kessler, *The Dissident Press.*

18. John Wilcox, quoted in editorial, "'Underground' Square?" *Seattle Post-Intelligencer,* January 28, 1971.

19. "Narcotics Officers Listed," *Los Angeles Free Press,* August 8-14, 1969.

20. McPherson, "Government Watchdogs."

21. Buchanan, *Conservative Votes, Liberal Victories,* 22.

22. Ibid., 87.

23. Michael Novak, "The Fire Last Time," *National Review,* August 3, 1998, 40.

24. Robert H. Bork, "The Fire Last Time," *National Review,* August 3, 1998, 42.

25. Armistead S. Pride, "Opening Doors for Minorities," *Quill,* November 1968, 24-27.

26. McPherson, *Journalism at the End of the American Century,* 10-16.

27. Paul M. Weyrich, "A Call for Knowledgeable Religion Reporters," Renew America, February 11, 2005, http://www.renewamerica.us/columns/weyrich/050211 (accessed March 23, 2006).

28. Davies, *Postwar Decline of American Newspapers.*

29. Editorial, "A Free Press Comes First," *Chicago Tribune,* July 1, 1971.

30. McPherson, *Journalism at the End of the American Century,* 52.

31. Seymour Hersh, "Huge C.I.A. Operation Reported in U.S. Against Antiwar Forces, Other Dissidents in Nixon Years," *New York Times,* December 22, 1974.

32. "Year of the Lions and Lingering Shadows," 1966–67 report of the New Enterprise Committee of the Associated Press Managing Editors Association, records of the Associated Press Managing Editors Association, State Historical Society of Wisconsin, Madison; Paul E. Kostyu, "Nothing More, Nothing Less: Case Law Leading to the Freedom of Information Act," *American Journalism* 12 (Fall 1995): 462–76.

33. Scott R. Maier, "The Digital Watchdog's First Byte: Journalism's First Computer Analysis of Public Records," *American Journalism* 17 (Fall 2000): 75–91; Sharon Hartin Iorio, "How State Open Meetings Laws Now Compare with Those of 1974," *Journalism Quarterly* 62 (Winter 1985): 741–49; Matthew D. Bunker, "Have It Your Way? Public Records Law and Computerized Government Information," *Journalism and Mass Communication Quarterly* 73 (Spring 1996): 90–101; Sigman L. Splichal and Bill F. Chamberlin, "The Fight for Access to Government Records Round Two: Enter the Computer," *Journalism Quarterly* 71 (Autumn 1994): 550–60.

34. Investigative Reporters and Editors, July 26, 2002, http://www.ire.org (accessed March 3, 2007).

35. Alex S. Jones, "News Watchdog Group to Vote on Its Future," *New York Times,* March 21, 1984; Jonathon Friendly, "National News Council Will Dissolve," *New York Times,* March 23, 1984.

36. Alfred E. Lewis, "5 Held in Plot to Bug Democrats' Offices Here," *Washington Post,* June 18, 1972; Bob Woodward and Carl Bernstein, "GOP Security Aide Among Five Arrested in Bugging Affair," *Washington Post,* June 19, 1972. See also Bob Woodward and Carl Bernstein, *The Final Days* (New York: Avon Books, 1976); and Louis W. Liebovich, *Richard Nixon, Watergate, and the Press: A Historical Perspective* (Westport, Conn.: Praeger, 2003).

37. Byron St. Dizier, "Republican Endorsements, Democratic Positions: An Editorial Page Contradiction," *Journalism Quarterly* 63 (Autumn 1986): 581–86; Haynes Johnson, "The Newspaper Guild's Identity Crisis," *Columbia Journalism Review,* November/December 1972, 44–48; Russell Watson, "Nixon and the Media," *Newsweek,* January 15, 1973, 42–48. See

also William Porter, *Assault on the Media: The Nixon Years* (Ann Arbor: University of Michigan Press, 1976); and James Keogh, *President Nixon and the Press* (New York: Funk and Wagnalls, 1972).

38. Paul L. Silver (characterizing the views of editor Frederick Charles Schwartz), "Christian Anti-Communism Crusade Newsletter," in Lora and Longton, *Conservative Press in Twentieth-Century America,* 495.

39. Heineman, *God Is a Conservative,* 66. Incidentally, Nixon was not found to have been involved in the bugging itself, just in helping try to cover it up afterward.

40. McPherson, *Journalism at the End of the American Century.*

41. Arthur Unger, "'Nightline' A Thinking Man's Alternative to Late Network Viewing," *Christian Science Monitor,* November 13, 1980. See also Ted Koppel and Kyle Gibson, *Nightline: History in the Making and the Making of Television* (New York: Times Books, 1996).

42. John F. Kennedy, news conference, May 9, 1962, reprinted in *Kennedy and the Press: The News Conferences,* ed. Harold W. Chase and Allen H. Lerman (New York: Thomas Y. Crowell, 1965), 239.

43. Howard Morland, "The H-Bomb Secret: How We Got It; Why We're Telling It," *Progressive,* November 1979, 14–23; Howard Morland, *The Secret That Exploded* (New York: Random House, 1981); A. DeVolpi and others, *Born Secret: The H-Bomb, the Progressive Case, and National Security* (New York: Pergamon, 1981); James Brian McPherson, "From 'Military Propagandist' to The Progressive: The Editorial Evolution of H-Bomb Battler Samuel H. Day, Jr." (doctoral dissertation, Washington State University, 1998).

44. Arlie Schardt, Frank Maier, and Lucy Howard, "A Surfeit of H-Bomb Secrets," *Newsweek,* June 25, 1979, 62.

45. Erwin Knoll, "Wrestling with Leviathan: The Progressive Knew It Would Win," *Progressive,* November 1979, 25.

46. Pew Research Center for the People and the Press, "News Media Differs with Public and Leaders on Watchdog Issues," May 22, 1995, http://people-press.org/reports/pdf/19950522.pdf (accessed October 3, 2006); Dorothy Bowles, "Missed Opportunity: Educating Newspaper Readers About First Amendment Values," *Newspaper Research Journal* 10 (Winter 1989): 39–53; McPherson, "Crosses Before a Government Vampire"; David Pritchard, "The Impact of Newspaper Ombudsmen

on Journalists' Attitudes," *Journalism Quarterly* 70 (Spring 1993): 77–86; Ronald Farrar, "News Councils and Libel Actions," *Journalism Quarterly* 63 (Autumn 1986): 509–16; Samuel P. Huntington, *American Politics: The Promise of Disharmony* (Cambridge, Mass.: Belknap, 1981).

47. Thomas E. Patterson, "Legitimate Beef: The Presidency and a Carnivorous Press," *Media Studies Journal,* Spring 1994, 21–26.

48. J. Herbert Altschull, *From Milton to McLuhan: The Ideas Behind American Journalism* (New York: Longman, 1990), 354.

49. Kristin McGrath and Cecilie Gaziano, "Dimensions of Media Credibility: Highlights of the 1985 ASNE Survey," *Newspaper Research Journal* 7 (Winter 1986): 57; Gerald Stone, Barbara Hartung, and Dwight Jensen, "Local TV News and the Good-Bad Dyad," *Journalism Quarterly* 64 (Spring 1987): 37–44; Jack B. Haskins and M. Mark Miller, "The Effects of Bad News and Good News on a Newspaper's Image," *Journalism Quarterly* 61 (Spring 1984): 3–13, 65; Cecilie Gaziano, "How Credible Is the Credibility Crisis?" *Journalism Quarterly* 65 (Summer 1988): 267–78, 375; Erika G. King, "The Flawed Characters in the Campaign: Prestige Newspaper Assessments of the 1992 Presidential Candidates' Integrity and Competence," *Journalism and Mass Communication Quarterly* 72 (Spring 1995): 84–97; Thomas E. Patterson, *Out of Order* (New York: Vintage, 1993); Dennis T. Lowry and Jon A. Shidler, "The Sound Bites, the Biters, and the Bitten: An Analysis of Network News Bias in Campaign '92," *Journalism and Mass Communication Quarterly* 72 (Spring 1995): 33–44; Huntington, *American Politics.*

50. David Weaver and LeAnne Daniels, "Public Opinion on Investigative Reporting in the 1980s," *Journalism Quarterly* 69 (Spring 1992): 146–55; K. Tim Wulfemeyer and Lori L. McFadden, "Anonymous Attribution in Network News," *Journalism Quarterly* 63 (Autumn 1986): 468–73; Jane Delano Brown and others, "Invisible Power: Newspaper News Sources and the Limits of Diversity," *Journalism Quarterly* 64 (Spring 1987): 44–54; S. Shyam Sundar, "Effect of Source Attribution on Perception of Online News Stories," *Journalism and Mass Communication Quarterly* 75 (Spring 1998): 55–68.

51. S. Elizabeth Bird, "Newspaper Editors' Attitudes Reflect Ethical Doubt on Surreptitious Reporting," *Journalism Quarterly* 62 (Summer 1985): 288; McPherson, *Journalism at the End of the American Century;*

Robert L. Spellman, "Tort Liability of the News Media for Surreptitious Reporting," *Journalism Quarterly* 62 (Summer 1985): 289–95.

52. William A. Henry III, "Why Journalists Can't Wear White," *Media Studies Journal,* Fall 1992, 16–29; Tom Goldstein, *The News at Any Cost: How Journalists Compromise Their Ethics to Shape the News* (New York: Simon and Schuster, 1985); Marie Dunne White, "Plagiarism and the News Media," *Journal of Mass Media Ethics* 4 (1989): 265–80.

53. Douglas A. Anderson and Marianne Murdock, "Effects of Communication Law Decisions on Daily Newspaper Editors," *Journalism Quarterly* 58 (Winter 1981): 525–28, 534; Donald M. Gillmor and others, *Mass Communication Law: Cases and Comment,* 5th ed. (St. Paul, Minn.: West, 1990); "Editorial Processes Are Opened," *News Media and the Law,* May/June 1979, 2.

54. Edward L. Carter and Brad Clark, "'Arrogance Cloaked as Humility' and the Majoritarian First Amendment: The Free Speech Legacy of Chief Justice William Rehnquist," *Journalism and Mass Communication Quarterly* 83 (Autumn 2006): 650–68.

55. Accuracy in Media, http://www.aim.org; Fairness and Accuracy in Reporting, http://www.fair.org (accessed March 3, 2007); Media Research Center, http://www.mediaresearch.org (accessed March 3, 2007); Center for Media and Public Affairs, http://www.cmpa.com (accessed March 3, 2007); McPherson, *Journalism at the End of the American Century.*

56. Sweeney, *Military and the Press,* 147. See also Phillip Knightley, *The First Casualty: From the Crimea to Vietnam: The War Correspondent as Hero, Propagandist, and Myth Maker* (New York: Harvest Books, 1975); William M. Hammond, *Reporting Vietnam: Media and Military at War* (Lawrence: University Press of Kansas, 1998); Daniel C. Hallin, *The "Uncensored War": The Media and Vietnam,* paperback ed. (Berkeley: University of California Press, 1989); Dan B. Curtis, "Vietnam War Coverage," in *Encyclopedia of Television News,* ed. Michael D. Murray (Phoenix: Oryx, 1999); James Landers, "Specter of Stalemate: Vietnam War Perspectives in *Newsweek, Time,* and *U.S. News and World Report,* 1965–1968," *Journalism History* 19 (Summer 2002): 13–38.

57. Sweeney, *Military and the Press,* 146.

58. Donald S. Kreger, *Press Opinion in the Eagleton Affair,* Journalism

Monographs 35 (Lexington, Ky.: Association for Education in Journalism and Mass Communication, 1974).

59. Marion Clark and Rudy Maxa, "Closed Session Romance on the Hill," *Washington Post,* May 23, 1976.

60. J. William Fulbright, "Fulbright on the Press," *Columbia Journalism Review,* November/December 1975, 79.

61. Leo Bogart, "Media and Democracy," *Media Studies Journal,* Summer 1995, 9.

62. "Facts About Newspapers," Newspaper Association of America, http://web.naa.org/info/facts04/readership-audience.html (accessed November 16, 2007). See also Richard Davis, *The Press and American Politics: The New Mediator,* 2nd ed. (Upper Saddle River, N.J.: Prentice Hall, 1996); Patterson, *Out of Order;* Doris A. Graber, *Mass Media and American Politics,* 4th ed. (Washington, D.C.: Congressional Quarterly, 1993).

63. "Morning in America" was a slogan for Reagan's second successful presidential campaign, in 1984.

CHAPTER FOUR

1. Rusher, *Rise of the Right.*

2. The text of the speech can be found in many places, including the Miller Center of Public Affairs Web site (linked to the Jimmy Carter Library and Museum's Web site), http://millercenter.virginia.edu/scripps/diglibrary/prezspeeches/carter/jec_1979_0715.html (accessed October 17, 2006).

3. Ibid.

4. Koppel and Gibson, *Nightline.* Conservative radio talk show host Rush Limbaugh used the "America held hostage" line to mark the passing of Bill Clinton's presidency, and liberal MSNBC host Keith Olbermann used a similar phrase daily during the Iraq War.

5. Heineman, *God Is a Conservative.*

6. Ibid., 106.

7. Editorial, "The Anti-Liberal Revolution," *National Review,* November 28, 1980, 1434–35.

8. Donald L. Barlett and James B. Steele, *America: What Went Wrong?* (Kansas City, Mo.: Andrews and McMeel, 1992).

9. Huntington, *American Politics.*

10. Wilbur Edel, *Defenders of the Faith: Religion and Politics from the Pilgrim Fathers to Ronald Reagan* (New York: Praeger, 1987).

11. Rusher, *Rise of the Right,* 297.

12. Sharon J. Alexander, "Implications of the White House Conference on Families for Family Life Education," *Family Relations* 30 (October 1981): 643. See also Leo P. Ribuffo, "Family Past as Prologue: Jimmy Carter, the White House Conference on Families, and the Mobilization of the New Christian Right," *Review of Policy Research* 23 (March 2006): 311–37.

13. Heineman, *God Is a Conservative,* 99–100; Edwards, *Conservative Revolution,* 197–98.

14. E. J. Dionne Jr., *Why Americans Hate Politics,* paperback ed. (New York: Touchstone, 1992), 227.

15. Mark Ward Sr., *Air of Salvation: The Story of Christian Broadcasting* (Grand Rapids, Mich.: Baker Books, 1994), 155.

16. Howard Zinn, *A People's History of the United States, 1492–Present,* rev. ed. (New York: HarperPerennial, 1995), 561.

17. Ronald Reagan, "A Time for Choosing," Ronald Reagan Presidential Foundation, http://www.reaganfoundation.org/reagan/speeches/rendezvous.asp (accessed October 17, 2006).

18. Ibid.

19. Paul Gavaghan, quoted in Garry Wills, *Reagan's America,* paperback ed. (New York: Penguin, 1988), 337.

20. Blumenthal, *Rise of the Counter-Establishment,* 249–50.

21. Dunn and Woodard, *American Conservatives,* 8.

22. Irving Kristol, "New Left, New Right," *Public Interest,* Summer 1966, 6.

23. Evans, *Future of Conservatism,* 265.

24. David North, "Ronald Reagan (1911–2004): An Obituary," World Socialist Web Site, http://www.wsws.org/articles/2004/jun2004/reag-jo9.shtml, June 9, 2004 (accessed October 24, 2006).

25. Fitzgerald, *Way Out There in the Blue.*

26. Michael Schudson and Susan E. Tifft, "American Journalism in Historical Perspective," in Overholser and Jamieson, *The Press,* 17–47.

27. "First Presidential Debate Draws Large Audience," Online Newshour, PBS, October 5, 2005, http://www.pbs.org/newshour/updates/campaigncover_10-05-04.html (accessed October 26, 2006).

28. Quoted in various sources, including "The Second 1984 Presidential Debate," PBS, http://www.pbs.org/newshour/debatingourdestiny/84debates/2prez2.html (accessed October 19, 2006).

29. J. Jeffery Auer, "Acting Like a President; or, What Has Ronald Reagan Done to Political Speaking?" in *Reagan and Public Discourse in America,* ed. Michael Weiler and W. Barnett Pearce (Tuscaloosa: University of Alabama Press, 1992), 102.

30. Rodger Streitmatter, "The Rise and Triumph of the White House Photo Opportunity," *Journalism Quarterly* 65 (Winter 1988): 984; Michael D. Murray, "The Contemporary Media, 1974–Present," in Sloan, *Media in America,* 465–90.

31. Bennett, *News: The Politics of Illusion.* See also Davis, *The Press and American Politics.*

32. David Sirota, "G. Walker Bush, Texas Ranger," Sirotablog, http://www.davidsirota.com/index.php/g-walker-bush-texas-ranger/ (accessed October 19, 2006).

33. Bennett, *News: The Politics of Illusion,* 168; Graber, *Mass Media and American Politics,* 256.

34. Louis W. Liebovich, *The Press and the Modern Presidency: Myths and Mindsets from Kennedy to Clinton* (Westport, Conn.: Praeger, 1998), 131.

35. Eve Pell, *The Big Chill: How the Reagan Administration, Corporate America, and Religious Conservatives Are Subverting Free Speech and the Public's Right to Know* (Boston: Beacon, 1984), 234. See also Eleanor Randolph, "White House Cuts Flow of Information; News Media Treated as an Alien Force," *Washington Post,* June 10, 1985; Richard Curry, ed., *Freedom at Risk: Secrecy, Censorship, and Repression in the 1980s* (Philadelphia: Temple University Press, 1988).

36. Eric Newton, "We Are One, but Mind Your Own Business," American Society of Newspaper Editors, http://www.asne.org/index.cfm?ID=514 (accessed November 25, 2007).

37. Mark Hertsgaard, *On Bended Knee: The Press and the Reagan Presidency* (New York: Farrar, Straus and Giroux, 1988). See also James T. Hamilton, "The Market and the Media," in Overholser and Jamieson, *The Press,* 351–71.

38. Philip Geyelin, "What He Doesn't Know," *Washington Post,* August 17, 1984. See also William J. Hughes, "The 'Not-So-Genial' Conspira-

cy: The *New York Times* and Six Presidential 'Honeymoons,' 1953–1993," *Journalism and Mass Communication Quarterly* 72 (Winter 1995): 841–50; Colman McCarthy, "Reagan and the Lie of the Land," *Washington Post,* December 7, 1986; John Tebbel and Sarah Miles Watts, *The Press and the Presidency: From George Washington to Ronald Reagan* (New York: Oxford University Press, 1985).

39. Elliot King and Michael Schudson, "The Myth of the Great Communicator," *Columbia Journalism Review,* November/December 1987, 37–39, http://archives.cjr.org/year/01/6/oldpieces/1987excerpt.asp (accessed October 20, 2006).

40. Liebovich, *The Press and the Modern Presidency,* 130.

41. Quoted in Haynes Johnson, *Sleepwalking Through History: America in the Reagan Years,* paperback ed. (New York: Anchor/Doubleday, 1991), 161.

42. Stacy Hirsh, "Reagan Presidency Pivotal for Unions," *Baltimore Sun,* June 8, 2004, http://www.baltimoresun.com/business/bal-bz.unions08jun08,0,1761456.story?coll=bal-business-headlines (accessed October 25, 2006).

43. Ibid.

44. D. W. Rajecki and others, "Documentation of Media Reflections of the Patriotic Revival in the United States in the 1980s," *Journal of Social Psychology* 131 (June 1991): 401–11.

45. Fitzgerald, *Way Out There in the Blue,* 22.

46. Lou Cannon, "President's Deeds Reveal His Real Opinion of Press Freedom," *Washington Post,* November 28, 1983.

47. Peter Braestrup, *Battle Lines: Report of the Twentieth Century Fund Task Force on the Military and the Media* (New York: Priority, 1985), 83–109; see also Sweeney, *Military and the Press,* 154–57.

48. Lou Cannon, "Media Chose Wrong Targets in Hitting Subordinates for Blackout," *Washington Post,* November 7, 1983. See also editorial, "When Is an Invasion Not an Invasion?" *Atlanta Constitution,* November 5, 1983; editorial, "Public and Press: 'Us' vs. 'Them'?" *Seattle Post-Intelligencer,* December 22, 1983.

49. Editorial, "The Press Gets a Bad Press," *Chicago Tribune,* December 11, 1983. See also editorial, "Press Needs Public Support," *Portland Oregonian,* December 2, 1983.

50. Charles R. Kesler, "The Reasonableness of Conservatism," *National Review*, December 31, 1980, 1592.

51. Tom Shales, "The Year of Roseanne, Saddam, Bart and PBS's 'Civil War,'" *Washington Post*, December 30, 1990.

52. Auer, "Acting Like a President," in Weiler and Pearce, *Reagan and Public Discourse*, 116.

53. Fitzgerald, *Way Out There in the Blue*, 53.

54. Zinn, *A People's History*, 574.

55. Lawrence E. Walsh, "Final Report of the Independent Counsel for Iran/Contra Matters," August 4, 1993, http://www.fas.org/irp/offdocs/walsh/ (accessed October 24, 2006).

56. Richard Stengel, "Bushwacked!" *Time*, February 8, 1988, 15, 17–20. See also Thomas J. Johnson, "Exploring Media Credibility: How Media and Nonmedia Workers Judged Media Performance in Iran/Contra," *Journalism Quarterly* 70 (Spring 1993): 87–97; and Scott Armstrong, "Iran-Contra: Was the Press Any Match for All the President's Men?" *Columbia Journalism Review*, May/June 1990, 27–35.

57. Walsh, "Final Report."

58. Christopher Layne, "Requiem for the Reagan Doctrine," in *Assessing the Reagan Years*, ed. David Boaz (Washington, D.C.: Cato Institute, 1988), 104.

59. Walsh, "Final Report."

60. Don Oberdorfer, "U.S. Moves to Prevent Iraqi Loss," *Washington Post*, January 1, 1984.

61. Bernard Gwertzman, "For First Time, Iraqis Bombard Iranian Citizens," *New York Times*, February 12, 1984.

62. McPherson, *Journalism at the End of the American Century*.

63. The missile defense program actually was named the Strategic Defense Initiative. Skeptical scientists called it "Star Wars." The focus of the program shifted with the end of the Reagan administration, until President George W. Bush renewed ballistic missile defense testing.

64. McPherson, *Journalism at the End of the American Century*. Without the destruction of the Berlin Wall and the breakup of the Soviet Union, Reagan's best-remembered speech likely would have been the one he gave eulogizing the seven astronauts killed when the space shuttle *Challenger* exploded shortly after takeoff in 1986. In the final sentence of the speech, Reagan said the astronauts had "slipped the surly bonds of earth"

to "touch the face of God." The key phrases came from "High Flight," a poem by a World War II Royal Canadian Air Force pilot and one popular with generations of pilots. For more about the poem and its author, see Nigel Rees, "High Flier," http://www.qunl.com/rees0008.html (accessed October 25, 2006).

65. Layne, "Requiem," in Boaz, *Assessing the Reagan Years,* 102.

66. Barlett and Steele, *America: What Went Wrong?* 18. The book is an expanded version of a 1991 *Philadelphia Inquirer* series.

67. Ibid.

68. Robert A. Bennett, "Another Crisis Engulfs the Thrifts," *New York Times,* July 22, 1984.

69. Editorial, "The 431 Insolvent S&Ls," *Washington Post,* November 8, 1985. See also Ernest Conine, "At a Time for Outrage on S&Ls and Takeovers, the Silence Is Deafening," *Los Angeles Times,* November 2, 1988.

70. Richard L. Berke, "Deregulation Has Gone Too Far, Many Tell the New Administration," *New York Times,* December 11, 1988.

71. Obituary, "Ronald Reagan, 1911–2004," CNN, http://www.cnn.com/SPECIALS/2004/reagan/stories/bio.part.one/index.html (accessed October 25, 2006).

72. Ronald Reagan, "Abortion and the Conscience of a Nation," *Human Life Review,* Spring 1983, reprinted on *National Review* Web site, http://www.nationalreview.com/document/reagan200406101030.asp (accessed October 25, 2006).

73. Irving Younger, "In Defense of the 'Litmus Test,'" *National Review,* November 14, 1980, 1393–94.

74. Grover Rees III, "The Constitution, the Court, and the President-Elect," *National Review,* December 31, 1980, 1595.

75. Dunn and Woodard, *American Conservatives,* 149.

76. Blumenthal, *Rise of the Counter-Establishment,* 241.

CHAPTER FIVE

1. Eric Alterman, "The Myth of the Liberal Media," in *News Incorporated: Corporate Media Ownership and Its Threat to Democracy,* ed. Elliot D. Cohen (New York: Prometheus, 2005), 111–12.

2. Gottfried, *Conservative Movement*.

3. Sean Hannity on *Hannity and Company,* Fox News transcript, April 5, 2001. For a few other examples of Hannity repeating the allegation, see *Hannity and Company,* Fox News transcript, February 15, 2005; *Hannity and Company,* Fox News transcript, November 9, 2004; and *Hannity and Colmes,* Fox News transcript, November 1, 2002. See also "Ingraham, Hannity Revived Claim That 'Al Gore Brought Up Willie Horton,'" Media Matters for America, February 16, 2005, http://mediamatters.org/items/200502160008 (accessed October 29, 2006); Bob Somerby, "Sean Happens! Dissembling Sean Played the Race Card," Daily Howler, November 1, 2002, http://www.dailyhowler.com/dh110102.shtml (accessed October 29, 2006). Gore did bring up the furlough program during a debate, but no evidence shows he had even heard of Horton.

4. Sean Hannity on *Hannity and Company,* Fox News transcript, July 13, 2000.

5. Bruce Porter, "So What? Pulitzer Prize-Winning Exposés and Their Sometimes Dubious Consequences," *Columbia Journalism Review,* March/April 1995, 41–47.

6. John Diamond, "Dukakis Changes Position on Furloughs for Murderers," Associated Press, March 22, 1988.

7. Mark Starr, "The Ballot Box Goes to Prison," *Newsweek,* January 25, 1988, 63.

8. Joseph Mianowany, "Remarkable Politics in '88," United Press International, December 12, 1988; Judy Woodruff on the *MacNeil/Lehrer Newshour,* PBS transcript, July 20, 1988; she made no mention of Gore.

9. Sandy Grady, "Even Mr. Clean Will Be Sullied by Mud-Slinging, Sex Scandals," *Philadelphia Daily News,* July 8, 1998.

10. Bill Kristol on *This Week,* ABC News transcript, October 24, 1999. Kristol repeated the allegation in later years; see Bill Kristol, *Fox on the Record,* Fox News transcript, February 16, 2004.

11. George Will, *This Week with David Brinkley,* ABC News transcript, July 12, 1992.

12. Ibid. Ironically, many liberals considered Gore to be too conservative, and some of them also repeated the Willie Horton myth. For example, see Alexander Cockburn and Jeffrey St. Clair, *Al Gore: A User's Manual* (New York: Verso, 2000).

13. Mary McGrory, "George Will Finds Being 'a Stablemate to States-men' Can Cost," *Washington Post,* July 12, 1983; George Will, "Backstage at the Presidential Debate," *Washington Post,* July 10, 1983. Will did say he would not repeat his earlier actions if given the opportunity.

14. William C. Berman, *America's Right Turn: From Nixon to Clinton,* 2nd ed. (Baltimore: Johns Hopkins University Press, 1998), 128.

15. John Micklethwait and Adrian Wooldridge, *The Right Nation: Conservative Power in America* (New York: Penguin, 1994), quoted in George Will, "Why America Leans Right," *Washington Post,* October 10, 1994.

16. Colin Powell on *Nightline,* ABC News transcript, January 25, 1993.

17. John Lancaster, "Many Allies Allow Gays in the Military," *Washington Post,* November 30, 1992; Chris Reidy, "Just Saying No," *Boston Globe,* January 31, 1993.

18. Margery Eagan, "Moral Hypocrites Make Political Hay," *Boston Herald,* July 16, 1996.

19. Howard Kurtz, "Ad on Christian Radio Touts Clinton's Stands," *Washington Post,* October 15, 1996.

20. Paul Starr, "What Happened to Health Care Reform?" *American Prospect,* Winter 1995, 20–31, http://www.princeton.edu/~starr/20starr .html (accessed November 1, 2006).

21. Ibid.

22. Derek Bok, "The Great Health Care Debate of 1993–94," *Public Talk: Online Journal of Discourse Leadership,* http://www.upenn.edu/pnc/ ptbok.html (accessed November 1, 2006).

23. Kenneth J. Cooper and Helen Dewar, "For Most Republicans on Hill, Last Week Was like No Other," *Washington Post,* November 20, 1994.

24. Howard Kurtz, "The Bad News About Clinton; Report Says Coverage Unfair to President," *Washington Post,* September 1, 1994.

25. Ibid.; Hughes, "The 'Not-So-Genial' Conspiracy," 841–50.

26. Neil MacNeil, "The American Congress: Its Troubled Role in the 1980's," *Modern Age,* Fall 1980, 373.

27. Editorial, "The Republican 'Contract,'" *Washington Times,* September 14, 1994.

28. Dan Balz and Charles R. Babcock, "Gingrich, Allies Made Waves

and Impression; Conservative Rebels Harassed the House," *Washington Post,* December 20, 1994; McPherson, *Journalism at the End of the American Century.*

29. MacNeil, "American Congress," 372.

30. Patterson, *Out of Order,* 156.

31. Davis, *The Press and American Politics.*

32. Kenneth R. Timmerman, "Has Clinton's China Policy Put U.S. National Security at Risk?" Cato Institute, Center for Trade Policy Studies, Insight Forum, November 6, 2000, http://www.freetrade.org/node/215 (accessed November 5, 2006).

33. Christopher Caldwell, "Should He Stay . . ." *Weekly Standard,* July 20, 1998, 20.

34. Committee of Concerned Journalists, "The Clinton Crisis and the Press: A Second Look," Committee of Concerned Journalists/Project for Excellence in Journalism, March 27, 1998, http://www.journalism.org/node/292 (accessed November 5, 2006). See also Kenton Bird, "White House Sex Scandal Absorbs the News Media," in Sloan, *Media in America,* 481.

35. Ben Wattenberg, "Refer, Impeach, Endure," *Washington Times,* December 16, 1998.

36. William F. Buckley Jr., "U.S. v. Clinton," *National Review,* September 28, 1998, 43.

37. David Gelernter, "U.S. v. Clinton," *National Review,* September 28, 1998, 44.

38. Michael Powell, "Buffalo Bill's Wild Road Show," *Washington Post,* January 22, 1999.

39. Will, "Why America Leans Right." Will was writing about *The Right Nation* by John Micklethwait and Adrian Wooldridge.

40. Viguerie and Franke, *America's Right Turn,* 58.

41. Ibid. America's Future, founded in 1946, actually still exists, though it was most active in the 1950s. See the organization's Web site at http://www.americasfuture.net (accessed November 6, 2006).

42. Viguerie and Franke, *America's Right Turn,* 59.

43. Robert Huberty, "Cultural Wellspring of the Conservative Movement," *Human Events,* February 9, 2004, http://www.findarticles.com/p/articles/mi_qa3827/is_200402/ai_n9386018 (accessed November 6, 2006).

44. Viguerie and Franke, *America's Right Turn,* 66.

45. Crawford, *Thunder on the Right,* 4.

46. American Conservative Union, http://www.conservative.org/about/default.asp (accessed November 7, 2006).

47. Ibid.

48. Crawford, *Thunder on the Right,* 8.

49. Conservative Caucus, http://www.conservativeusa.org (accessed November 7, 2006).

50. Ibid.

51. Viguerie and Franke, *America's Right Turn,* 126.

52. Heritage Foundation, http://www.heritage.org/About/about Heritage.cfm (accessed November 7, 2006).

53. David Brock, *The Republican Noise Machine: Right-Wing Media and How It Corrupts Democracy* (New York: Crown, 2004), 58.

54. Heritage Foundation.

55. American Legislative Exchange Council, http://www.alec.org (accessed November 8, 2006).

56. Mark J. Ambinder, "Inside the Council for National Policy," ABC News, May 2, 2006, http://abcnews.go.com/Politics/story?id=121170&page=1 (accessed November 8, 2006).

57. Ibid.

58. Ibid.

59. Viguerie and Franke, *America's Right Turn.*

60. Crawford, *Thunder on the Right.*

61. Myra MacPherson, "The New Right Brigade," *Washington Post,* August 10, 1980.

62. Brock, *Republican Noise Machine,* 92.

63. Elizabeth Kastor, "The Cautious Closet of the Gay Conservative," *Washington Post,* May 11, 1987.

64. Leadership Institute, http://www.leadershipinstitute.org (accessed November 6, 2006).

65. Ibid.

66. Viguerie and Franke, *America's Right Turn,* 167–68.

67. Leadership Institute.

68. Viguerie and Franke, *America's Right Turn,* 168.

69. Leadership Institute, Bi-Partisan Congressional Advisory Board,

http://www.leadershipinstitute.org/about/includes/board.pdf (accessed November 6, 2006).

70. Helen Dewar and Vivian Aplin-Brownlee, "Rep. McDonald Hailed as Right-Wing Martyr," *Washington Post,* September 2, 1983.

71. Bob Morgan, "Conservatives: A Well-Financed Network," *Washington Post,* January 4, 1981.

72. Paul L. Martin, "The Conservatives' Drive for a Stronger Voice," *U.S. News and World Report,* July 11, 1977, 47.

73. Ibid.

CHAPTER SIX

1. Viguerie and Franke, *America's Right Turn,* 87–88.

2. Ibid., 94.

3. Himmelstein, *To the Right,* 69.

4. Thomas Frank, *What's the Matter with Kansas? How Conservatives Won the Heart of America* (New York: Metropolitan, 2004), 5.

5. Ibid.

6. Hardisty, *Mobilizing Resentment.*

7. Hal Malchow, quoted in Viguerie and Franke, *America's Right Turn,* 160.

8. Ibid., 165.

9. Shanto Ivengar, quoted in Michael Grunwald, "The Year of Playing Dirtier," *Washington Post,* October 27, 2006.

10. Berman, *America's Right Turn,* 128; Himmelstein, *To the Right,* 201.

11. William F. Buckley, "Publisher's Statement," *National Review,* November 19, 1955, 5.

12. William F. Buckley, "The Magazine's Credenda," *National Review,* November 19, 1955, 6.

13. Ibid.

14. Mrs. S. P. Wallich, letter to the editor, *National Review,* December 21, 1955, 17.

15. Mabel E. Karm, letter to the editor, *National Review,* December 21, 1955, 16.

16. Irving Kristol, "American Conservatism 1945–1995," *Public Interest,* Fall 1995, 83.

17. Ronald Lora, "National Review," in Lora and Longton, *Conservative Press in Twentieth-Century America,* 515.

18. Ibid., 517.

19. William Rusher, "The First Ten Years Are the Hardest," *National Review,* November 30, 1965, 1116.

20. Ibid.

21. Quoted in Blumenthal, *Rise of the Counter-Establishment,* 26.

22. Viguerie and Franke, *America's Right Turn,* 64.

23. Kristol, "American Conservatism," 83.

24. Ibid.

25. Lora, "National Review."

26. George A. Panichas, "Modern Age," in Lora and Longton, *Conservative Press in Twentieth-Century America,* 531.

27. Jacob H. Dorn, "University Bookman," in Lora and Longton, *Conservative Press in Twentieth-Century America,* 547–58.

28. Jacob H. Dorn, "Intercollegiate Review," in Lora and Longton, *Conservative Press in Twentieth-Century America,* 559–71.

29. Daniel Bell and Irving Kristol, "What Is the Public Interest?" *Public Interest,* Fall 1965, 4.

30. Charles Krauthammer, "Our Own Cool Hand Luke," *Washington Post,* April 29, 1995.

31. John M. Elliott, "Public Interest," in Lora and Longton, *Conservative Press in Twentieth-Century America,* 651.

32. Edwin J. Feulner Jr., David I. Meiselman, and Robert L. Schuettinger, "Introducing *Policy Review,*" *Policy Review,* Summer 1977, 5.

33. John Ehrman, "Commentary," in Lora and Longton, *Conservative Press in Twentieth-Century America,* 617–27.

34. Steven J. Fitch, "Conservative Digest," in Lora and Longton, *Conservative Press in Twentieth-Century America,* 668.

35. Barry D. Riccio, "Continuity," in Lora and Longton, *Conservative Press in Twentieth-Century America,* 591–604.

36. Viguerie and Franke, *America's Right Turn,* 257. See also Scott McConnell, "The Weekly Standard's War," *American Conservative,* Novem-

ber 21, 2005, http://amconmag.com/2005/2005_11_21/article.html (accessed November 16, 2006).

37. Project for Excellence in Journalism, "The State of the News Media 2006," http://www.stateofthenewsmedia.org/2006/narrative_magazines_audience.asp?cat=3&media=8 (accessed November 16, 2006).

38. Ibid.

39. Quote from a Moon Web site entitled "True Love King," http://www.revsunmyungmoon.net (accessed November 14, 2006).

40. American Family Coalition, http://www.americanfamilycoalition.org (accessed November 14, 2006). The site makes little actual mention of Moon, repeatedly referring to the coalition as a grassroots organization.

41. "The Healing of the World: An Introduction to the Life and Teachings of Sun Myung Moon," Unification Church, http://www.unification.org/healing_of_world.html (accessed November 14, 2006). Moon has had two legal marriages and one common-law wife.

42. Dante Chinni, "The Other Paper," *Columbia Journalism Review,* September/October 2002, 47. See also Ken McIntyre, "Surviving, and Thriving, as a First Source of News," *Washington Times,* May 17, 2002; and Lee Edwards, ed., *Our Times: The Washington Times 1982–2002* (Washington, D.C.: Regnery, 2002).

43. Roxanne Roberts, "Moon Eclipses Birthday Bash for Times," *Washington Post,* May 22, 2002.

44. Brock, *Republican Noise Machine,* 2.

45. Frank Ahrens, "Moon Speech Raises Old Ghosts as the Times Turns 20," *Washington Post,* May 23, 2002.

46. Dorothy Kidd, "Clear Channel and the Public Airwaves," in Cohen, *News Incorporated,* 267–85.

47. Streitmatter, *Mightier Than the Sword;* Gary W. Larson, "Radio Journalism," in Sloan and Parcell, *American Journalism,* 277–85.

48. Peter Johnson, "Fox Ratings Rise Despite Recent Harsh Criticism," *USA Today,* July 26, 2004; Frazier Moore, "Fox News Channel: Not Playing Fair With Its 'Fair and Balanced' Slogan?" Associated Press, July 20, 2004; Dorothy Bowles, "Missed Opportunity: Educating Newspaper Readers About First Amendment Values," *Newspaper Research Journal* 10 (Winter 1989): 39–53.

49. Project for Excellence in Journalism, "The State of the News Media 2006," http://www.stateofthenewsmedia.org/2006/journalist _survey_prc.asp (accessed November 16, 2006).

50. Steffano DellaVigna and Ethan Kaplan, "The Fox News Effect: Media Bias and Voting," March 30, 2006, http://elsa.berkeley.edu/ ~sdellavi/wp/foxvote06-03-30.pdf#search=%22fox%20news%20studies %22 (accessed November 16, 2006).

51. Howard Kurtz, "Bush Cousin Made Florida Vote Call for Fox News," *Washington Post,* November 14, 2000.

52. John Ellis, "Why I Won't Write Anymore About the 2000 Campaign," *Boston Globe,* July 3, 2000. Ellis announced his resignation from the newspaper a few weeks later: John Ellis, "Thank You for Reading," *Boston Globe,* July 29, 2000. See also McPherson, *Journalism at the End of the American Century,* 156.

53. "Networks Largely Called Election Results with Caution, but Differed on Ohio and Nevada," Online Newshour, PBS, http://www .pbs.org/newshour/vote2004/politics101/politics101_covering campaign.html (accessed November 15, 2006). The Ohio projection actually left Bush one vote short of the majority needed for reelection, and Fox News waited longer than most other networks to declare Nevada— the state that formally pushed him over the top—in his favor.

54. Paul Apostolidis, "Scanning the 'Stations of the Cross': Christian Right Radio in Post-Fordist Society," in *Radio Reader: Essays in the Cultural History of Radio,* ed. Michel Hilmes and Jason Loiglio (New York: Routledge, 2002), 461–83.

55. American Family Association, http://www.afa.net (accessed March 25, 2006); the ownership numbers are from Apostolidis, "Scanning the 'Stations of the Cross,'" in Hilmes and Loiglio, *Radio Reader,* and from the Project for Excellence in Journalism's 2004 "State of the News Media" report, http://www.stateofthenewsmedia.org/narrative_radio_ownership .asp?cat=5&media=8 (accessed March 25, 2006). See also Lora and Longton, *Conservative Press in Twentieth-Century America.*

56. David Copeland, "Religion and Colonial Newspapers," in *Media and Religion in American History,* ed. William David Sloan (Northport, Ala.:Vision, 2000), 54–67; David A. Copeland, *Colonial American Newspapers: Character and Content* (Newark: University of Delaware Press, 1997).

See also Mark Silk, *Unsecular Media: Making News of Religion in America* (Urbana: University of Illinois Press, 1995).

57. A few religious newspapers did appear, as noted in Marvin Olasky, "Democracy and the Secularization of the American Press," in *American Evangelicals and the Mass Media,* ed. Quentin J. Schultz (Grand Rapids, Mich.: Academie Books, 1990), 47–67.

58. Carol Sue Humphrey, "Religious Newspapers and Antebellum Reform," in Sloan, *Media and Religion in American History,* 104–18.

59. Julie Hedgepeth Williams, "The Founding of *The Christian Science Monitor,*" in Sloan, *Media and Religion in American History,* 149–65.

60. "A Revived Monitor," *Presstime,* August 2002, http://www.naa .org/Home/PressTime/2002/August/PressTimeContent/Special -Report-Local-Stories-Far-From-Home.aspx (accessed March 23, 2006).

61. Silk, *Unsecular Media;* Doug Underwood, *From Yahweh to Yahoo! The Religious Roots of the Secular Press* (Champaign: University of Illinois Press, 2002); Doug Underwood and Keith Stamm, "Are Journalists Really Irreligious? A Multidimensional Analysis," *Journalism and Mass Communication Quarterly* 78 (Winter 2001): 771–86; Peter A. Kerr and Patricia Moy, "Newspaper Coverage of Fundamentalist Christians, 1980–2000," *Journalism and Mass Communication Quarterly* 79 (Spring 2002): 54–72.

62. David Gibson, "Do Editors Care About Religion Coverage?" Religion Newswriters Association, http://www.rna.org/faq3.php (accessed March 24, 2006).

63. Warren L. Vinz, "Sword of the Lord," in Lora and Longton, *Conservative Press in Twentieth-Century America,* 131–32.

64. Thomas J. Ferris, "Christian Beacon," in Lora and Longton, *Conservative Press in Twentieth-Century America,* 147.

65. Ibid.

66. Vinz, "Sword of the Lord," in Lora and Longton, *Conservative Press in Twentieth-Century America,* 131–32.

67. Kenneth W. Shipps, "Christianity Today," in Lora and Longton, *Conservative Press in Twentieth-Century America,* 171–80.

68. Tona Hangen, "Man of the Hour: Walter A. Maier and Religion by Radio on the *Lutheran Hour,*" in Hilmes and Loiglio, *Radio Reader,* 113–34.

69. Ward, *Air of Salvation,* 15.

70. Dennis N. Voskuil, "The Power of the Air: Evangelicals and the

Rise of Religious Broadcasting," in Schultz, *American Evangelicals and the Mass Media,* 69–95; Stuart Brooks Keith III, "It's Not That Simple: A Survey of Televangelism," in *Religion as Entertainment,* ed. C. K. Robertson (New York: Peter Lang, 2002), 121–35; Hangen, "Man of the Hour," in Hilmes and Loiglio, *Radio Reader.*

71. Voskuil, "Power of the Air," in Schultz, *American Evangelicals and the Mass Media,* 85–88; Tona J. Hangen, *Redeeming the Dial: Radio, Religion, and Popular Culture in America* (Chapel Hill: University of North Carolina Press, 2002), 122–24.

72. Hangen, *Redeeming the Dial,* 152.

73. Stewart M. Hoover, "Ten Myths About Religious Broadcasting," in *Religious Television: Controversies and Conclusions,* by Robert Abelman and Stewart M. Hoover (Norwood, N.J.: Ablex, 1990), 23–39; Ward, *Air of Salvation;* Quentin J. Schultz, "Defining the Electronic Church," in Abelman and Hoover, *Religious Television,* 41–51.

74. Himmelstein, *To the Right.*

75. Maralee Schwartz and Kenneth J. Cooper, "Equal Rights Initiative in Iowa Attacked," *Washington Post,* August 23, 1992; "Pat Robertson Says Feminists Want to Kill Kids, Be Witches," *Atlanta Constitution,* August 26, 1992.

76. Thomas B. Edsall, "Forecasting Havoc for Orlando," *Washington Post,* June 10, 1998.

77. "In Annual Predictions, Robertson Predicts Terrorist Attack on U.S. Soil in '07," *USA Today,* January 3, 2007.

78. David Brooks on the *NewsHour with Jim Lehrer,* PBS, November 9, 2007.

CHAPTER SEVEN

1. Pew Research Center for the People and the Press, "Self Censorship: How Often and Why," April 30, 2000, http://people-press.org/reports/display.php3?ReportID=39 (accessed December 11, 2006).

2. Shoemaker and Reese, *Mediating the Message;* Doris A. Graber, *News and Democracy: Are Their Paths Diverging?* Roy W. Howard Public Lecture, 3 (Bloomington: Indiana University School of Journalism, 1992); Ardyth B. Sohn, "Newspaper Agenda-Setting and Community Expectations," *Journalism Quarterly* 61 (1984): 892–97.

3. Samuel Day (former editor of *Lewiston Morning Tribune* and of *The Progressive*), interview with author, August 18, 1995.

4. Glenn Lee Papers, Washington State University Manuscripts, Archives and Special Collections, Pullman, Wash.

5. Norman Solomon, "Big Money, Self-Censorship, and Corporate Media," in Cohen, *News Incorporated,* 54.

6. Ibid., 57.

7. Gottfried, *Conservative Movement.*

8. Michael Schudson and Susan E. Tifft, "American Journalism in Historical Perspective," in Overholser and Jamieson, *The Press,* 17–47.

9. Everette E. Dennis and Huntington Williams III, "Preface," *Gannett Center Journal,* Spring 1987, 4.

10. Dane S. Claussen, "Economics, Business, and Financial Motivations," in Sloan and Parcell, *American Journalism,* 106.

11. James McManus, "How Objective Is Local Television News?" *Mass Comm Review* 18 (1991): 21–30, 48.

12. John F. Berry, "Skepticism Greets Hype Surrounding Cable News Debut," *Washington Post,* June 1, 1980.

13. John C. Busterna, "Trends in Daily Newspaper Ownership," *Journalism Quarterly* 65 (Winter 1988): 831–38; McPherson, *Journalism at the End of the American Century,* 108.

14. John C. Busterna and Robert G. Picard, *Joint Operating Agreements: The Newspaper Preservation Act and Its Application* (Norwood, N.J.: Ablex, 1993), 2–3.

15. Stephen R. Barnett, "The JOA Scam," *Columbia Journalism Review,* November/December 1991, 47–48.

16. William B. Blankenburg, "Predicting Newspaper Circulation After Consolidation," *Journalism Quarterly* 64 (Summer/Autumn 1987): 585–87.

17. Panel discussion, "Merger and Acquisition Frenzy in the News Business: Where Will It End?" in *Proceedings of the 1986 Convention of the American Society of Newspaper Editors, 1986* (Washington, D.C.: American Society of Newspaper Publishers, 1986), 225–39. See also Busterna, "Trends in Daily Newspaper Ownership," 831–38; Richard McCord, *The Chain Gang: One Newspaper versus the Gannett Empire* (Columbia: University of Missouri Press, 2001); Eugene Roberts, Thomas Kunkel, and

Charles Layton, eds., *Leaving Readers Behind: The Age of Corporate News-papering* (Fayetteville: University of Arkansas Press, 2001); Philip Gaunt, *Choosing the News: The Profit Factor in News Selection* (New York: Green-wood, 1990), 67–68; Jim McPherson, "Mergers, Chains, Monopoly, and Competition," in Sloan and Parcell, *American Journalism,* 116–24; and Martha N. Matthews, "How Public Ownership Affects Publisher Au-tonomy," *Journalism Quarterly* 73 (Summer 1996): 343–53.

18. Quoted in Victor Jose, "Do Newspapermen Really Want Compe-tition?" *Quill,* August 1965, 21.

19. John C. Busterna, "Price Discrimination as Evidence of News-paper Chain Market Power," *Journalism Quarterly* 68 (Spring/Summer 1991): 5–14; John C. Busterna, "National Advertising Pricing: Chain vs. Independent Newspapers," *Journalism Quarterly* 65 (Summer 1988): 307–12, 334.

20. Dennis and Williams, "Preface," 4.

21. Peter W. Kaplan, "Plan for a Fox Network Intrigues TV Industry," *New York Times,* October 11, 1985; Eric Barnouw and others, *Conglomer-ates and the Media* (New York: New Press, 1997).

22. Ben H. Bagdikian, "News as a Byproduct," *Columbia Journalism Review,* Spring 1967, 5–12.

23. Ben H. Bagdikian, *The Media Monopoly* (Boston: Beacon, 1983); David Croteau and William Hoynes, *The Business of Media: Corporate Me-dia and the Public Interest* (Thousand Oaks, Calif.: Pine Oaks, 2001); Co-hen, *News Incorporated;* William A. Hachten, *The Troubles of Journalism: A Critical Look at What's Right and Wrong with the Press,* 3rd ed. (Mahwah, N.J.: Lawrence Erlbaum, 2005).

24. Janine Jaquet, "Broadcast Ownership: A Gift to Big Media," in *The Success and Failure of the 1996 Telecommunications Act* (Cambridge, Mass.: Massachusetts Institute of Technology's Center for Reflective Community Practice, and the Leadership Conference Education Fund, 2002), http://www.civilrights.org/publications/reports/1996_telecommunications/telecom.html (accessed March 5, 2006).

25. Sharon Walsh, "Tomorrow's Merger Today: Multimedia Combina-tions Are the Future, Analysts Say," *Washington Post,* March 14, 2000.

26. Mark Jurkowitz, "Tribune's Deal Would Create 'Old Media' Gi-ant," *Boston Globe,* March 14, 2000.

27. Martin Kasindorf, "Modern L.A. Reflects 'Times,'" *USA Today,* March 14, 2000.

28. Daniel B. Wood, "L.A. Prepares for Life Without a 'Local' Paper," *Christian Science Monitor,* March 15, 2000.

29. Leonard Downie Jr. and Robert G. Kaiser, *The News About the News: American Journalism in Peril* (New York: Vintage, 2003), 68.

30. L. Paul Husselbee, "How Newspapers Covered the Telecommunications Act of 1996," conference paper for the 1997 convention of the Association for Education in Journalism and Mass Communication, http://list.msu.edu/cgi-bin/wa?A2=ind9710a&L=aejmc&F=&S=&P= 6953 (accessed March 6, 2006). Most of the coverage that did appear focused on the implementation of a new TV program rating system similar to that used for movies in theaters and the "V-chip" that would be added to all new televisions so that parents could block objectionable content.

31. Jerry Walker, "Newspaper Alliance Sought for Television," *Editor and Publisher,* March 22, 1947, 48.

32. Michael L. McKean and Vernon A. Stone, "Deregulation and Competition: Explaining the Absence of Local Broadcast News Operations," *Journalism Quarterly* 69 (Autumn 1992): 713–23. See also Herbert H. Howard, "Group and Cross-Media Ownership of TV Stations: A 1989 Update," *Journalism Quarterly* 66 (Winter 1989): 785–92; McPherson, *Journalism at the End of the American Century;* and Elliot D. Cohen, "Corporate Media's Betrayal of America," in Cohen, *News Incorporated,* 17–32.

33. Robert G. Picard, "Money, Media, and the Public Interest," in Overholser and Jamieson, *The Press,* 341.

34. Media Regulation Timeline, PBS, http://www.pbs.org/now/ politics/mediatimeline.html (accessed December 11, 2006); McPherson, *Journalism at the End of the American Century,* 159.

35. Stephen Lacy and Alan Blanchard, "The Impact of Public Ownership, Profits, and Competition on Number of Newsroom Employees and Starting Salaries in Mid-Sized Newspapers," *Journalism and Mass Communication Quarterly* 80 (Winter 2003): 949–68.

36. Project for Excellence in Journalism, "The State of the News Media 2006," http://www.stateofthenewsmedia.com/2006/narrative _overview_eight.asp?cat=2&media=1 (accessed January 2, 2007).

37. Downie and Kaiser, *News About the News,* 69.

38. Joseph R. Dominick, "Impact of Budget Cuts on CBS News," *Journalism Quarterly* 65 (Summer 1988): 469–73.

39. Doug Underwood, *When MBAs Rule the Newsroom: How the Marketers and Managers Are Reshaping Today's Media* (New York: Columbia University Press, 1993).

40. Bonnie M. Anderson, *News Flash: Journalism, Infotainment, and the Bottom-Line Business of Broadcast News* (San Francisco: Jossey-Bass, 2004), 9.

41. George Lewis, quoted in Anderson, *News Flash,* 13.

42. Project for Excellence in Journalism, "The State of the News Media 2006," http://www.stateofthenewsmedia.com/2006/narrative_overview_eight.asp?cat=2&media=1 (accessed January 2, 2007).

43. Doug Grow, "Now Journalists Are Sharing the Pain of Industries They've Been Covering," *Minneapolis Star-Tribune,* December 8, 2006.

44. Bill Kovach and Tom Rosenstiel, *The Elements of Journalism: What Newspeople Should Know and the Public Should Expect* (New York: Crown, 2001), 59.

45. Christiane Amanpour, keynote address to Radio-Television News Directors Association, Minneapolis, September 13, 2000, quoted in Anderson, *News Flash,* 9.

46. Downie and Kaiser, *News About the News,* 100.

47. Ibid.

48. Jay T. Harris, quoted in Downie and Kaiser, *News About the News,* 109.

49. Carolyn Said, "McClatchy to Sell San Jose, Contra Costa Papers as Part of Knight Ridder Deal," *San Francisco Chronicle,* March 13, 2006.

50. Ibid.

51. Peter Carey, "Knight Ridder Sold to McClatchy," *San Jose Mercury News,* March 13, 2006.

52. Joe Strupp, "'San Jose Mercury News' Strikes Contract with Guild," *Editor and Publisher,* December 4, 2006, http://www.editorandpublisher.com/eandp/news/article_display.jsp?vnu_content_id=1003468087 (accessed December 15, 2006).

53. Anderson, *News Flash.*

54. Glen T. Cameron and David Blount, "VNRs and Air Checks: A Content Analysis of the Video News Release in Television Newscasts," *Journalism and Mass Communication Quarterly* 73 (Winter 1996): 890–904.

55. Downie and Kaiser, *News About the News,* 244.

56. Kovach and Rosenstiel, *Elements of Journalism,* 60.

57. Anderson, *News Flash,* 11.

58. Tom Fenton, *Bad News: The Decline of Reporting, the Business of News, and the Danger to Us All* (New York: ReganBooks, 2005), 76–77.

59. Scotti Williston, "Global News and the Vanishing American Foreign Correspondent," *Transnational Broadcasting Studies,* Spring/Summer 2001, http://www.tbsjournal.com/Archives/Spring01/Williston.html (accessed March 5, 2006). See also Richard A. Schwarzlose, "Cooperative News Gathering," in Sloan and Parcell, *American Journalism,* 153–62; and Graber, *Mass Media and American Politics,* 364.

60. Arthur Kent, "Preface," in Cohen, *News Incorporated,* 12.

61. Fenton, *Bad News,* 74.

62. Ibid.

63. Lee B. Becker, Vernon A. Stone, and Joseph D. Graf, "Journalism Labor Force Supply and Demand: Is Oversupply an Explanation for Low Wages?" *Journalism and Mass Communication Quarterly* 73 (Autumn 1996): 519–33; Stuart Goldberg, "Then and Now," *Columbia Journalism Review,* November/December 1986, 47.

64. James F. Tracy, "The News About the Newspapers: Press Coverage of the 1965 American Newspaper Strike Against the *New York Times,*" *Journalism Studies* 5 (2004): 451–67, http://web.ebscohost.com/ehost/pdf?vid=4&hid=8&sid=5c38fc6a-10c4-43dc-9214-c34ac36b969e%40sessionmgr9 (accessed December 16, 2006).

65. In 1987 the ITU merged with the Communication Workers of America, which represented telephone and cable workers.

66. Michael Emery and Edwin Emery, *The Press and America: An Interpretive History of the Mass Media,* 6th ed. (Englewood Cliffs, N.J.: Prentice Hall, 1988).

67. Tracy, "News About the Newspapers," 458.

68. Ibid.

69. Ibid., 465.

70. Solomon, "Big Money, Self-Censorship, and Corporate Media," in Cohen, *News Incorporated,* 61.

71. Claussen, "Economics, Business, and Financial Motivations," in Sloan and Parcell, *American Journalism,* 113.

CHAPTER EIGHT

1. Robert M. Press, "Nonstop News for TV Buffs Who Think They've Seen It All," *Christian Science Monitor,* June 16, 1980.

2. Tom Shales, "Ted Turner's Nonstop Gamble: CNN Sets Sail; In Arlington, the Show," *Washington Post,* June 2, 1980.

3. Thomas F. Baldwin, Marianne Barrett, and Benjamin Bates, "Influence of Cable on Television News Audiences," *Journalism Quarterly* 69 (Fall 1992): 651–58.

4. Peter Arnett, "Speech at the National Press Club," in *The Media and the Gulf War: The Press and Democracy in Wartime,* ed. Hedrick Smith (Washington, D.C.: Seven Locks, 1992), 315–29; Peter Arnett, *Live from the Battlefield: From Vietnam to Baghdad; 35 Years in the World's War Zones* (New York: Simon and Schuster, 1994); Jeff Kamen, "CNN's Breakthrough in Baghdad," in Smith, *Media and the Gulf War,* 350–57.

5. Kamen, "CNN's Breakthrough," in Smith, *Media and the Gulf War.*

6. "The Week," *National Review,* January 26, 1998, 8.

7. Both networks claim ratings supremacy, and both are right, depending on measures used. Fox tends to have higher overall viewership, with fewer viewers watching for more hours at a time, while CNN has more individual viewers who spend less time watching.

8. Project for Excellence in Journalism, "The State of the News Media 2006," http://www.stateofthenewsmedia.com/2006/narrative_cabletv _intro.asp?media=6 (accessed January 2, 2007).

9. Anderson, *News Flash,* 166.

10. Ibid.

11. "CBS News Special Report," CBS News transcript, September 12, 2001.

12. *NBC Nightly News with Brian Williams,* MSNBC news transcript, September 13, 2001.

13. David Pryce-Jones, "Containing Saddam," *National Review,* April 2, 2001, 29.

14. Ibid.

15. Thomas M. DeFrank, "Powell Pounds Iraq at UN Show and Tell," *New York Daily News,* February 6, 2003.

16. Ted Gup, "Useful Secrets," *Columbia Journalism Review,* March/April 2003, 15.

17. Chris Mooney, "The Editorial Pages and the Case for War," *Columbia Journalism Review,* March/April 2004, 33.

18. Editor's note, *New York Times,* May 26, 2004.

19. Daniel Okrent, "Weapons of Mass Destruction? Or Mass Distraction?" *New York Times,* May 30, 2004.

20. Ibid.

21. Liza Featherstone, "Parallel Universe at the *Times,*" *Columbia Journalism Review,* July/August 2003, 60.

22. Paul Freidman, "TV: A Missed Opportunity," *Columbia Journalism Review,* May/June 2003, 29–30.

23. William Branigin, "A Gruesome Scene on Highway 9," *Washington Post,* April 1, 2003.

24. John Stossel, *Give Me a Break: How I Exposed Hucksters, Cheats, and Scam Artists and Became the Scourge of the Liberal Media* (New York: HarperCollins, 2004).

25. Rick Perlstein, "Eyes Right," *Columbia Journalism Review,* March/April 2003, 52–55; Eric Alterman, *What Liberal Media? The Truth About Bias and the News* (New York: Basic Books, 2003).

26. Brock, *Republican Noise Machine,* 11.

27. Following widespread complaints, the Sinclair Broadcasting Group decided to air a more balanced program that excerpted the documentary (McPherson, *Journalism at the End of the American Century,* 179).

28. Ibid.

29. Editorial, "The Fictional Path to 9/11," *New York Times,* September 12, 2006.

30. A. J. Liebling, *The Press,* rev. ed. (New York: Ballantine, 1964), 225.

31. Ted Koppel, *Nightline,* ABC News transcript, January 24, 1995. On that day, two stories did dominate the network news programs: O. J. Simpson's trial for murder during the day, and Bill Clinton's 1995 State of the Union Address in the evening.

32. Project for Excellence in Journalism, "The State of the News Media 2006," http://www.stateofthenewsmedia.com/2006/narrative_overview_eight.asp?cat=2&media=1 (accessed January 2, 2007).

33. McPherson, *Journalism at the End of the American Century.*

34. Unnamed reporter quoted in Trotta, *Fighting for Air,* 25.

35. Quoted in Charles R. Novitz, "The TV News Turn-off and What Can Be Done About It," *Quill,* December 1969, 14.

36. James T. Hamilton, "The Market and the Media," in Overholser and Jamieson, *The Press,* 351–71.

37. Jonathon Friendly, "Questions Remain After *USA Today's* First Year," *New York Times,* September 16, 1983.

38. Don Hatfield, "Leisure Sections: Are They Worth the Expense?" September 1978 report of the Modern Living Committee of the Associated Press Managing Editors Association, records of the Associated Press Managing Editors Association, State Historical Society of Wisconsin, Madison. See also Walter D. Scott, "Today's Journalism: A Candid Appraisal," *Quill,* June 1965, 32; and John C. Merrill and Harold A. Fisher, *The World's Great Dailies: Profiles of Fifty Newspapers* (New York: Hastings House, 1980).

39. Davis Merritt, "Public Journalism—Defining a Democratic Art," *Media Studies Journal,* Summer 1995, 125–32. Merritt was editor of the *Wichita Eagle* and one of the founders of the civic journalism movement. See also Edmund B. Lambeth, Philip E. Meyer, and Esther Thorson, eds., *Assessing Public Journalism* (Columbia: University of Missouri Press, 1998).

40. Pew Center for Investigative Journalism, http://www.pewcenter.org (accessed December 31, 2006).

41. Mike Hoyt, "Are You Now, or Will You Ever Be, a Civic Journalist?" *Columbia Journalism Review,* September/October 1995, 27. See also George Everett and W. Joseph Campbell, "The Age of New Journalism 1883–1900," in Sloan, *Media in America,* 247; Robert M. Entman, *Democracy Without Citizens: Media and the Decay of American Politics* (New York: Oxford University Press, 1989); and Public Journalism Network, http://www.pjnet.org (accessed December 31, 2006).

42. Michael Hoyt, "The Wichita Experiment," *Columbia Journalism Review,* July/August 1992, http://archives.cjr.org/year/92/4/wichita.asp (accessed December 31, 2006); Jay Rosen, "Public Journalism as a Democratic Art," in *Public Journalism: Theory and Practice,* ed. Cheryl Gibbs (Dayton, Ohio: Kettering Foundation, 1997); John C. Merrill, Peter J. Gade, and Frederick R. Blevens, *Twilight of Press*

272 NOTES TO PAGES 195-99

Freedom: The Rise of People's Journalism (Mahwah, N.J.: Lawrence Erlbaum, 2001); and Davis Merritt, *Public Journalism and Public Life: Why Telling the Truth Is Not Enough,* 2nd ed. (Hillsdale, N.J.: Lawrence Erlbaum, 1997).

43. David D. Kurpius, "Sources and Civic Journalism: Changing Patterns of Reporting?" *Journalism and Mass Communication Quarterly* 79 (Winter 2002): 853–66; Tom Dickson, Wanda Brandon, and Elizabeth Topping, "Editors, Educators Agree on Outcomes but Not Goals," *Newspaper Research Journal* 22 (Fall 2001): 44–56.

44. Project for Excellence in Journalism, "The State of the News Media 2006," http://www.stateofthenewsmedia.com/2006/narrative_overview _intro.asp?media=1 (accessed January 4, 2007).

45. Karen Carlson, e-mail to author, December 2, 2006.

46. Joseph R. Dominick, Alan Wurtzel, and Guy Lometti, "Television Journalism vs. Show Business: A Content Analysis of Eyewitness News," *Journalism Quarterly* 52 (Summer 1975): 213–18.

47. Fox News, http://www.foxnews.com/story/0,2933,238042,00 .html (accessed December 31, 2006).

48. Ford died at the end of the year, after the Associated Press poll was conducted.

49. Noam N. Levey, "Anti-Foley Blogger Speaks Out," *Los Angeles Times,* November 10, 2006. Other bloggers managed to find out and reveal the identity of the blogger, Lane Hudson.

50. Jeff Gremillion, "Star School: On the Fast Track to Network News," *Columbia Journalism Review,* January/February 1995, http://www .cjr.org/archives.asp?url=/95/1/star.asp (accessed March 3, 2007).

51. Dan Rather, *The Camera Never Blinks: Adventures of a TV Journalist* (New York: William Morrow, 1977), 272.

52. Gloria Goodale, "Evening News' Trump Card: Katie Couric," *Christian Science Monitor,* September 5, 2006.

53. Anderson, *News Flash,* 6.

54. Deborah Potter, "Conflicts of Interest," *American Journalism Review,* December 2004, 64; Jules Witcover, "Revolving-Door Journalists," *Washington Journalism Review,* April 1990, 32.

55. Richard L. Berke, "The 1992 Campaign: The Media; Why Candidates Like Public's Questions," *New York Times,* August 15, 1992.

56. Anderson, *News Flash,* xiii.

57. Quoted in Geneva Overholser and Kathleen Hall Jamieson, "Afterword," in Overholser and Jamieson, *The Press,* 436.

58. Anderson, *News Flash,* 150–51.

59. Lawrence C. Soley, "Pundits in Print: 'Experts' and Their Use in Newspaper Stories," *Newspaper Research Journal* 15 (Spring 1994): 65–75.

60. Trudy Lieberman, *Slanting the Story: The Forces That Shape the News* (New York: New Press, 2000), 13.

61. Ibid.

62. Maxwell McCombs, "The Agenda-Setting Function of the Press," in Overholser and Jamieson, *The Press,* 156–68.

63. Thomas Patterson and Philip Seib, "Informing the Public," in Overholser and Jamieson, *The Press,* 193.

64. Ibid., 194.

65. Jack Cafferty, quoted in Peter Johnson, "Brit Hume's Fox News Exclusive with Cheney Draws Criticism," *USA Today,* February 15, 2006.

66. Robert D. Kaplan, "The Media and Medievalism," *Policy Review,* December 2004/January 2005, 51.

67. McPherson, *Journalism at the End of the American Century.*

68. Gary Lee, "Kuwait's Campaign on the PR Front," *Washington Post,* November 29, 1990.

69. Arthur E. Rowse, "How to Build Support for a War," *Columbia Journalism Review,* September/October 1992, 28–29. See also John R. MacArthur, *Second Front: Censorship and Propaganda in the Gulf War* (Berkeley: University of California Press, 1992), 58–61, 245–49; John Stauber and Sheldon Rampton, *Toxic Sludge Is Good for You: Lies, Damn Lies and the Public Relations Industry* (Monroe, Maine: Common Courage, 1995), 173–74; McPherson, *Journalism at the End of the American Century,* 121–25; and James W. Tankard Jr. and Bill Israel, "PR Goes to War: The Effects of Public Relations Campaigns on Media Framing of the Kuwaiti and Bosnian Crises," conference paper for the 1997 convention of the Association for Education in Journalism and Mass Communication, http://list.msu.edu/cgi-bin/wa?A2=ind9709c&L=aejmc&F=&S=&P= 3857 (accessed March 3, 2007).

70. George H. W. Bush, excerpts from speech given November 22,

1990, at a Marine outpost in Saudi Arabia, *New York Times,* November 23, 1990; George H. W. Bush, speech at Hickam Air Force Base, Hawaii, October 28, 1990, obtained via Federal Information Systems Corporation, Federal News Service.

71. Bush speech at Hickam Air Force Base; George H. W. Bush, fundraising speech in Iowa, October 16, 1990, obtained via Federal Information Systems Corporation, Federal News Service.

72. George H. W. Bush, presidential press conference, White House, October 9, 1990; Paul Bedard, "Bush Talks of Atrocity Trial for Saddam," *Washington Times,* October 16, 1990.

73. Judith Miller, "Standoff in the Gulf; Atrocities by Iraqis in Kuwait: Numbers Are Hard to Verify," *New York Times,* December 16, 1990.

74. William Branigin and Nora Boustany, "Groups Probe Torture in Kuwait," *Washington Post,* April 2, 1991.

75. John R. MacArthur, "Remember Nayirah, Witness for Kuwait," *New York Times,* January 6, 1992; Editorial, "Deception on Capital Hill," *New York Times,* January 15, 1992.

76. Rowse, "How to Build Support."

CHAPTER NINE

1. Paul Weyrich, "A Desultory and Distressing Campaign," Renew America, November 7, 2006, http://www.renewamerica.us/columns/weyrich/061107 (accessed November 7, 2006).

2. William E. Leuchtenburg, "New Faces of 1946," *Smithsonian,* November 2006, 54.

3. Fred Barnes, "Six Isn't Great," *American Standard,* November 1, 2006, http://www.weeklystandard.com/Content/Public/Articles/000/000/012/887qxgjm.asp (accessed November 5, 2006).

4. "Which Candidate Is the Republican?" *Human Events,* November 6, 2006, http://www.humanevents.com/sarticle.php?id=17862 (accessed November 6, 2006).

5. "Moderate Republicans Try to Blur Party Lines," *Washington Post,* November 6, 2006.

6. Frank, *What's the Matter with Kansas?* 242.

7. Dionne, *Why Americans Hate Politics,* 12.

8. Julie Rawe, "Underreported Stories," *Time,* http://www.time.com/time/topten/2006/underreported/10.html (accessed January 1, 2007).

9. Frank, *What's the Matter with Kansas?* 241. See also Frank's book for a fuller exploration of the connection between capitalism and culture.

10. Steven Malloy, "Top Ten Junk Science Stories of the Past Decade," Fox News, April 6, 2006, http://www.foxnews.com/story/0,2933,189706,00.html (accessed January 1, 2007).

11. Quoted on *American Conservative* magazine's Web site, http://amconmag.com/aboutus.html (accessed January 3, 2007). The magazine was founded in 2002.

12. Frank, *What's the Matter with Kansas?*

13. Carey Gillam, "In Kansas, 9 Former Republicans Run as Democrats," Reuters, http://today.reuters.com/news/aticlenews.aspx?type=politicsNews&storyID=2006-11-02T185745Z_01_N02244815_RTRUKOC_0_US-USA-ELECTIONS-KASAS.xml&WTmodLoc=PolNewsHome_C1_%5bFeed%5d-6 (accessed November 2, 2006).

14. Diane Sawyer, "Mea Culpa: Diane Apologizes for Misrepresenting Dean," *Good Morning America,* ABC News transcript, January 29, 2004; David Bauder, "CNN Says It Overplayed Dean's Iowa Scream," Associated Press, February 8, 2004.

15. George Will, "Why America Leans Right," *Washington Post,* October 10, 1994. Will was writing about *The Right Nation* by John Micklethwait and Adrian Wooldridge.

16. Ibid.

17. Frank, *What's the Matter with Kansas?* 247.

18. Book review from the *Washington Post*'s Book World/washingtonpost.com, posted on http://www.amazon.com/gp/product/product-description/0307237699/ref=dp_proddesc_0/002-8553218-8835204?ie=UTF8&n=283155&s=books (accessed October 26, 2006). See also Barack Obama, *The Audacity of Hope: Thoughts on Reclaiming the American Dream* (New York: Crown, 2006).

19. Crawford, *Thunder on the Right,* 113.

20. Cal Thomas, "Wanted: A Leader by Example," Spokane *Spokesman-Review,* September 2, 2006.

21. Liebling, *The Press,* 71.

22. Joe Strupp, "Papers Use Web to Cover '06 Campaign from All Angles," Society of Professional Journalists, http://www.spj.org/pressnotes.asp?REF=16856 (accessed January 3, 2007).

23. League of Women Voters Education Fund (a voter education site), http://www.vote411.org (accessed January 3, 2007); Project Vote Smart, http://www.vote-smart.org/index.htm (accessed January 3, 2007).

24. Yuvul Levin, "Politics After the Internet," *Public Interest,* Fall 2002, 84.

25. Accuracy in Media, http://www.aim.org/static/20_0_7_0_C (accessed January 10, 2007).

26. "Evidence Proving Foster Was Murdered," Accuracy in Media, http://www.aim.org/aim_report/A2212_0_4_0_C/ (accessed January 10, 2007). See also Joseph Farah, "The Unquiet Death of the American Spectator," *WorldNetDaily,* November 18, 1997, http://www.worldnetdaily.com/news/article.asp?ARTICLE_ID=14372 (accessed January 10, 2007).

27. Accuracy in Media, "Stop Al-Jazeera" Web site, http://www.stopaljazeera.org (accessed January 10, 2007).

28. Media Research Center, http://www.mediaresearch.org/about/aboutwelcome.asp (accessed January 10, 2007).

29. Media Research Center, http://www.mrc.org/archive/nq/best.asp (accessed January 10, 2007).

30. L. Brent Bozell III, "Vicious Liberal Media Bias Sways Elections," The Watchdog, November 2006, http://www.mrc.org/flash/2006/Watchdog-nov06PDF.pdf (accessed January 10, 2007).

31. News release, "MSNBC's Keith Olbermann Preaches Hate Speech and Liberal Media Are Silent," Media Research Center, November 2, 2006, http://www.mrc.org/press/2007/press20070104.asp (accessed January 10, 2007); news release, "Bozell Challenges Union of Concerned Scientists to Prove Charges That MRC Studies Are Stifling Climate Change Debate," Media Research Center, January 4, 2007, http://www.mrc.org/press/2007/press20070104.asp (accessed January 10, 2007).

32. Julie Mitchell Corbett, "The Family as Seen Through the Eyes of the New Religious-Political Right," in Abelman and Hoover, *Religious Television,* 285–94.

33. American Family Association, http://www.afa.net (accessed March 26, 2006).

34. Constance G. Mackey, "Saving Public Broadcasting," Family Re-

search Council, http://www.frc.org/get.cfm?i=PV05F01 (accessed January 10, 2007).

35. News release, "In the War Against Obscenity, CBS-TV's '60 Minutes' Has Put Its Money and Hopes on the Hardcore Pornographers," Morality in Media, November 24, 2003, http://www.moralityinmedia .org (accessed January 10, 2007); news release, "Porn Starlet Gets Free Plug in the New York Times and a Three-Story-Tall Billboard in Times Square," Morality in Media, http://www.moralityinmedia.org, August 21, 2003 (accessed November 17, 2007).

36. News release, "MRC Launches Culture and Media Institute," Media Research Center, October 18, 2006, http://www.mrc.org/ press/2007/press20070104.asp (accessed January 10, 2007).

37. Poynter Institute, http://www.poynter.org; Project for Excellence in Journalism, http://www.journalism.org; Committee of Concerned Journalists, http://www.concernedjournalists.org; Association for Education in Journalism and Mass Communication, http://www.aejmc.org; Dow Jones Newspaper Fund, http://djnewspaperfund.dowjones.com/ fund/default.asp; International Center for Journalists, http://www.icfj .org; Investigative Reporters and Editors, Inc., http://www.ire.org (all accessed January 10, 2007).

38. Of course, a phalanx of Fox News commentators try to help viewers "decide" along conservative lines, and the network offers little of the variety of perspectives that a true "marketplace" would require.

39. Peter Phillips and Project Censored, *Censored 2007* (New York: Seven Stories, 2006).

40. Geneva Overholser and Kathleen Hall Jamieson, "Afterword," in Overholser and Jamieson, *The Press,* 440.

41. Sheldon Rampton and John Stauber, *Weapons of Mass Deception: The Uses of Propaganda in Bush's War on Iraq* (New York: Jeremy P. Tarcher/Penguin, 2003), 155–56; Daniel Franklin, "Official Secrets," *Mother Jones,* January/February 2003, http://www.motherjones.com/news/ outfront/2003/01/ma_219_01.html (accessed January 9, 2007).

42. House Committee on Oversight and Government Reform, Minority Office, "Secrecy in the Bush Administration," September 14, 2004, http://www.democrats.reform.house.gov/features/secrecy_report/ index.asp (accessed January 3, 2007).

43. Phillips and Project Censored, *Censored 2007,* 62–64.

44. Quoted in news release, "Bush Administration Press Strategy: TGIF," Center for Media and Public Affairs, May 5, 2006, http://www.cmpa.com/BushWhiteHousePressStrategyTGIF.htm (accessed January 9, 2007).

45. Charlie Savage, "Bush Challenges Hundreds of Laws," *Boston Globe,* April 30, 2006; Michael Abramowitz, "Bush's Tactic of Refusing Laws Is Probed," *Washington Post,* July 24, 2006; Dan Froomkin, "Bush Signing Statements: Constitutional Crisis or Empty Rhetoric?" *Nieman Watchdog,* June 27, 2006, http://www.niemanwatchdog.org/index.cfm?fuseaction=ask_this.view&askthisid=00211 (accessed January 9, 2007). A panel of the American Bar Association reported that Bush challenged more than eight hundred provisions of laws passed by Congress, despite Bush administration claims that he had issued only eighty signing statements.

46. Savage, "Bush Challenges."

47. House Committee on Oversight and Government Reform, Minority Office, "About Politics and Science," August 2003, http://oversight.house.gov/features/politics_and_science/index.htm (accessed January 10, 2007).

48. Larry Margasak, "Government Watchdogs Under Attack from Bosses," Associated Press, December 27, 2006, http://www.startribune.com/587/story/900907.html and http://www.guardian.co.uk/uslatest/story/0,,-6305744,00.html (accessed January 3, 2007).

49. Phillips and Project Censored, *Censored 2007,* 54–57.

50. Frank S. Meyer, "The Revolt Against Congress," *National Review,* May 30, 1956, 10.

51. Later popularized by political activists, used as the name of an international center promoting human rights, and used in the title of at least four books during the past decade, the phrase "speak truth to power" came from a 1955 Quaker pamphlet about dealing with the cold war. The American Friends Service Committee produced the pamphlet, titled *Speak Truth to Power* and subtitled *A Quaker Search for an Alternative to Violence.* The pamphlet can be seen online at http://www.quaker.org/sttp.html (accessed January 11, 2007). See also Larry Ingle, "Living the Truth, Speaking to Power," http://www2.gol.com/users/quakers/

living_the_truth.htm (accessed January 11, 2007); Speak Truth to Power, http://www.speaktruth.org (accessed January 11, 2007); Kerry Kennedy Cuoma and Eddie Adams, *Speak Truth to Power: Human Rights Defenders Who Are Changing Our World* (New York: Crown, 2000); Anita Hill, *Speaking Truth to Power* (New York: Anchor, 1998); Darlene Clark Hine, *Speak Truth to Power: Black Professional Class in United States History* (New York: Carlson, 1996); and Manning Marable, *Speaking Truth to Power: Essays on Race, Resistance, and Radicalism* (Boulder, Colo.: Westview, 1996).

52. Bradley A. Smith, "Power to the Swift Boaters!" *Los Angeles Times,* January 3, 2007. Smith, who was critical of the FEC ruling, had served as FEC chairman in 2004.

53. Theodore Roosevelt, "The Man with the Muckrake," *New York Tribune,* April 15, 1906, reprinted in Weinberg and Weinberg, *The Muckrakers,* 61.

54. Project for Excellence in Journalism, "The State of the News Media 2006," http://www.stateofthenewsmedia.com/2006/narrative _overview_eight.asp?cat=2&media=1 (accessed January 2, 2007).

55. Project for Excellence in Journalism, "The State of the News Media 2006," http://www.stateofthenewsmedia.org/2006/journalist_survey _prc.asp (accessed January 3, 2007).

SELECTED BIBLIOGRAPHY

Abelman, Robert, and Stewart M. Hoover. *Religious Television: Controversies and Conclusions.* Norwood, N.J.: Ablex, 1990.

Accuracy in Media. http://www.aim.org.

Alterman, Eric. *What Liberal Media? The Truth About Bias and the News.* New York: Basic Books, 2003.

Altschull, J. Herbert. *Agents of Power: The Role of the News Media in Human Affairs.* New York: Longman, 1984.

————. *From Milton to McLuhan: The Ideas Behind American Journalism.* New York: Longman, 1990.

American Conservative Union. http://www.conservative.org.

American Legion. http://www.legion.org.

American Legislative Exchange Council. http://www.alec.org.

American Society of Newspaper Editors. http://www.asne.org.

Anderson, Bonnie M. *News Flash: Journalism, Infotainment, and the Bottom-Line Business of Broadcast News.* San Francisco: Jossey-Bass, 2004.

Anderson, Douglas A., and Marianne Murdock. "Effects of Communication Law Decisions on Daily Newspaper Editors." *Journalism Quarterly* 58 (Winter 1981): 525–28, 534.

Ansolabehere, Stephen, Rebecca Lessem, and James M. Snyder Jr. "The Orientation of Newspaper Endorsements in U.S. Elections, 1940–2002." *Quarterly Journal of Political Science* 1 (2006): 393–404.

Arnett, Peter. *Live from the Battlefield: From Vietnam to Baghdad; 35 Years in the World's War Zones.* New York: Simon and Schuster, 1994.

Associated Press. http://www.ap.org.

Bagdikian, Ben H. *The Media Monopoly.* Boston: Beacon, 1983.

Barlett, Donald L., and James B. Steele. *America: What Went Wrong?* Kansas City, Mo.: Andrews and McMeel, 1992.

Barnouw, Erik. *Tube of Plenty: The Evolution of American Television.* 2nd rev. ed. New York: Oxford University Press, 1990.

Barnouw, Erik, and others. *Conglomerates and the Media*. New York: New Press, 1997.

Becker, Lee B., Vernon A. Stone, and Joseph D. Graf. "Journalism Labor Force Supply and Demand: Is Oversupply an Explanation for Low Wages?" *Journalism and Mass Communication Quarterly* 73 (Autumn 1996): 519–33.

Bennett, W. Lance. *News: The Politics of Illusion*. 2nd ed. New York: Longman, 1988.

Berman, William C. *America's Right Turn: From Nixon to Clinton*. 2nd ed. Baltimore: Johns Hopkins University Press, 1998.

Bernstein, Carl, and Bob Woodward. *All the President's Men*. New York: Simon and Schuster, 1974.

Bird, S. Elizabeth. "Newspaper Editors' Attitudes Reflect Ethical Doubt on Surreptitious Reporting." *Journalism Quarterly* 62 (Summer 1985): 284–88.

Blankenburg, William B. "Predicting Newspaper Circulation After Consolidation." *Journalism Quarterly* 64 (Summer/Autumn 1987): 585–87.

Blumenthal, Sidney. *The Rise of the Counter-Establishment: From Conservative Ideology to Political Power*. New York: Times Books, 1986.

Boaz, David, ed. *Assessing the Reagan Years*. Washington, D.C.: Cato Institute, 1988.

Bowles, Dorothy. "Missed Opportunity: Educating Newspaper Readers About First Amendment Values." *Newspaper Research Journal* 10 (Winter 1989): 39–53.

Bozell, L. Brent, III, and Brent H. Baker, eds. *And That's the Way It Is(n't): A Reference Guide to Media Bias*. Alexandria, Va.: Media Research Center, 1990.

Braestrup, Peter. *Battle Lines: Report of the Twentieth Century Fund Task Force on the Military and the Media*. New York: Priority, 1985.

Brasch, Walter M. *Forerunners of Revolution: Muckrakers and the American Social Conscience*. Lanham, Md.: University Press of America, 1990.

Brock, David. *The Republican Noise Machine: Right-Wing Media and How It Corrupts Democracy*. New York: Crown, 2004.

Brown, Jane Delano, Carl R. Bybee, Stanley T. Wearden, and Dulcie

Murdock Straughan. "Invisible Power: Newspaper News Sources and the Limits of Diversity." *Journalism Quarterly* 64 (Spring 1987): 44–54.

Buchanan, Patrick J. *Conservative Votes, Liberal Victories: Why the Right Has Failed.* New York: Quadrangle/New York Times Book Co., 1975.

Buckley, William F., and L. Brent Bozell Jr. *McCarthy and His Enemies: The Record and Its Meaning.* Washington, D.C.: Henry Regnery, 1954.

Bunker, Matthew D. "Have It Your Way? Public Records Law and Computerized Government Information." *Journalism and Mass Communication Quarterly* 73 (Spring 1996): 90–101.

Busterna, John C. "National Advertising Pricing: Chain vs. Independent Newspapers." *Journalism Quarterly* 65 (Summer 1988): 307–12, 334.

———. "Price Discrimination as Evidence of Newspaper Chain Market Power." *Journalism Quarterly* 68 (Spring/Summer 1991): 5–14.

———. "Trends in Daily Newspaper Ownership." *Journalism Quarterly* 65 (Winter 1988): 831–38.

Busterna, John C., and Robert G. Picard. *Joint Operating Agreements: The Newspaper Preservation Act and Its Application.* Norwood, N.J.: Ablex, 1993.

Cameron, Glen T., and David Blount. "VNRs and Air Checks: A Content Analysis of the Video News Release in Television Newscasts." *Journalism and Mass Communication Quarterly* 73 (Winter 1996): 890–904.

Carter, Edward L., and Brad Clark. "'Arrogance Cloaked as Humility' and the Majoritarian First Amendment: The Free Speech Legacy of Chief Justice William Rehnquist." *Journalism and Mass Communication Quarterly* 83 (Autumn 2006): 650–68.

CBS News. http://www.cbsnews.com.

Center for Media and Public Affairs. http://www.cmpa.com.

Chase, Harold W., and Allen H. Lerman, eds. *Kennedy and the Press: The News Conferences.* New York: Thomas Y. Crowell, 1965.

Clear Channel Communications. http://www.clearchannel.com.

Clor, Harry M., ed. *The Mass Media and Modern Democracy.* Chicago: Rand McNally, 1974.

CNN. http://cnn.com.

Cockburn, Alexander, and Jeffrey St. Clair. *Al Gore: A User's Manual.* New York: Verso, 2000.

Cohen, Elliot D., ed. *News Incorporated: Corporate Media Ownership and Its Threat to Democracy.* New York: Prometheus, 2005.

Committee of Concerned Journalists/Project for Excellence in Journalism. http://www.journalism.org.

Conservative Caucus. http://www.conservativeusa.org.

Copeland, David A. *Colonial American Newspapers: Character and Content.* Newark: University of Delaware Press, 1997.

Crawford, Alan. *Thunder on the Right: The "New Right" and the Politics of Resentment.* New York: Pantheon, 1980.

Croteau, David, and William Hoynes. *The Business of Media: Corporate Media and the Public Interest.* Thousand Oaks, Calif.: Pine Oaks, 2001.

Curry, Richard, ed. *Freedom at Risk: Secrecy, Censorship, and Repression in the 1980s.* Philadelphia: Temple University Press, 1988.

Davies, David R. *The Postwar Decline of American Newspapers, 1945–1965.* Westport, Conn.: Praeger, 2006.

Davis, Richard. *The Press and American Politics: The New Mediator.* 2nd ed. Upper Saddle River, N.J.: Prentice Hall, 1996.

DeVolpi, A., G. E. Marsh, T. A. Postol, and G. S. Stanford. *Born Secret: The H-Bomb, the Progressive Case, and National Security.* New York: Pergamon, 1981.

Dickson, Tom, Wanda Brandon, and Elizabeth Topping. "Editors, Educators Agree on Outcomes but Not Goals." *Newspaper Research Journal* 22 (Fall 2001): 44–56.

Dionne, E. J., Jr. *Why Americans Hate Politics.* Paperback ed. New York: Touchstone, 1992.

Dominick, Joseph R., Alan Wurtzel, and Guy Lometti. "Television Journalism vs. Show Business: A Content Analysis of Eyewitness News." *Journalism Quarterly* 52 (Summer 1975): 213–18.

Dorrien, Gary. *The Neoconservative Mind: Politics, Culture, and the War of Ideology.* Philadelphia: Temple University Press, 1993.

Downie, Leonard, Jr., and Robert G. Kaiser. *The News About the News: American Journalism in Peril.* New York: Vintage, 2003.

Dudman, Richard. *Men of the Far Right*. New York: Pyramid Books, 1962.

Dunn, Charles W., and J. David Woodard. *American Conservatives from Burke to Bush: An Introduction*. Lanham, Md.: Madison Books, 1991.

Eagle Forum. http://www.eagleforum.org.

Edel, Wilbur. *Defenders of the Faith: Religion and Politics from the Pilgrim Fathers to Ronald Reagan*. New York: Praeger, 1987.

Edwards, Lee. *The Conservative Revolution: The Movement That Remade America*. New York: Free Press, 1999.

———, ed. *Our Times: The Washington Times 1982–2002*. Washington, D.C.: Regnery, 2002.

Emery, Edwin, and Michael Emery. *The Press and America: An Interpretive History of the Mass Media*. 6th ed. Englewood Cliffs, N.J.: Prentice Hall, 1988.

Engelhardt, Tom. *The End of Victory Culture: Cold War America and the Disillusioning of a Generation*. New York: Basic Books, 1995.

Entman, Robert M. *Democracy Without Citizens: Media and the Decay of American Politics*. New York: Oxford University Press, 1989.

Equal Rights Amendment. http://www.equalrightsamendment.org.

Evans, M. Stanton. *The Future of Conservatism: From Taft to Reagan and Beyond*. New York: Holt, Rinehart and Winston, 1968.

Fairness and Accuracy in Reporting. http://www.fair.org.

Farrar, Ronald. "News Councils and Libel Actions." *Journalism Quarterly* 63 (Autumn 1986): 509–16.

Farrell, Amy Erdman. *Yours in Sisterhood: Ms. Magazine and the Promise of Popular Feminism*. Chapel Hill: University of North Carolina Press, 1998.

Fenton, Tom. *Bad News: The Decline of Reporting, the Business of News, and the Danger to Us All*. New York: ReganBooks, 2005.

Fitzgerald, Frances. *Way Out There in the Blue: Reagan, Star Wars and the End of the Cold War*. New York: Simon and Schuster, 2000.

Frank, Thomas. *What's the Matter with Kansas? How Conservatives Won the Heart of America*. New York: Metropolitan, 2004.

Fukuyama, Francis. *America at the Crossroads: Democracy, Power, and the Neoconservative Legacy*. New Haven, Conn.: Yale University Press, 2006.

Gans, Herbert J. *Deciding What's News: A Study of CBS Evening News, NBC Nightly News, Newsweek and Time.* New York: Pantheon, 1979.

Gaunt, Philip. *Choosing the News: The Profit Factor in News Selection.* New York: Greenwood, 1990.

Gaziano, Cecilie. "How Credible Is the Credibility Crisis?" *Journalism Quarterly* 65 (Summer 1988): 267–78, 375.

Germond, Jack W., and Jules Witcover. *Blue Smoke and Mirrors: How Reagan Won and Why Carter Lost the Election of 1980.* New York: Viking, 1981.

Gibbs, Cheryl, ed. *Public Journalism: Theory and Practice.* Dayton, Ohio: Kettering Foundation, 1997.

Gillmor, Donald M., Jerome A. Barron, Todd F. Simon, and Herbert A. Terry. *Mass Communication Law: Cases and Comment.* 5th ed. St. Paul, Minn.: West, 1990.

Glessing, Robert J. *The Underground Press in America.* Bloomington, Ind.: Midland, 1971.

Goldstein, Tom. *The News at Any Cost: How Journalists Compromise Their Ethics to Shape the News.* New York: Simon and Schuster, 1985.

Gottfried, Paul. *The Conservative Movement.* Rev. ed. New York: Twayne, 1993.

Graber, Doris A. *Mass Media and American Politics.* 4th ed. Washington, D.C.: Congressional Quarterly, 1993.

———. *News and Democracy: Are Their Paths Diverging?* Roy W. Howard Public Lecture, 3. Bloomington: Indiana University School of Journalism, 1992.

Haarsager, Sandra. "Choosing Silence: A Case of Reverse Agenda Setting in Depression Era News Coverage." *Journal of Mass Media Ethics* 6 (1991): 35–46.

Hachten, William A. *The Troubles of Journalism: A Critical Look at What's Right and Wrong with the Press.* 3rd ed. Mahwah, N.J.: Lawrence Erlbaum, 2005.

Halberstam, David. *The Fifties.* New York: Villard Books, 1993.

Hallin, Daniel C. *The "Uncensored War": The Media and Vietnam.* Paperback ed. Berkeley: University of California Press, 1989.

Hammond, William M. *Reporting Vietnam: Media and Military at War.* Lawrence: University Press of Kansas, 1998.

Hangen, Tona J. *Redeeming the Dial: Radio, Religion, and Popular Culture in America.* Chapel Hill: University of North Carolina Press, 2002.

Hardisty, Jean. *Mobilizing Resentment: Conservative Resurgence from the John Birch Society to the Promise Keepers.* Boston: Beacon, 1999.

Hartsock, John C. *A History of American Literary Journalism: The Emergence of a Modern Narrative Form.* Amherst: University of Massachusetts Press, 2000.

Haskins, Jack B., and M. Mark Miller. "The Effects of Bad News and Good News on a Newspaper's Image." *Journalism Quarterly* 61 (Spring 1984): 3–13, 65.

Hayek, Friedrich A. *The Road to Serfdom.* Chicago: University of Chicago Press, 1944.

Heineman, Kenneth J. *God Is a Conservative: Religion, Politics, and Morality in Contemporary America.* New York: New York University Press, 1998.

Henry, William A., III. "Why Journalists Can't Wear White." *Media Studies Journal* (Fall 1992): 16–29.

Heritage Foundation. http://www.heritage.org.

Hertsgaard, Mark. *On Bended Knee: The Press and the Reagan Presidency.* New York: Farrar, Straus and Giroux, 1988.

Hilmes, Michel, and Jason Loiglio, eds. *Radio Reader: Essays in the Cultural History of Radio.* New York: Routledge, 2002.

Himmelstein, Jerome L. *To the Right: The Transformation of American Conservatism.* Berkeley: University of California Press, 1990.

Hoeveler, J. David, Jr. *Watch on the Right: Conservatives in the Reagan Era.* Madison: University of Wisconsin Press, 1991.

Howard, Herbert H. "Group and Cross-Media Ownership of TV Stations: A 1989 Update." *Journalism Quarterly* 66 (Winter 1989): 785–92.

Hughes, William J. "The 'Not-So-Genial' Conspiracy: The *New York Times* and Six Presidential 'Honeymoons,' 1953–1993." *Journalism and Mass Communication Quarterly* 72 (Winter 1995): 841–50.

Huntington, Samuel P. *American Politics: The Promise of Disharmony.* Cambridge, Mass.: Belknap, 1981.

Huntzicker, William E. *The Popular Press, 1833–1865.* Westport, Conn.: Greenwood, 1999.

Iorio, Sharon Hartin. "How State Open Meetings Laws Now Compare with Those of 1974." *Journalism Quarterly* 62 (Winter 1985): 741–49.

Johnson, Haynes. *Sleepwalking Through History: America in the Reagan Years.* Paperback ed. New York: Anchor/Doubleday, 1991.

Johnson, Michael L. *The New Journalism: The Underground Press, the Artists of Nonfiction, and Changes in the Established Media.* Lawrence: University Press of Kansas, 1971.

Johnson, Thomas J. "Exploring Media Credibility: How Media and Nonmedia Workers Judged Media Performance in Iran/Contra." *Journalism Quarterly* 70 (Spring 1993): 87–97.

Keogh, James. *President Nixon and the Press.* New York: Funk and Wagnalls, 1972.

Kerr, Peter A., and Patricia Moy. "Newspaper Coverage of Fundamentalist Christians, 1980–2000." *Journalism and Mass Communication Quarterly* 79 (Spring 2002): 54–72.

Kessler, Lauren. *The Dissident Press: Alternative Journalism in American History.* Beverly Hills, Calif.: Sage, 1984.

King, Erika G. "The Flawed Characters in the Campaign: Prestige Newspaper Assessments of the 1992 Presidential Candidates' Integrity and Competence." *Journalism and Mass Communication Quarterly* 72 (Spring 1995): 84–97.

Knightley, Phillip. *The First Casualty: From the Crimea to Vietnam: The War Correspondent as Hero, Propagandist, and Myth Maker.* New York: Harvest Books, 1975.

Koppel, Ted, and Kyle Gibson. *Nightline: History in the Making and the Making of Television.* New York: Times Books, 1996.

Kostyu, Paul E. "Nothing More, Nothing Less: Case Law Leading to the Freedom of Information Act." *American Journalism* 12 (Fall 1995): 462–76.

Kovach, Bill, and Tom Rosenstiel. *The Elements of Journalism: What Newspeople Should Know and the Public Should Expect.* New York: Crown, 2001.

Kreger, Donald S. *Press Opinion in the Eagleton Affair.* Journalism Monographs 35. Lexington, Ky.: Association for Education in Journalism and Mass Communication, 1974.

Kurpius, David D. "Sources and Civic Journalism: Changing Patterns of Reporting?" *Journalism and Mass Communication Quarterly* 79 (Winter 2002): 853–66.

Kusnetz, Marc, William M. Arkin, Montgomery Meigs, and Neal Shapiro. *Operation Iraqi Freedom.* Kansas City, Mo.: Andrews McMeel, 2003.

Lacy, Stephen, and Alan Blanchard. "The Impact of Public Ownership, Profits, and Competition on Number of Newsroom Employees and Starting Salaries in Mid-Sized Newspapers." *Journalism and Mass Communication Quarterly* 80 (Winter 2003): 949–68.

Landers, James. "Specter of Stalemate: Vietnam War Perspectives in *Newsweek, Time,* and *U.S. News and World Report, 1965–1968.*" *Journalism History* 19 (Summer 2002): 13–38.

Leadership Institute. http://www.leadershipinstitute.org.

League of Women Voters Education Fund. http://www.vote411.org.

Lee, Martin A., and Norman Solomon. *Unreliable Sources: A Guide to Detecting Bias in News Media.* New York: Carol, 1990.

Lieberman, Trudy. *Slanting the Story: The Forces That Shape the News.* New York: New Press, 2000.

Liebling, A. J. *The Press.* Rev. ed. New York: Ballantine, 1964.

Liebovich, Louis W. *The Press and the Modern Presidency: Myths and Mindsets from Kennedy to Clinton.* Westport, Conn.: Praeger, 1998.

———. *Richard Nixon, Watergate, and the Press: A Historical Perspective.* Westport, Conn.: Praeger, 2003.

Lora, Ronald, and William Henry Longton, eds. *The Conservative Press in Twentieth-Century America.* Westport, Conn.: Greenwood, 1999.

Lowry, Dennis T., and Jon A. Shidler. "The Sound Bites, the Biters, and the Bitten: An Analysis of Network News Bias in Campaign '92." *Journalism and Mass Communication Quarterly* 72 (Spring 1995): 33–44.

MacArthur, John R. *Second Front: Censorship and Propaganda in the Gulf War.* Berkeley: University of California Press, 1992.

Maier, Scott R. "The Digital Watchdog's First Byte: Journalism's First Computer Analysis of Public Records." *American Journalism* 17 (Fall 2000): 75–91.

Martin, William. *With God on Our Side: The Rise of the Religious Right in America.* Paperback ed. New York: Broadway, 1997.

Matthews, Martha N. "How Public Ownership Affects Publisher Autonomy." *Journalism Quarterly* 73 (Summer 1996): 343–53.

McCord, Richard. *The Chain Gang: One Newspaper versus the Gannett Empire.* Columbia: University of Missouri Press, 2001.

McGrath, Kristin, and Cecilie Gaziano. "Dimensions of Media Credibility: Highlights of the 1985 ASNE Survey." *Newspaper Research Journal* 7 (Winter 1986): 57.

McKean, Michael L., and Vernon A. Stone. "Deregulation and Competition: Explaining the Absence of Local Broadcast News Operations." *Journalism Quarterly* 69 (Autumn 1992): 713–23.

McManus, James. "How Objective Is Local Television News?" *Mass Comm Review* 18 (1991): 21–30, 48.

McPherson, James Brian. "Crosses Before a Government Vampire: How Four Newspapers Addressed the First Amendment in Editorials, 1962–1991." *American Journalism* 13 (Summer 1996): 304–17.

———. "Government Watchdogs: How Four Newspapers Expressed Their First Amendment Responsibilities in Editorials." Master's thesis, Washington State University, May 1993.

———. *Journalism at the End of the American Century, 1965–Present.* Westport, Conn.: Praeger, 2006.

Media Matters for America. http://mediamatters.org.

Merrill, John C., and Harold A. Fisher. *The World's Great Dailies: Profiles of Fifty Newspapers.* New York: Hastings House, 1980.

Merrill, John C., Peter J. Gade, and Frederick R. Blevens. *Twilight of Press Freedom: The Rise of People's Journalism.* Mahwah, N.J.: Lawrence Erlbaum, 2001.

Merritt, Davis. *Public Journalism and Public Life: Why Telling the Truth Is Not Enough.* 2nd ed. Hillsdale, N.J.: Lawrence Erlbaum, 1997.

Meyer, Philip. *The Vanishing Newspaper: Saving Journalism in the Information Age.* Columbia: University of Missouri Press, 2004.

Miller Center of Public Affairs. http://millercenter.virginia.edu.

Mindich, David T. Z. *Tuned Out: Why Americans Under 40 Don't Follow the News.* New York: Oxford University Press, 2005.

Morland, Howard. *The Secret That Exploded.* New York: Random House, 1981.

Murray, Michael D., ed. *Encyclopedia of Television News.* Phoenix: Oryx, 1999.

National News Council. *An Open Press*. New York: National News Council, 1977.

New York Times. *The Pentagon Papers*. New York: Bantam, 1971.

Niven, David. *The Search for Media Bias*. Westport, Conn.: Praeger, 2002.

Novick, Peter. *That Noble Dream: The "Objectivity Question" and the American Historical Profession*. New York: Cambridge University Press, 1988.

Obama, Barack. *The Audacity of Hope: Thoughts on Reclaiming the American Dream*. New York: Crown, 2006.

Overholser, Geneva, and Kathleen Hall Jamieson, eds. *The Press*. Oxford: Oxford University Press, 2005.

Patterson, Thomas E. *Out of Order*. New York: Vintage, 1993.

PBS. http://www.pbs.org.

Peck, Abe. *Uncovering the Sixties: The Life and Times of the Underground Press*. New York: Citadel Underground, 1991.

Pell, Eve. *The Big Chill: How the Reagan Administration, Corporate America, and Religious Conservatives Are Subverting Free Speech and the Public's Right to Know*. Boston: Beacon, 1984.

Pew Research Center for the People and the Press. http://people-press.org/.

Phillips, Kevin P. *The Emerging Republican Majority*. New Rochelle, N.Y.: Arlington House, 1969.

Phillips, Peter, and Project Censored. *Censored 2007*. New York: Seven Stories, 2006.

Porter, William. *Assault on the Media: The Nixon Years*. Ann Arbor: University of Michigan Press, 1976.

Pritchard, David. "The Impact of Newspaper Ombudsmen on Journalists' Attitudes." *Journalism Quarterly* 70 (Spring 1993): 77–86.

Project for Excellence in Journalism. http://www.journalism.org.

Project Vote Smart. http://www.vote-smart.org.

Rajecki, D. W., Cheryl Halter, Andrew Everts, and Chris Feghali. "Documentation of Media Reflections of the Patriotic Revival in the United States in the 1980s." *Journal of Social Psychology* 131 (June 1991): 401–11.

Rampton, Sheldon, and John Stauber. *Weapons of Mass Deception: The Uses of Propaganda in Bush's War on Iraq*. New York: Jeremy P. Tarcher/Penguin, 2003.

Rather, Dan. *The Camera Never Blinks: Adventures of a TV Journalist.* New York: William Morrow, 1977.

Renew America. http://www.renewamerica.us.

Reuters. http://today.reuters.com.

Roberts, Eugene, Thomas Kunkel, and Charles Layton, eds. *Leaving Readers Behind: The Age of Corporate Newspapering.* Fayetteville: University of Arkansas Press, 2001.

Robertson, C. K., ed. *Religion as Entertainment.* New York: Peter Lang, 2002.

Ronald Reagan Presidential Foundation. http://www.reaganfoundation.org.

Ruschmann, Paul. *Point/Counterpoint: Media Bias.* Philadelphia: Chelsea House, 2006.

Rusher, William A. *The Rise of the Right.* New York: William Morrow, 1984.

Russell Kirk Center for Cultural Renewal. http://www.kirkcenter.org.

Sandel, Michael, ed. *Liberalism and Its Critics.* New York: New York University Press, 1984.

Schneider, Gregory L., ed. *Conservatism in America Since 1930.* New York: New York University Press, 2003.

Schultz, Quentin J., ed. *American Evangelicals and the Mass Media.* Grand Rapids, Mich.: Academie Books, 1990.

Shoemaker, Pamela J., and Stephen D. Reese. *Mediating the Message: Theories of Influences on Mass Media Content.* 2nd ed. White Plains, N.Y.: Longman, 1996.

Siebert, Fred S., Theodore Peterson, and Wilbur Schram, eds. *Four Theories of the Press.* Reprint, Freeport, N.Y.: Books for Libraries Press, 1973.

Sifry, Micah L., and Christopher Cerf, eds. *The Iraq War Reader: History, Documents, Opinions.* New York: Touchstone, 2003.

Silk, Mark. *Unsecular Media: Making News of Religion in America.* Urbana: University of Illinois Press, 1995.

Sims, Norman, ed. *The Literary Journalists.* New York: Ballantine, 1984.

Sinclair, Upton. *The Brass Check: A Study of American Journalism.* Rev. ed. Girard, Kan.: Haldeman Julius, 1919.

Sirotablog. http://www.davidsirota.com.

Sloan, William David. *The Media in America: A History.* 6th ed. Northport, Ala.: Vision, 2005.

———, ed. *Media and Religion in American History.* Northport, Ala.: Vision, 2000.

Sloan, William David, and Lisa Mullikin Parcell, eds. *American Journalism: History, Principles, Practices.* Jefferson, N.C.: McFarland, 2002.

Sloan, William David, and Julie Hedgepeth Williams. *The Early American Press, 1690–1783.* Westport, Conn.: Greenwood, 1994.

Smith, Hedrick, ed. *The Media and the Gulf War: The Press and Democracy in Wartime.* Washington, D.C.: Seven Locks, 1992.

Smith, Jeffery A. *Printers and Press Freedom: The Ideology of Early American Journalism.* New York: Oxford University Press, 1988.

Sohn, Ardyth B. "Newspaper Agenda-Setting and Community Expectations." *Journalism Quarterly* 61 (1984): 892–97.

Soley, Lawrence C. "Pundits in Print: 'Experts' and Their Use in Newspaper Stories." *Newspaper Research Journal* 15 (Spring 1994): 65–75.

Spellman, Robert L. "Tort Liability of the News Media for Surreptitious Reporting." *Journalism Quarterly* 62 (Summer 1985): 289–95.

Splichal, Sigman L., and Bill F. Chamberlin. "The Fight for Access to Government Records Round Two: Enter the Computer." *Journalism Quarterly* 71 (Autumn 1994): 550–60.

Startt, James D., and William David Sloan, eds. *The Significance of the Media in American History.* Northport, Ala.: Vision, 1994.

Stauber, John, and Sheldon Rampton. *Toxic Sludge Is Good for You: Lies, Damn Lies and the Public Relations Industry.* Monroe, Maine: Common Courage, 1995.

St. Dizier, Byron. "Republican Endorsements, Democratic Positions: An Editorial Page Contradiction." *Journalism Quarterly* 63 (Autumn 1986): 581–86.

Stephens, Mitchell. *A History of News from the Drum to the Satellite.* New York: Viking, 1988.

Stone, Gerald, Barbara Hartung, and Dwight Jensen. "Local TV News and the Good-Bad Dyad." *Journalism Quarterly* 64 (Spring 1987): 37–44.

Stossel, John. *Give Me a Break: How I Exposed Hucksters, Cheats, and Scam Artists and Became the Scourge of the Liberal Media.* New York: HarperCollins, 2004.

Streitmatter, Rodger. *Mightier Than the Sword: How the News Media Have Shaped American History.* Boulder, Colo.: Westview, 1997.

———. "The Rise and Triumph of the White House Photo Opportunity." *Journalism Quarterly* 65 (Winter 1988): 981–85.

Sundar, S. Shyam. "Effect of Source Attribution on Perception of Online News Stories." *Journalism and Mass Communication Quarterly* 75 (Spring 1998): 55–68.

Sweeney, Michael S. *The Military and the Press: An Uneasy Truce.* Evanston, Ill.: Northwestern University Press, 2006.

Tebbel, John, and Sarah Miles Watts. *The Press and the Presidency: From George Washington to Ronald Reagan.* New York: Oxford University Press, 1985.

Teel, Leonard Ray. *The Public Press, 1900–1945.* Westport, Conn.: Praeger, 2006.

Trilling, Lionel. *The Liberal Imagination: Essays on Literature and Society.* New York: Doubleday, 1950.

Trotta, Liz. *Fighting for Air: In the Trenches with Television News.* New York: Simon and Schuster, 1991.

Twentieth Century Fund Task Force. *A Free and Responsive Press.* New York: Twentieth Century Fund, 1973.

Underwood, Doug. *From Yahweh to Yahoo! The Religious Roots of the Secular Press.* Champaign: University of Illinois Press, 2002.

———. *When MBAs Rule the Newsroom: How the Marketers and Managers Are Reshaping Today's Media.* New York: Columbia University Press, 1993.

Underwood, Doug, and Keith Stamm. "Are Journalists Really Irreligious? A Multidimensional Analysis." *Journalism and Mass Communication Quarterly* 78 (Winter 2001): 771–86.

Viguerie, Richard A., and David Franke. *America's Right Turn: How Conservatives Used New and Alternative Media to Take Power.* Chicago: Bonus Books, 2004.

Ward, Mark, Sr. *Air of Salvation: The Story of Christian Broadcasting.* Grand Rapids, Mich.: Baker Books, 1994.

Weaver, David, and LeAnne Daniels. "Public Opinion on Investigative Reporting in the 1980s." *Journalism Quarterly* 69 (Spring 1992): 146–55.

Weaver, Paul H. *News and the Culture of Lying.* New York: Free Press, 1994.

Weiler, Michael, and W. Barnett Pearce, eds. *Reagan and Public Discourse in America.* Tuscaloosa: University of Alabama Press, 1992.

Weinberg, Arthur, and Lila Weinberg, eds. *The Muckrakers.* New York: Capricorn Books, 1964.

White, Marie Dunne. "Plagiarism and the News Media." *Journal of Mass Media Ethics* 4 (1989): 265–80.

Wills, Garry. *Reagan's America.* Paperback ed. New York: Penguin, 1988.

Wolfe, Tom. *The New Journalism.* New York: Harper and Row, 1973.

Woodward, Bob, and Carl Bernstein. *The Final Days.* New York: Avon Books, 1976.

World Public Opinion. http://www.worldpublicopinion.org.

World Socialist Web Site. http://www.wsws.org.

Wulfemeyer, K. Tim, and Lori L. McFadden. "Anonymous Attribution in Network News." *Journalism Quarterly* 63 (Autumn 1986): 468–73.

Zinn, Howard. *A People's History of the United States, 1492–Present.* Rev. ed. New York: HarperPerennial, 1995.

INDEX

James Brian McPherson is an associate professor of communication studies at Whitworth University and the author of *Journalism at the End of the American Century, 1965–Present.*

Sidney Blumenthal is a former editor and writer for the *New Republic,* the *Washington Post,* and the *New Yorker.* A former senior adviser to President Bill Clinton, he is the author of several books, including *The Clinton Wars* and *How Bush Rules.*